Patrick County Virginia

BIRTH RECORDS

1853–1869

I0129893

— Volume I ·

by
Barbara C. Baughan
and
Betty A. Pilson

Lord, help me dig into the past
And sift the sands of time
That I might find the roots that made
This family tree of mine...

HERITAGE BOOKS
2015

HERITAGE BOOKS

AN IMPRINT OF HERITAGE BOOKS, INC.

Books, CDs, and more—Worldwide

For our listing of thousands of titles see our website
at
www.HeritageBooks.com

Published 2015 by
HERITAGE BOOKS, INC.
Publishing Division
5810 Ruatan Street
Berwyn Heights, Md. 20740

International Standard Book Numbers
Paperbound: 978-1-888265-68-2
Clothbound: 978-0-7884-3427-3

TABLE OF CONTENTS

Each Section Alphabetical

INTRODUCTION

Birth records are an important research area for genealogists. Although Patrick County was formed from Henry County in 1791, birth records were not recorded for the county until 1853.

We have attempted to abstract these records as accurately as possible. We have used original spellings from the records even though some entries are questionable. Also, writing styles from this era make it extremely difficult to abstract all entries with complete accuracy. Unless otherwise indicated after the Father's name, you may assume that his occupation was farmer. Also, unless otherwise indicated after the child's name, you may assume that the birthplace was Patrick County. Any abnormality or other comments are also indicated after the child's name.

Some of the black birth records indicate one person as Father\Owner and another person as Informant\Master. In these cases, the child and\or its mother was owned by one person and either leased or employed by another. Also, if you have a question as to the race of your ancestor you should check the original birth records in the Patrick County Clerk's Office and BVS Reel #52 microfilm in the Virginia State Library. In this time frame if you were not Caucasian, you could be listed as "colored", "mulatto", or "black".

Neither the Patrick County Clerk's Office or BVS Reel #52 have recorded births for the years 1856 and 1863. Since the Clerk's Office has no birth records for 1869, the births listed herein for that year were copied from the Virginia State Library Microfilm. Therefore, there is a good possibility that some of these recordations may be in error by one year. If your ancestor's birth record seems questionable to you, we suggest that you check the original information in the Clerk's Office or on the microfilm.

We have chosen to publish these records in two sections. Section I covers the years 1853-1865, from the instigation of these recordings until the end of the War Between the States. Section II covers the years 1866-1869. The first County Court held after Lee's surrender at Appomattox on April 24, 1865, expressed its great concern about the "outrages" that were being committed in the county. The Underwood Constitution for the Commonwealth of Virginia went into effect in 1870. The court system that had served Patrick County since its formation some 70 years earlier was completely changed. The last County Court was held on February 28, 1870. Following some names in Section II, you will see (F M). This abbreviation was used for free black males.

Hopefully this compilation will provide information on individuals who do not appear on census records or other public records, and provide some insight into your personal search for your ancestors.

Betty A. Pilson
P. O. Box 742
Stuart, Virginia 24171

Barbara C. Baughan
216 Glenwood Terrace
Stuart, Virginia 24171

SECTION I

```
CHILD'S NAME                            RACE  SEX    BIRTH DATE
FATHER\OWNER                            MOTHER
               INFORMANT
------------------------------------------------------------------------
AARON                                   B/S   M    28 Dec 1855
HUGHS, James M                          Amanda
               Owner

AARON                                   B/S   M     9 Oct 1860
ALLEN, Creed                            Sarah
               Joshua Adams, Master

AARON                                   B/S   M     9 Oct 1860
ALLEN, Creed                            Sarah
               Joshua Adams, Master

ABAGAL                                  B/S   F    18 Dec 1858
MOIR, J W                               Emily
               Master

ABE LINCOLN                             B     M    10 Aug 1864
Not Given                               Charlotte
               Martha Brown, Former Owner

ABRAM                                   B/S   M    26 Oct 1854
CORN, John                              Catherine
               Elizabeth Corn, Mistress

ADALINE                                 B/S   F    -- Sept 1854
EDWARDS, Joseph H                       Lucy
               Owner

ADALINE                                 B/S   F    -- May 1854
VIA, James Sr                           Susan
               Owner

ADALINE                                 B/S   F    10 Sept 1858
FLIPPEN, Joseph                         Rhoda
               Owner

ADAMS, A  J                             W     M    15 May 1861
Illegitimate                            ADAMS, Mary
               R H Adams, Grandfather

ADAMS, Charles E                        W     M    26 Sept 1858
ADAMS, I C                              ADAMS, Oney D
               Father

ADAMS, Dotia A                          W     F    14 Feb 1862
ADAMS, Thomas L                         ADAMS, Mazy E
               Mother

ADAMS, Elizabeth R                      W     F    22 Mar 1854
ADAMS, J T                              ADAMS, Elizabeth S
               Father
```

1

CHILD'S NAME FATHER\OWNER		RACE SEX BIRTH DATE MOTHER
	INFORMANT	

ADAMS, Isaac W		W M 4 Feb 1855
ADAMS, Abram		ADAMS, Ruth
	Father	

ADAMS, John A		W M 4 Feb 1857
ADAMS, Abram		ADAMS, Ruth
	Father	

ADAMS, John W		W M 30 Nov 1859
ADAMS, William		ADAMS, Elizabeth
	Father	

ADAMS, Joshua J T		W M 8 May 1862
ADAMS, J T		ADAMS, Elizabeth
	Father	

ADAMS, Manervia		W F 30 Jan 1862
ADAMS, James		ADAMS, Mary J
	Father	

ADAMS, Mary		W F 7 Apr 1859
ADAMS, James		ADAMS, Mary
	Father	

ADAMS, Mary		W F -- Apr 1859
ADAMS, Josiah		ADAMS, Nancy
	Father	

ADAMS, Mary J		W F 20 July 1860
ADAMS, J T		ADAMS, Elizabeth
	Father	

ADAMS, Maze A		W F 10 Nov 1860
ADAMS, Josiah		ADAMS, Nancy
	Father	

ADAMS, Moses Turner		W M 20 Mar 1854
ADAMS, Paul C		ADAMS, Easter
	Father	

ADAMS, Not Named		W M 30 Sept 1865
ADAMS, Joshua		ADAMS, Lucinda F
	Mother	

AGEE, John E		W M 24 Oct 1862
AGEE, D J		AGEE, Louisa M
	Father	

AGEE, Stafford B		W M 22 Oct 1854
AGEE, Samuel		AGEE, Mary
	Father	

```
CHILD'S NAME                          RACE  SEX    BIRTH DATE
FATHER\OWNER                          MOTHER
          INFORMANT
-----------------------------------------------------------------------
AGER (AGEE?), Ellen                   W     F     9 Oct 1860
AGER, D J                             AGER, Lucy
          Father

AGNAS                                 B/S   F     5 Aug 1860
TERRY, N B                            Grace
          Master

AGNESS                                B/S   F     19 Feb 1853
PENN, Thomas Sr                       Margarite
          Owner

AILSEY                                B/S   F     20 Mar 1857
PENN, Jackson                         Easter
          Master

AKENS, Sarah A                        W     F     31 May 1858
AKENS, George W                       AKENS, Virginia
          Father

AKERS, E J                            W     F     27 Feb 1860
AKERS, Elisha                         AKERS, A J
          Father

AKERS, Elizabeth                      W     F     16 Feb 1857
AKERS, Elisha                         AKERS, Ailsey J
          Father

AKERS, John T                         W     M     25 Sept 1860
AKERS, George W                       AKERS, Virginia
          Father

AKERS, Louisa                         W     F     16 Jan 1865
AKERS, Elisha                         AKERS, Aley J
          Father

AKERS, Mary Ann                       W     F     29 June 1862
AKERS, Elisha                         AKERS, E  J
          Father

AKERS, Samuel                         B/S   M     10 Mar 1853
AKERS, Featherston                    Not Given
          E F Jefferson, Present Master

ALEXANDER                             B/S   M     25 June 1855
ROBERTSON, William J                  Not Given
          Master

ALEXANDER STEPHEN                     B/S   M     1 July 1861
CRITZ, James P                        Mary
          Owner


                          3
```

CHILD'S NAME / FATHER\OWNER / INFORMANT	RACE	SEX	BIRTH DATE / MOTHER

ALICE
MURPHY, William L
    Owner
B/S F 3 Aug 1854
Lucinda (Slave)

ALICE
TUGGLE, John
    Master
B/S F 5 Jan 1862
Milly

ALICE
JOYCE, Hamilton
    Elizabeth Joyce, Mistress
B/S F -- June 1862
Martha

ALLEN
STAPLES, Col A
    Clairborne Mills, Overseer
B/S M -- -- 1854
Not Given

ALLEN, A J
ALLEN, Daniel
    Father
W M -- June 1859
ALLEN, Sarah

ALLEN, Fatha Ann
ALLEN, Robert
    Mother
W F 22 Mar 1853
ALLEN, Elvira

ALLEN, Sarah Avaline
ALLEN, Robert (Wheelwright)
    Father
W F 1 June 1854
ALLEN, Elvera

ALLEN, Statira
ALLEN, Creed
    Father
W F 29 Oct 1857
ALLEN, Nancy E

ALLEN, Victor
ALLEN, J
    Father
W M 27 May 1854
ALLEN, Nancy

ALLEN, Victoria E
ALLEN, Creed
    Father
W F 10 June 1860
ALLEN, Nancy E

ALLICE
SIMMONS, Sarah
    Owner
B/S F 10 May 1854
Slave Mahala

ALLIS
CRITZ, Gabriel
    Owner
B/S F 5 May 1853
Mary

ALLISON
SCALES, Ab
    Owner
B/S F 27 July 1859
Virginia

```
CHILD'S NAME                              RACE  SEX    BIRTH DATE
FATHER\OWNER                              MOTHER
                    INFORMANT
-------------------------------------------------------------------------
ALSEY                                     B/S   F      24 June 1854
PENN, Clark                               Not Given
                    Owner

AMAMDA                                    B/S   F      -- Jan 1854
MINIFEE, Wiley                            Mariah
                    Owner

AMANDA                                    B/S   F      20 July 1862
PANNILL, Joseph                           Mary
                    Sarah Pannill, Mistress

AMANDA (Twin)                             B/S   F      5 Apr 1859
TURNER, John                              Susan
                    Master

AMERICA                                   B/S   F      30 Oct 1857
HUGHS, James                              Hannah
                    Master

AMERICA                                   B/S   F      -- Apr 1859
ZEGLER, Richard                           Ann
                    Owner

AMERICA                                   B/S   F      1 Aug 1860
BROWN, N                                  Martha
                    Master

AMERICA                                   B/S   F      10 May 1860
HYLTON, George                            Bet
                    Thomas Winn, Overseer

AMERICA                                   B/S   F      7 June 1860
ALLEN, Creed                              Matilda
                    Elizabeth Akers, Mistress

AMY                                       B/S   F      29 Nov 1858
VIA, C A                                  Pocohontas
                    J C Moir, Guardian for C A Via

ANDERSON                                  B/S   M      1 Oct 1860
HYLTON, A                                 Bettie
                    Master

ANDY                                      B/S   M      12 Sept 1862
PACK, Martha                              Judith
                    Mistress

ANGIN, James (One Thumb Off)              W     M      -- Jan 1855
ANGLIN, John L                            ANGLIN, Mary
                    Father
```

5

```
CHILD'S NAME                          RACE  SEX   BIRTH DATE
FATHER\OWNER                          MOTHER
            INFORMANT
---------------------------------------------------------------------------
ANGLIN, Adrain                        W     M    1 July 1861
ANGLIN, John L                        ANGLIN, Mary
            Father

ANGLIN, Betty                         B     F    31 Mar 1865
Not Given                             ANGLIN, Ann
            E Anglin, Former Master

ANGLIN, Parthenia                     W     F    15 Dec 1853
ANGLIN, Philip                        ANGLIN, Parthenia
            Father

ANN                                   B/S   F    2 Oct 1854
BARNARD, Isham                        Ruth
            Owner

ANN                                   B/S   F    1 Oct 1855
WILSON, Samuel P                      Sarah Ann
            Jesse M Giles, Overseer

ANN                                   B/S   F    -- Dec 1857
SMITH, Sarah                          Matilda
            Mistress

ANN                                   B/S   F    -- Sept 1857
MARTIN, Joseph                        Mariah
            Anthony Satterfield

ANN                                   B/S   F    30 Oct 1858
AKERS, Eliza                          Matilda
            Mistress

ANN                                   B/S   F    4 May 1859
MURPHY, A                             May
            Owner

ANN                                   B/S   F    10 Aug 1859
SHELTON, William H                    Mary
            Owner

ANTHONY, William H                    W     M    1 July 1855
ANTHONY, Benjamin A                   ANTHONY, Martha
            Father

ANY P                                 B/S   F    4 Mar 1854
DeHART, Aaron                         Rhoda
            Owner

ARCH                                  B/S   M    30 July 1862
YATES, John Y                         Caroline
            Master
```

```
CHILD'S NAME                              RACE  SEX    BIRTH DATE
FATHER\OWNER                              MOTHER
               INFORMANT
------------------------------------------------------------------------
ARCHIBALD                                 B/S   M      31 Mar 1857
MORRIS, William                           Caroline
               Master

ARMANDO                                   B/S   F      5 June 1853
SMITH, Susannah                           Sarah
               Marshall Smith, Son of Owner

ARMSTEAD                                  B/S   M      27 July 1855
WALLER, Edmond                            May
               Owner

ARMSTEAD                                  B/S   M      -- July 1859
VIA, C A                                  Susan
               James C Moir, Guardian

ARNOLD, Emily                             W     F      24 Feb 1860
ARNOLD, M                                 ARNOLD, Dolly
               Fathr

ARNOLD, Martha                            W     F      29 Nov 1857
ARNOLD, A J                               ARNOLD, Elizabeth
               Father

ARRINGTON, Not Named                      W     M      27 Dec 1855
ARRINGTON, John H                         ARRINGTON, Ann T
               Father

ARRINGTON, Ruth A                         W     F      12 May 1854
ARRINGTON, Leroy                          ARRINGTON, Rachel
               Mother

ARRINGTON, Sarah A                        W     F      21 Oct 1858
ARRINGTON, Leroy                          ARRINGTON, Rachael
               Mother

ARRINGTON, William P                      W     M      29 May 1854
ARRINGTON, Daniel                         ARRINGTON, Sarah Ann
               Father

ARTHUR                                    B     M      2 Sept 1864
Not Given                                 Nancy
               H W Reynolds, Former Owner

ASHLEY, John L                            W     M      4 Feb 1854
ASHLEY, Lafayette                         ASHLEY, America
               Father

ASHWORTH, B  L                            W     M      20 Sept 1865
ASHWORTH, G  H                            ASHWORTH, Nancy
               Father
```

7

```
CHILD'S NAME                            RACE  SEX    BIRTH DATE
FATHER\OWNER                            MOTHER
            INFORMANT
----------------------------------------------------------------------
ASHWORTH, George L                      W     M   10 Jan 1860
ASHWORTH, G H                           ASHWORTH, Nancy
            Father

ASHWORTH, George Lafayette              W     M   14 Jan 1861
ASHWORTH, G H                           ASHWORTH, Nancy
            Father

ASHWORTH, Nancy C                       W     F   -- Mar 1857
ASHWORTH G H                            ASHWORTH, Nancy
            Father

ATKINS, Nancy F                         W     F   27 Nov 1861
ATKINS, Booker M                        ATKINS, Judith C
            Mother

AUGUSTIN                                B/S   F   -- Aug 1859
PENN, Susan                             Lucinda
            Owner

AUSTIN                                  B/S   M   25 Nov 1853
KOGER, John Sr                          Milly
            Owner

AUSTIN, John W (Born Floyd Co)          W     M   -- Aug 1857
AUSTIN, David                           AUSTIN, Anna
            Father

AVALINE                                 B/S   F   - July 1853
THOMAS, Washington                      Avaline
            Master

AVALINE                                 B/S   F   10 Mar 1857
MURPHY, William                         Lucinda
            Master

AVALINE                                 B/S   F   22 Nov 1857
TURNER, John                            Susannah
            Master

AVALINE                                 B/S   F   -- Sept 1859
PENN, Susan                             Ruth
            Father

AYERS, Catherine                        W     F   22 June 1854
AYERS, James J                          AYERS, Elizabeth
            Father

AYERS, James M                          W     M   20 Oct 1854
AYERS, William M                        AYERS, Emily E
            Father
```

```
CHILD'S NAME                            RACE  SEX    BIRTH DATE
FATHER\OWNER                            MOTHER
            INFORMANT
-----------------------------------------------------------------------
AYERS, Martha E                         W    F    9 Sept 1862
AYRES, William H                        AYERS, Emaline
            Father

AYERS, Thomas J                         W    M    1 Sept 1860
AYRES, Thomas                           AYERS, Rachael
            Father

AYRES, Amos J                           W    M   23 July 1855
AYRES, Madison H                        AYRES, Orlean
            Mother

AYRES, Ann                              W    F   25 Apr 1858
AYRES, M D                              AYRES, Paulina
            Father

AYRES, Columbea                         W    F    1 Jan 1864
AYRES, William                          AYRES, Emily
            James Shepherd, Grandfather

AYRES, Elizabeth                        W    F   -- June 1861
AYRES, William                          AYERS, Ann
            Father

AYRES, Louisa E                         W    F   16 Feb 1855
AYRES, Green                            AYRES, Elizabeth
            Father

AYRES, William Giles                    W    M   25 Sept 1859
AYRES, W H                              AYRES, Emily
            Father

BAILY, Amillar                          W    F   25 Sept 1855
BAILY, Jesse (Res - Montgomery Co)      BAILY, Julia A
            Father

BALILES, J B M                          W    M   28 Aug 1865
BALILES, Lee                            BALILES, Nancy
            Father

BARBARY                                 B/S  F    2 Nov 1861
PENN, Polly                             Sally
            Owner

BARBOUR, Mary Jane                      W    F    8 Oct 1860
BARBOUR, Jones                          BARBOUR, Susan
            Father

BARNARD, Daman Leonedus                 W    M   25 Jan 1854
BARNARD, Charles                        BARNARD, Delila
            Mother
```

9

```
CHILD'S NAME                          RACE  SEX    BIRTH DATE
FATHER\OWNER                          MOTHER
             INFORMANT
--------------------------------------------------------------------------
BARNARD, Eletha                        W    F    10 Jan 1857
BARNARD, Isham                         BARNARD, Caroline
             Father

BARNARD, Ellen                         W    F    5 July 1859
BARNARD, William P                     BARNARD, Ceany
             Father

BARNARD, George                        B    M    21 Mar 1865
BARNARD, Henderson                     BARNARD, Judy
             Isham Barnard, Neighbor

BARNARD, Hillory                       W    M    1 Oct 1857
BARNARD, James                         BARNARD, Elizabeth
             Father

BARNARD, Jathenia                      W    F    27 June 1860
BARNARD, James                         BARNARD, Elizabeth
             Farmer

BARNARD, Lucinda E                     W    F    22 Feb 1861
BARNARD, Thomas                        BARNARD, Caroline
             Father

BARNARD, Not Named                     W    M    15 Apr 1855
BARNARD, James                         BARNARD, Elizabeth
             Fathr

BARNARD, Not Named                     W    M    29 Dec 1857
BARNARD, Charles                       BARNARD, Delila
             Father

BARNARD, Not Named                     W    F    20 Dec 1859
BARNARD, Charles                       BARNARD, Delila
             Father

BARNARD, Ruth                          W    F    6 June 1862
BARNARD, R J                           BARNARD, Bethaniah
             Father

BARNARD, Thomas B                      W    M    -- Apr 1861
BARNARD, Charles Jr                    BARNARD, Mary
             Tyree Barnard, Grandfather

BARNES, Charles A                      W    M    13 Jan 1859
BARNES, Shad                           BARNES, Lucinda
             Father

BARNES, Elizabeth J                    W    F    29 Dec 1857
BARNES, Shadrack                       BARNES, Lucinda
             Father
```

10

```
CHILD'S NAME                               RACE  SEX     BIRTH DATE
FATHER\OWNER                               MOTHER
              INFORMANT
--------------------------------------------------------------------------
BARNES, Mary Ann (Born Stokes Co, NC)      W     F     1 Mar 1854
BARNES, Sanford                            BARNES, Frances
              Father

BARNES, Mary L                             W     F     9 Aug 1861
BARNES, Shadrack                           BARNES, Lucinda
              Father

BARNES, Richard J                          W     M    11 Nov 1853
BARNES, Emanuel                            BARNES, Exoney
              Father

BARNES, Sarah E                            W     F     -- May 1855
BARNES, Abner                              BARNES, Hannah
              Father

BARNES, Sarah F                            W     F     3 July 1854
BARNES, John M                             BARNES, Leathy S
              Father

BARNES, Thomas                             W     M     2 Apr 1858
BARNES, Abner                              BARNES, Hannah
              Father

BARNETT, William J                         W     M    11 July 1855
BARNETT, Thomas A                          BARNETT, Caroline
              Father

BARNS, Louisa                              W     F     7 May 1862
BARNS, Abner                               BARNS, Hanah
              Father

BARTEE, James B                            W     M    20 Dec 1854
BARTEE, James                              BARTEE, Elizabeth
              Father

BARTER, Martin V                           W     M    19 May 1860
BARTER, James                              BARTER, Elizabeth
              Father

BAXTER, Not Named                          W     F    15 Mar 1862
BAXTER, William D (Tinner)                 BAXTER, Martha H
              Father

BAXTER, Samuel                             W     M     -- Jan 1859
BAXTER, William D                          BAXTER, Martha
              Father

BEASLEY, Mary F                            W     F    30 Feb 1853?
None Given                                 BEASLEY, Hannah
              Polly Beasley, Grandmother
```

11

```
CHILD'S NAME                            RACE  SEX    BIRTH DATE
FATHER\OWNER                            MOTHER
          INFORMANT
-----------------------------------------------------------------------
BECKY                                   B/S   F    -- -- 1857
WILSON, Not Given                       Rachael
          Jesse Giles, Master

BELCHER, Benjamin                       W     M    12 Mar 1858
BELCHER, Jno                            BELCHER, Nancy
          Father

BELCHER, Edward J                       W     M    12 Dec 1853
BELCHER, Hardin                         BELCHER, Elizabeth
          Father

BELCHER, L  P                           W     M    14 Apr 1861
BELCHER, Noah                           BELCHER, Catherine
          Sarah Belcher, Grandmother

BELCHER, Moses W                        W     M     9 May 1858
BELCHER, Hardin                         BELCHER, Elizabeth
          Father

BELCHER, Nancy Ann                      W     F    11 Mar 1861
BELCHER, John                           BELCHER, Nancy
          Father

BELCHER, Noah S                         W     M    18 Jan 1859
BELCHER, Noah                           BELCHER, Catherine
          Mother

BELCHER, Sarah E                        W     F    30 Oct 1855
BELCHER, Hardin                         BELCHER, Elizabeth
          Father

BELISLE, Allice                         W     F    10 Dec 1854
BELISLE, Barnabas                       BELISLE, Mary J
          Father

BELTON, Lucy Ann                        W     F    15 Jan 1860
BELTON, H B                             BELTON, Elizabeth
          Father

BENNETT, M Thomas                       W     M    20 Nov 1861
BENNETT, John H                         BENNETT, Mary
          Father

BENNETT, Not Named                      W     F    -- Nov 1861
BENNETT, Alex C                         BENNETT, Elizabeth A
          Father

BENNETT, Venson A                       W     M     1 Apr 1860
BENNETT, A C                            BENNETT, Elizabeth
          Father
```

12

```
CHILD'S NAME                          RACE  SEX    BIRTH DATE
FATHER\OWNER                          MOTHER
          INFORMANT
----------------------------------------------------------------------
BESSY                                 B/S    F    -- July 1857
GUNTER, Elizabeth                     Martha
          B L Gunter, Master

BETTIE                                B/S    F    15 Dec 1855
BURNETT, Mary                         Leathy
          Henry Hines, Old Master

BETTIE                                B/S    F    10 Aug 1855
SMITH, M Estate of                    Sarah
          William D Smith, Young Master

BETTIE                                B/S    F    12 Feb 1859
ROBERTSON, William J                  Martha
          Master

BETTIE                                B      F    15 Jan 1864
Father Not Given                      Susan
          H W Reynolds, Former Owner

BETTIE ANN                            B/S    F    24 Nov 1855
CLARK, Alex B                         Judy
          Owner

BETTY                                 B/S    F    -- Dec 1862
CLARK, Jane                           Matilda
          Owner

BILLY                                 B/S    M    27 June 1853
WILSON, Samuel P                      Margaret
          Benjamin G Walker, Overseer

BINGHAM                               B/S    M    4 June 1855
VIA, James D                          Mary
          Master

BLACKARD, Gabriel A                   W      M    10 Dec 1855
BLACKARD, William                     BLACKARD, Susannah M
          Father

BLACKARD, John C A                    W      M    31 Mar 1854
BLACKARD, Willoby                     BLACKARD, America
          Mother

BLACKARD, Joseph B                    W      M    -- Dec 1859
BLACKARD, Willoughby                  BLACKARD, America
          Father

BLACKARD, Lucinda E                   W      F    24 Jan 1858
BLACKARD, William                     BLACKARD, Susan
          Father
```

13

```
CHILD'S NAME                            RACE  SEX    BIRTH DATE
FATHER\OWNER                            MOTHER
             INFORMANT
-------------------------------------------------------------------------
BLACKARD, Sarah E                       W    F    9 Nov 1854
BLACKARD, Enoch                         BLACKARD, Mary Jane
             Father

BLACKARD, Stephen T DeHeart             W    M    29 Nov 1853
BLACKARD, William                       BLACKARD, Susannah M
             Mother

BLACKARD, Susan                         W    F    15 Apr 1860
BLACKARD, William                       BLACKARD, Susan M
             Father

BLACKARD, Virginia E                    W    F    3 Feb 1858
BLACKARD, W                             BLACKARD, America
             Father

BLANCARD, Charles                       W    M    10 Jan 1859
BLANCARD, Samuel                        BLANCARD, Eliza Ann
             Father

BLANCET, Mintoria                       W    F    10 Feb 1862
BLANCET, J  M                           BLANCET, Sarah A
             James Barnard, Grandfather

BLANCETT, Martha J                      W    F    27 Sept 1858
BLANCETT, J M                           BLANCETT, Sarah A
             Father

BLANCETT, Mary E                        W    F    6 Nov 1855
BLANCETT, James M                       BLANCETT, Sarah A
             Father

BLANCETT, Mary Virginia                 W    F    22 Feb 1855
BLANCETT, Enoch                         BLANCETT, Mary Jane
             Father

BLANCETT, Susan E                       W    F    30 Mar 1853
BLANCETT, Samuel                        BLANCETT, Eliza Ann
             William Blancett, Grandfather

BLANCETT, William G                     W    M    18 Jan 1855
BLANCETT, Samuel                        BLANCETT, Eliza A
             Father

BOAZ, Charles M                         W    M    3 May 1860
BOAZ, Robert                            BOAZ, Rebecca
             Father

BOAZ, James                             W    M    12 Oct 1862
BOAZ, James                             BOAZ, Terfina
             Mother
```

14

```
CHILD'S NAME                            RACE  SEX     BIRTH DATE
FATHER\OWNER                            MOTHER
              INFORMANT
------------------------------------------------------------------------
BOAZ, Not Named                         W     F    10 Mar 1864
BOAZ, T J                               BOAZ, Martha
              Father

BOAZE, Mat D                            W     M     1 Apr 1858
BOAZE, S                                BOAZE, Lucretia
              Father

BOB SAMPSON                             B/S   M    15 Mar 1853
POINDEXTER, Judith                      Not Given
              James R. Poindexter, Son of Owner

BOND, Nathan Dudley                     W     M    15 Mar 1854
BOND, Reuben                            BOND, Mary
              Isaac Bond, Brother-in-law

BOOTHE, Mary J (Born Botetourt Co)      W     F     4 May 1865
BOOTHE, Jesse                           BOOTHE, Elizabeth
              Father

BOWLIN, George F                        W     M    16 Oct 1862
BOWLIN, William                         BOWLIN, Joanah
              Father

BOWLING                                 B/S   M    12 Nov 1859
ZIGLER, C                               Noney
              Owner

BOWLING, Enona C                        W     F    17 Mar 1854
BOWLING, Gabriel                        BOWLING, Alaminty
              Father

BOWLING, Florenline T                   W     F     7 May 1857
BOWLING, James M                        BOWLING, Mary
              Father

BOWLING, Gabriel P                      W     M    19 Mar 1861
BOWLING, Gabriel                        BOWLING, Alminta
              Father

BOWLING, Harriett                       W     F    10 Nov 1854
BOWLING, William (Carpenter)            BOWLING, Joannah
              Father

BOWLING, Henrietta                      W     F    25 Mar 1859
BOWLING, Gabriel                        BOWLING, Almenta
              Father

BOWLING, Henry G                        W     M    27 Apr 1861
BOWLING, Henry T                        BOWLING, Elizabeth E
              Father
```

15

```
CHILD'S NAME                              RACE  SEX    BIRTH DATE
FATHER\OWNER                              MOTHER
             INFORMANT
-------------------------------------------------------------------------
BOWLING, Hester Ann E                     W    F     9 Apr 1854
BOWLING, William W                        BOWLING, Nancy
             Father

BOWLING, Joseph                           W    M    -- Feb 1857
BOWLING, William                          BOWLING, Jane
             Father

BOWLING, N  C                             W    M     6 July 1865
BOWLING, Gabriel                          BOWLING, Aleminta
             Father

BOWLING, Nancy V                          W    F    29 May 1853
BOWLING, Henry F                          BOWLING, Elizabeth
             Father

BOWLING, Not Named                        W    F    -- June 1855
BOWLING, Gabriel                          BOWLING, Alamenta
             Father

BOWLING, Not Named                        W    M    28 July 1859
BOWLING, James M (Mechanic)               BOWLING, Mary
             Father

BOWLING, Presina                          W    F    21 Nov 1858
BOWLING, H T                              BOWLING, Elizabeth E
             Father

BOWLING, Sarah A                          W    F    -- July 1857
BOWLING, Gabe                             BOWLING, Elamanda
             Father

BOWLING, Susan                            W    F     4 Mar 1865
BOWLING, William                          BOWLING, Susanah
             Father

BOWLING, Tazewell R                       W    M    15 Dec 1854
BOWLING, James M (Mechanic)               BOWLING, Mary
             Father

BOWMAN, America E                         W    F    21 July 1853
BOWMAN, William                           BOWMAN, Mary
             Claron Bowman, Relative

BOWMAN, Austin F                          W    M    27 July 1859
BOWMAN, William                           BOWMAN, Matilda
             Father

BOWMAN, Catherine                         W    F    26 June 1855
BOWMAN, Gabriel                           BOWMAN, Ruth
             Mother
```

16

```
CHILD'S NAME                              RACE  SEX    BIRTH DATE
FATHER\OWNER                              MOTHER
              INFORMANT
---------------------------------------------------------------------------
BOWMAN, Charles H                         W     M     4 Aug 1854
BOWMAN, Joel                              BOWMAN, Ann E
              Father

BOWMAN, Daniel                            W     M    27 Aug 1855
BOWMAN, Austin                           BOWMAN, Mary
              Father

BOWMAN, Eletha                            W     F    15 Mar 1853
None Given                               BOWMAN, Matilda
              John Hensley, Neighbor

BOWMAN, Gilly                             W     F    11 July 1853
BOWMAN, Gilbert                          BOWMAN, Ruth
              Gilbert Bowman, Neighbor (?)

BOWMAN, Hancil V                          W     M     8 Feb 1853
BOWMAN, Austin                           BEASLEY, Polly Arrington
              Father

BOWMAN, James                             W     M    21 Sept 1858
BOWMAN, John                             BOWMAN, Milly
              Father

BOWMAN, Jane                              W     F    10 June 1858
BOWMAN, G F                              BOWMAN, Elizabeth
              Father

BOWMAN, Joseph A                          W     M    -- Nov 1857
BOWMAN, William                          BOWMAN, Matilda
              Father

BOWMAN, Mahala                            W     F    22 Dec 1860
BOWMAN, Austin                           BOWMAN, Mary
              Leroy Arrington, Grandfather

BOWMAN, Mahala                            W     F    29 Dec 1860
BOWMAN, Austin                           BOWMAN, Mary
              Leroy Arrington, Grandfather

BOWMAN, Mary                              W     F    23 July 1855
BOWMAN, Ewell                            BOWMAN, Martha J
              Father

BOWMAN, Mary                              W     F    13 Jan 1858
BOWMAN, C F                              BOWMAN, Mahala
              Father

BOWMAN, Not Named                         W     M    16 Nov 1854
BOWMAN, Peter                            BOWMAN, Nancy
              Father
```

```
CHILD'S NAME                          RACE  SEX    BIRTH DATE
FATHER\OWNER                          MOTHER
          INFORMANT
--------------------------------------------------------------------
BOWMAN, Not Named                     W     M    20 Sept 1855
BOWMAN, Roland                        BOWMAN, Rebecca
          Father

BOWMAN, Not Named                     W     F    10 Apr 1855
BOWMAN, Pleasant                      BOWMAN, Mary
          Father

BOWMAN, Not Named                     W     F     7 July 1857
BOWMAN, William                       BOWMAN, Polly
          Father

BOWMAN, Not Named                     W     F     7 July 1857
BOWMAN, William                       BOWMAN, Polly
          Father

BOWMAN, Not Named                     W     M    11 Sept 1859
BOWMAN, William                       BOWMAN, Mary
          E Bowman, Uncle

BOWMAN, Queen Victoria                W     F    16 Apr 1860
BOWMAN, G F                           BOWMAN, Lucy
          Father

BOWMAN, Rachel                        W     F     9 May 1853
BOWMAN, William                       BOWMAN, Lilla
          Father

BOWMAN, Samuel B                      W     M    27 Apr 1858
BOWMAN, Austin                        BOWMAN, Mary
          Father

BOWMAN, Sarah F                       W     F    11 May 1860
BOWMAN, John                          BOWMAN, Nancy
          Father

BOWMAN, Susan                         W     F     3 Sept 1864
BOWMAN, John                          BOWMAN, Matilda
          John Duncan, Father(?)

BOWMAN, William Alexander             W     M    22 Mar 1864
BOWMAN, Isham                         BOWMAN, Malenda
          Mother

BOWMAN, William T                     W     M    28 Apr 1855
BOWMAN, Sanders                       BOWMAN, Fanny
          Father

BOYD, Alvertia                        W     F     7 Oct 1860
BOYD, Charles                         BOYD, June
          Father
```

```
CHILD'S NAME                              RACE  SEX     BIRTH DATE
FATHER\OWNER                              MOTHER
                    INFORMANT
-----------------------------------------------------------------------
BOYD, Isaac                               W     M    15 Sept 1858
BOYD, Isaac                               BOYD, Nancy
                    Father

BOYD, Joa                                 W     F    13 Mar 1862
BOYD, Charles                             BOYD, Melisa J
                    Father

BOYD, John W                              W     M    15 July 1854
BOYD, William                             BOYD, Jane
                    Mother

BOYD, Lucinda                             W     F    -- Dec 1853
BOYD, Isaac                               BOYD, Elizabeth
                    Father

BOYD, Martha                              W     F    7 July 1854
BOYD, Samuel                              BOYD, Ruth
                    Father

BOYD, Peoria                              W     F    -- Oct 1854
BOYD, Caleb                               BOYD, Rachael
                    Father

BOYD, Putnam                              W     M    -- June 1853
BOYD, Caleb                               BOYD, Rachel
                    Mother

BOYD, Reverdy                             W     M    10 Aug 1854
BOYD, James                               BOYD, Massey
                    Father

BOYD, Samuel P                            W     M    28 July 1859
BOYD, C J                                 BOYD, Nancy E
                    Father

BOYD, Susan (?)                           W     F    16 Jan 1859
BOYD, Caleb                               BOYD, Rachael
                    Father

BOZE, Joshua                              W     M    27 Sept 1859
BOZE, John                                BOZE, Polly
                    Father

BRADLEY, Sarah S                          W     F    22 May 1860
BRADLEY, M W                              BRADLEY, Sarah
                    Father

BRADSON, Not Named                        W     M    -- -- 1855
BRADSON, Samuel G (Tailor)                BRADSON, Mariha
                    Father
```

19

```
CHILD'S NAME                           RACE  SEX    BIRTH DATE
FATHER\OWNER                           MOTHER
              INFORMANT
-------------------------------------------------------------------------
BRAMMER, America                       W     F     3 May 1860
BRAMMER, William D                     BRAMMER, Lucinda
              Father

BRAMMER, B. F                          W     M     22 Mar 1858
BRAMMER, William D                     BRAMMER, Lucinda
              Father

BRAMMER, James J                       W     M     14 Jan 1858
BRAMMER, Jeff D                        BRAMMER, Elizabeth J
              Father

BRAMMER, John J                        W     M     3 Dec 1861
BRAMMER, John                          BRAMMER, Nancy J
              Father

BRAMMER, John J                        W     M     4 Jan 1862
BRAMMER, John                          BRAMMER, M  J
              Father

BRAMMER, Pencanna                      W     F     4 July 1865
BRAMMER, H  L                          BRAMMER, Sallie
              Mother

BRAMMER, Permelia A                    W     F     8 Sept 1859
BRAMMER, J H                           BRAMMER, Eliza J
              Father

BRAMMER, Samuel J                      W     M     16 Oct 1861
BRAMMER, Jeff H                        BRAMMER, E  J
              Father

BRAMMER, Samuel J                      W     M     -- Jan 1862
BRAMMER, Jeff H                        BRAMMER, Elizabeth
              Father

BRAMMER, Sarah L                       W     F     10 Aug 1865
BRAMMER, Perry                         BRAMMER, Lucinda
              Mother

BRAMMER, Sarah M (Born Floyd Co)       W     F     27 Apr 1860
BRAMMER, J L                           BRAMMER, Julina F
              Father

BRAMMER, Sarah M (Born Floyd Co)       W     F     27 Apr 1860
BRAMMER, J L                           BRAMMER, Julina F
              Father

BRAMMER, Susan A                       W     F     22 Mar 1853
BRAMMER, William D                     BRAMMER, Lucinda
              Father
```

```
CHILD'S NAME                              RACE  SEX     BIRTH DATE
FATHER\OWNER                              MOTHER
            INFORMANT
--------------------------------------------------------------------------
BRAMMER, William H                        W     M    30 Jan 1860
BRAMMER, John                             BRAMMER, Nancy
            Father

BRAMMER, William H                        W     M    30 Jan 1860
BRAMMER, John                             BRAMMER, Nancy
            Fathre

BRANCH, John W  L                         W     M    17 June 1862
BRANCH, John                              BRANCH, Louisa E
            Mother

BRANCH, Martha E                          W     F    10 May 1860
BRANCH, Olive                             BRANCH, Pelinia
            Father

BRANCH, Not Named                         W     M    1 Aug 1857
BRANCH, John                              BRANCH, Luvenia
            Father

BRECKENRIDGE                              B/S   M    26 Sept 1860
CRITZ, J P                                Ruth
            Master

BRIM, John W                              W     M    12 Sept 1853
BRIM, Philip W                            BRIM, Mary
            Father

BRIM, Mary E F                            W     F    8 Aug 1855
BRIM, Rice A                              BRIM, Martha N
            Father

BRIM, Not Named                           W     M    18 Mar 1855
BRIM, William                             BRIM, Mahala A
            Father

BRIM, Not Named                           W     F    20 Nov 1860
BRIM, William                             BRIM, Mahala Ann
            Father

BRIM, Philip                              W     M    27 Apr 1859
BRIM, Philip                              BRIM, Mary
            Father

BROOKS, Martha L E M S F                  W     F    29 Apr 1853
BROOKS, John M                            BROOKS, Mary A
            Father

BROWN, C C                                W     M    13 Dec 1853
BROWN, Jonathan R (Practicing Medicine)   BROWN, Nancy H
            Father
```

21

```
CHILD'S NAME                              RACE  SEX     BIRTH DATE
FATHER\OWNER                              MOTHER
                INFORMANT
-----------------------------------------------------------------------
BROWN, George Robert                      W     M   10 June 1857
BROWN, Samuel                             BROWN, Mary Jane
                Mother

BROWN, Sally                              W     F    -- June 1859
BROWN, John                               BROWN, Frances
                Father

BROWN, Sarah R                            W     F   13 June 1853
BROWN, Nicholas (Manufactory)             BROWN, Sarah C
                Father

BROWN, Susan M                            W     F   24 Oct 1855
BROWN, John                               BROWN, Frances
                Father

BRYAN, Abner J                            W     M   16 Oct 1865
BRYAN, H  L                               BRYAN, Mary
                Father

BRYANT, Charles R                         W     M   21 Mar 1862
BRYANT, Richard                           BRYANT, July A
                Mother

BRYANT, Cinthy E                          W     F    -- Apr 1853
BRYANT, John                              BRYANT, Rachel
                Father

BRYANT, Jane                              W     F    8 June 1859
BRYANT, H L                               BRYANT, Mary
                Father

BRYANT, John W                            W     M   21 Sept 1859
Illegitimate                              BRYANT, Ruth
                James N Bryant, Grandpa

BRYANT, Josiah                            W     M    1 Feb 1860
BRYANT, John T                            BRYANT, Rachael
                Father

BRYANT, Lelia A                           W     F    2 June 1862
BRYANT, R  T                              BRYANT, Mary
                Mother

BRYANT, Martha E                          W     F   17 June 1854
BRYANT, Henry L                           BRYANT, Mary
                Father

BRYANT, Nancy J                           W     F   12 Mar 1861
BRYANT, James W                           BRYANT, Mahaly J
                Father
```

```
CHILD'S NAME                                 RACE  SEX    BIRTH DATE
FATHER\OWNER                                 MOTHER
            INFORMANT
-----------------------------------------------------------------------
BRYANT, Not Named                            W     M     27 Sept 1859
BRYANT, John Jr                              BRYANT, Lucinda
            Father

BRYANT, Not Named                            W     F     27 Sept 1860
BRYANT, John Jr                              BRYANT, Lucinda
            Father

BRYANT, Not Named                            W     F     27 Sept 1860
BRYANT, Jno Jr                               BRYANT, Lucinda
            Father

BRYANT, Not Named                            W     F     -- Apr 1861
BRYANT, John Jr                              BRYANT, Lucinda
            Father

BRYANT, Not Named                            W     F     19 Mar 1862
BRYANT, John                                 BRYANT, Lucinda
            Mother

BRYANT, Sarah (Twin)                         W     F     18 Sept 1857
BRYANT, Robert                               BRYANT, Mary
            Father

BRYANT, Sarah J                              W     F     22 Feb 1857
BRYANT, Richard                              BRYANT, Julia A
            Father

BRYANT, William (Twin)                       W     M     18 Sept 1857
BRYANT, Robert                               BRYANT, Mary
            Father

BRYANT, William F                            W     M     8 Sept 1859
BRYANT, Richard                              BRYANT, July Ann
            Father

BULLIN, Tempy M                              W     F     14 Mar 1855
BULLIN, Jacob                                BULLIN, Betsy
            Father

BURGE, Nancy                                 W     F     25 Mar 1854
BURGE, Robert                                BURGE, Elizabeth
            Joseph Morefield, Neighbor\Uncle

BURNETT, Abram P                             W     M     29 Mar 1855
BURNETT, Fleming (Cabinetmaker)              BURNETT, Matilda
            Father

BURNETT, Ann W                               W     F     13 Jan 1859
BURNETT, A                                   BURNETT, Eliz A Onanna
            Father
```

```
CHILD'S NAME                            RACE  SEX    BIRTH DATE
FATHER\OWNER                            MOTHER
            INFORMANT
-------------------------------------------------------------------------
BURNETT, Elmira                          B    F    17 Apr 1865
BURNETT, Busta                          BURNETT, Julia A
            Father

BURNETT, Florence                        W    F    13 Dec 1857
BURNETT, Lewis                          BURNETT, Susan
            Father

BURNETT, Judith E J                      W    F    16 Oct 1853
BURNETT, Ben F                          BURNETT, Mary E
            Father

BURNETT, Malessa A                       W    F    18 Mar 1857
BURNETT, J J                            BURNETT, Mary E
            Father

BURNETT, Mary E                          W    F    17 June 1859
BURNETT, D B                            BURNETT, Exony
            Father

BURNETT, Nancy                           W    F    28 Jan 1855
BURNETT, Jacob J                        BURNETT, Mary E
            Father

BURNETT, Napolean                        W    M    22 May 1860
BURNETT, Flem H (Carpenter)             BURNETT, Matilda
            Father

BURNETT, Not Named                       W    F     5 Apr 1861
BURNETT, Jacob J                        BURNETT, Mary C
            Father

BURNETT, Stephen B                       W    M     4 Dec 1853
BURNETT, Lewis                          BURNETT, Susan
            Father

BURNETT, Susan E                         W    F     6 Aug 1857
BURNETT, F H                            BURNETT, Matilda
            Father

BURNETT, Thomas G                        W    M     9 Jan 1859
BURNETT, J J                            BURNETT, Mary E
            Father

BURNETT, Thomas P                        W    M    19 Sept 1857
BURNETT, Alexander                      BURNETT, Elizabeth
            Father

BURNETT, Virgil T                        W    M    31 Oct 1862
BURNETT, Lewis                          BURNETT, Susan
            Mother
```

```
CHILD'S NAME                           RACE  SEX     BIRTH DATE
FATHER\OWNER                           MOTHER
            INFORMANT
----------------------------------------------------------------------
BURNETT, William                       W     M     5 Nov 1858
BURNETT, John                          BURNETT, Martha
            Father

BURWELL                                B/S   M     -- Jan 1855
ADAMS, Notley P                        Not Given
            Master

BURWELL                                B/S   M     -- June 1858
VIA, Mary                              Jenett
            Mistress

BURWELL                                B/S   M     7 May 1859
CLARK, Robert                          Avaline
            Master

BUSTER                                 B/S   M     19 Aug 1854
KOGER, Henry                           Not Given
            Owner

CALEB                                  B/S   M     -- Nov 1855
PENN, Thomas                           Not Given
            Master

CALEB                                  B/S   M     -- July 1855
McCABE, Mary M                         Ruth
            Mistress

CALLAHAN, Jefferson                    W     M     18 Aug 1859
CALLAHAN, M C                          CALLAHAN, Nancy Ann
            Father

CALVIN                                 B/S   M     1 Oct 1862
DAVIS, B  A                            Eliza
            Master

CANADAY, Not Named                     W     F     6 June 1860
CANADAY, Constant                      CANADAY, Sarah
            Father

CANNADAY, Benjamin                     W     M     -- Sept 1858
CANNADAY, Pleasant                     CANNADAY, Deborah
            Father

CANNADAY, C M                          W     M     12 Jan 1855
CANNADAY, J B                          CANNADAY, Elender
            Father

CANNADAY, Elizabeth                    W     F     27 Nov 1860
CANNADAY, Ferdinand                    CANNADAY, Elizabeth
            Father


                            25
```

```
CHILD'S NAME                          RACE  SEX    BIRTH DATE
FATHER\OWNER                          MOTHER
              INFORMANT
-----------------------------------------------------------------------
CANNADAY, Elizabeth                    W     F     19 Apr 1861
CANNADAY, M  D                         CANNADAY, Ann
              Mother

CANNADAY, Emeline V                    W     F     28 Aug 1854
CANNADAY, Constant                     CANNADAY, Sarah
              Father

CANNADAY, Emily A                      W     F     26 June 1853
CANNADAY, Pleasant                     CANNADAY, Deborah
              Father

CANNADAY, Naaman R                     W     M     27 May 1854
CANNADAY, Joshue                       CANNADAY, Lydia
              Father

CANNADAY, Not Named                    W     F     -- Jan 1858
CANNADAY, Furdon                       CANNADAY, Elizabeth
              Father

CANNADAY, Not Named                    W     M     30 July 1859
CANNADAY, F                            CANNADAY, Elizabeth
              Father

CANNADAY, Not Named (Born Dead)        W     M     30 Mar 1858
CANNADAY, Const                        CANNADAY, Sarah
              Father

CANNADAY, Rachael                      W     F     15 Jan 1859
CANNADAY, Rand                         CANNADAY, Mary J
              Father

CANNADAY, Sarah E                      W     F     4 Mar 1854
CANNADAY, Jacob B                      CANNADAY, Elenor
              Father

CANNADY, Jo A R                        W     M     27 Dec 1859
CANNADY, Pleasant                      CANNADY, Delora
              Father

CAROLINE                               B/S   F     15 Feb 1853
KING, George W                         Jane
              Master

CAROLINE                               B/S   F     16 May 1854
AKERS, Elizabeth                       Matilda
              Owner

CAROLINE                               B/S   F     -- Dec 1862
HANBY, H  H                            Martha
              Master
```

```
CHILD'S NAME                              RACE  SEX     BIRTH DATE
FATHER\OWNER                              MOTHER
             INFORMANT
---------------------------------------------------------------------
CARRIE LEE                                B     F    1 Nov 1864
Father Not Given                          Susan
             William F Tatum, Former Owner

CARTER, Banes                             W     M    16 Sept 1865
CARTER, John P                            CARTER, America
             Father

CARTER, Caroline                          W     F    15 Feb 1861
CARTER, John P                            CARTER, America
             Father

CARTER, E E                               W     M    26 oct 1858
CARTER, S T                               CARTER, Sarah G
             Father

CARTER, Elizabeth Jane                    W     F    9 July 1857
CARTER, John                              CARTER, Mary
             Father

CARTER, Gabriel T                         W     M    25 June 1858
CARTER, R                                 CARTER, Rhoda
             Father

CARTER, J W                               W     M    19 Jan 1859
CARTER, J P                               CARTER, Amelia
             Father

CARTER, John M                            W     M    8 Apr 1861
CARTER, John J                            CARTER, Mary
             Father

CARTER, Julia                             W     F    -- Feb 1857
CARTER, John P                            CARTER, America
             Father

CARTER, Mary H                            W     F    3 Oct 1859
CARTER, C C                               CARTER, Martha
             Father

CARTER, Meralean P                        W     M    25 Oct 1860
CARTER, Robert                            CARTER, Rhoda
             Mother

CARTER, Nancy H                           W     F    18 July 1854
CARTER, John J                            CARTER, Nancy
             Father

CARTER, Not Named                         W     F    21 Nov 1854
CARTER, Jerman W (Merchant)               CARTER, Sophia
             Father
```

```
CHILD'S NAME                              RACE  SEX    BIRTH DATE
FATHER\OWNER                              MOTHER
              INFORMANT
-----------------------------------------------------------------------
CARTER, Not Named                         W     M    10 Dec 1859
CARTER, John                              CARTER, Mary
              Father

CARTER, Tempy                             W     F    15 July 1854
CARTER, Robert                            CARTER, Rhoda
              Mother

CARTER, Thomas                            W     M    28 June 1853
CARTER, John J                            CARTER, Nancy
              Father

CARTER, Thomas T                          W     M    -- -- 1853
CARTER, J P                               CARTER, America
              Father

CASSADAY, John A                          W     M     4 Oct 1855
CASSADAY, William                         CASSADAY, Jane
              Father

CASSADAY, Not Named                       W     F     1 Jan 1855
Legitimate                                CASSADAY, Nancy
              Mother

CASSADAY, Not Named                       W     M    20 Sept 1859
CASSADAY, William                         CASSADAY, Jane
              Father

CASSADAY, Not Named                       W     M    23 Feb 1862
Not Given                                 CASSADAY, Nancy
              Mother

CASSEL, Frances                           W     F     1 Oct 1865
CASSEL, Peter                             CASSEL, Nancy J
              Father

CASSELL, George P  J                      W     M    26 Aug 1862
CASSELL, Peter (Trader)                   CASSELL, Nancy J
              Father

CASSELL, George W Mc                      W     M    20 Jan 1854
CASSELL, Rev A J (Farmer & Preacher)      CASSELL, Luvenia
              Father

CASSELL, Lewis Shelton                    W     M     8 May 1861
CASSELL, A  J                             CASSELL, L
              Father

CASSELL, Mary M                           W     F    24 Mar 1862
CASSELL, B  W                             CASSELL, Martha J
              Father


                          28
```

```
CHILD'S NAME                              RACE  SEX    BIRTH DATE
FATHER\OWNER                              MOTHER
            INFORMANT
--------------------------------------------------------------------------
CASSELL, Not Named                        W     F      -- Aug 1857
CASSELL, Peter                            CASSELL, Mary Jane
            Father

CASTLE, Sarah F                           W     F      5 Dec 1853
CASTLE, Michael                           CASTLE, Mary
            Father

CATHANERN                                 B/S   F      14 Mar 1855
GUNTER, Elizabeth                         Jane
            Beverly Gunter, Young Master

CATHERINE                                 B/S   F      -- Mar 1855
ROGERS, John S                            Dinah
            Master

CATHERINE                                 B/S   F      -- Oct 1859
CRITZ, Gabriel                            Polly
            Owner

CELIA                                     B/S   F      -- Aug 1855
HUGHS, James M                            Violet
            Owner

CELTY                                     B/S   F      -- Nov 1854
HAGOOD, George                            Martha
            Owner

CHAINEY, Jefferson D                      W     M      24 Sept 1861
CHAINEY, Stephen B                        CHAINEY, Margaret
            Mother

CHAINEY, Jno                              W     M      27 Feb 1858
CHAINEY, A C                              CHAINEY, Hester A
            Father

CHAINEY, Not Named                        W     M      10 Mar 1861
CHAINEY, Alexander C                      CHAINEY, Hester A
            Father

CHAINEY, Sally                            W     F      8 May 1853
CHAINEY, Mathers H (Miller)               CHAINEY, Charlott
            Father

CHANDLER, Andrew J                        W     M      3 Jan 1858
CHANDLER, James                           CHANDLER, Susan
            Father

CHANDLER, James R                         W     M      5 Mar 1854
CHANDLER, John                            CHANDLER, Malinda
            Mother
```

29

CHILD'S NAME FATHER\OWNER		RACE SEX BIRTH DATE MOTHER
	INFORMANT	

CHILD'S NAME		RACE	SEX	BIRTH DATE	MOTHER
CHANEY VIA, James Sr Owner		B/S	F	5 Feb 1853	Cinda
CHANEY, Judith A CHANEY, S B Father		W	F	15 Aug 1858	CHANEY, Margaret
CHARITY SNEED, E A W Houchins		B/S	F	20 Mar 1858	Lucinda
CHARLES BURNETT, Adaline Owner		B/S	M	1 Apr 1853	Emily
CHARLES WILSON, Samuel P Jesse Giles, Overseer		B/S	M	1 Oct 1855	Malinda
CHARLES PENN, Peter P Owner		B/S	M	-- Feb 1855	Mary
CHARLES CLARK, Jacob Owner		B/S	M	-- -- 1855	America
CHARLES CONNER, William Master		B/S	M	24 May 1858	Purlina
CHARLES HYLTON, Gabriel Owner		B/S	M	11 Jan 1859	Jane
CHARLES HYLTON, V owner		B/S	M	24 July 1859	Ruth
CHARLES MOIR, James C Master		B/S	M	17 May 1859	Kitty
CHARLES PUCKETT, Robert Jackson Penn, Master		B/S	M	-- June 1860	Esther
CHARLES TATUM, Prior Master		B/S	M	29 Mar 1862	Eady

```
CHILD'S NAME                        RACE  SEX    BIRTH DATE
FATHER\OWNER                        MOTHER
            INFORMANT
---------------------------------------------------------------------
CHARLES                             B/S   M      17 Apr 1862
LANGHORNE, James S                  Sally
            Master

CHARLES A                           B/S   M      24 Dec 1855
REYNOLDS, James                     Zina
            Master

CHARLES JEFFERSON                   B/S   M      15 Dec 1854
CLARK, Jacob                        America
            Master

CHARLOTT                            B/S   F      15 Oct 1855
CRITZ, Gabriel                      Mary
            Owner

CHARLOTT                            B/S   F      -- Nov 1857
PENN, Jefferson                     Jane
            Master

CHARLOTTE                           B/S   F      -- May 1857
JOYCE, Hamilton                     Juda
            Owner

CHARLOTTE                           B/S   F      1 Apr 1859
SMITH, W D                          Sarah
            Owner

CHARLOTTE                           B/S   F      5 Mar 1859
CONNER, G R                         Amanda
            Master

CHATMAN (CHAPMAN?), Robert J        W     M      7 Mar 1865
CHATMAN, William                    CHATMAN, Sarah E
            Father

CHERRY, Susannah A                  W     F      12 Feb 1853
CHERRY, Benjamin R                  CHERRY, Mary
            Father

CHILDRESS, Frances                  W     F      6 Mar 1860
CHILDRESS, Martin                   CHILDRESS, Frances
            Father

CHILDRESS, Not Named                W     M      15 Nov 1853
CHILDRESS, William                  CHILDRESS, Mary Ann
            Richard Childress, Grandfather

CHILDRESS, Osborne F                W     M      23 oct 1853
CHILDRESS, Martin                   CHILDRESS, Frances
            Father
```

31

```
CHILD'S NAME                              RACE  SEX    BIRTH DATE
FATHER\OWNER                              MOTHER
              INFORMANT
---------------------------------------------------------------------
CHILDRESS, Posey                          W    M     17 Sept 1853
CHILDRESS, Robert                         CHILDRESS, Massey
              Jessey Boyd, Neighbor

CHILDRESS, Ruberda Francis                W    F     -- Nov 1854
CHILDRESS, William                        CHILDRESS, Mary A E
              Richard Stanley, Grandfather

CLAIBORNE                                 B/S  M     6 May 1855
WILSON, Samuel P                          Sophy
              Jesse M Giles, Overseer

CLARA                                     B/S  F     25 Apr 1853
SCALES, Absalom                           Everline
              Caroline Scales, Wife of Owner

CLARA                                     B/S  F     -- May 1854
HAGOOD, Anderson                          Caroline
              Elizabeth Hagood, Owner

CLARK, Arthur                             W    M     4 June 1855
CLARK, Alex B                             CLARK, Sallie
              Father

CLARK, Davis L                            W    M     12 Nov 1861
CLARK, R  M                               CLARK, Exony
              Father

CLARK, George H                           W    M     9 Aug 1865
CLARK, Jacob S                            CLARK, Mary A
              Father

CLARK, Green                              W    M     3 Jan 1859
CLARK, Robert                             CLARK, Exona
              Father

CLARK, Henry C                            W    M     19 May 1853
CLARK, Robert M                           CLARK, Enona
              Father

CLARK, John H                             W    M     22 Nov 1855
CLARK, Robert M                           CLARK, Enona
              Father

CLARK, Mary                               W    F     21 June 1860
CLARK, John                               CLARK, Susan A
              Father

CLARK, Mary J                             W    F     19 May 1853
CLARK, George W                           CLARK, Elizabeth
              Father
```

```
CHILD'S NAME                        RACE  SEX    BIRTH DATE
FATHER\OWNER                        MOTHER
            INFORMANT
-----------------------------------------------------------------------
CLARK, McHenry                      W     M      18 Jan 1860
CLARK, Thomas J                     CLARK, Mary J
            Father

CLARK, Nancy E                      W     F      -- Dec 1853
CLARK, William C                    CLARK, Catherine
            Father

CLARK, Nora Ann                     W     F      22 Feb 1855
CLARK, George W (Physician)         CLARK, Bettie
            Father

CLARK, Not Named                    W     M      4 Feb 1859
CLARK, A B                          CLARK, Sally
            Father

CLARK, Not Named                    W     M      23 Feb 1862
CLARK, Jos M                        CLARK, Ella V
            Father

CLARK, Not Named                    W     F      18 Nov 1864
CLARK, Robert                       CLARK, Exony
            Father

CLARK, Robert G                     W     M      22 Mar 1855
CLARK, Jerman                       CLARK, Frances
            Father

CLARK, Sarah A V                    W     F      25 June 1854
CLARK, John R                       CLARK, Sarah J
            Father

CLARK, Thomas H                     W     M      6 May 1859
CLARK, Jacob                        CLARK, Mary Ann
            Father

CLARK, William                      B     M      5 Sept 1865
CLARK, Joe                          CLARK, Jestin
            T J Clark, Former Owner

CLARK, William H                    W     M      13 Mar 1854
CLARK, Jacob S                      CLARK, Mary Ann
            Father

CLARK, William S                    W     M      27 Mar 1859
CLARK, John                         CLARK, Susan
            Father

CLARY                               B/S   F      6 Nov 1861
ZIGLER, Chriss                      Lucinda
            Owner
```

```
CHILD'S NAME                             RACE  SEX    BIRTH DATE
FATHER\OWNER                             MOTHER
             INFORMANT
-------------------------------------------------------------------------
CLEM                                     B/S   M    2 Mar 1853
SPENCER, Martin S                        America
             Owner

CLIFTON, Andrew J                        W     M    13 Nov 1861
CLIFTON, A  J                            CLIFTON, Martha J
             Mother

CLIFTON, Elizabeth Jane                  W     F    20 June 1857
CLIFTON, William                         CLIFTON, Rachael
             Father

CLIFTON, Ellen                           W     F    2 Apr 1859
CLIFTON, William                         CLIFTON, Rachael
             Father

CLIFTON, Not Named                       W     F    10 June 1855
CLIFTON, William                         CLIFTON, Rachel
             Father

CLIFTON, Sally                           W     F    -- Sept 1854
CLIFTON, Emanuel                         CLIFTON, Ruth
             Father

CLIFTON, T G W                           W     M    20 June 1865
CLIFTON, R  W                            CLIFTON, Mary M
             Mother

CLIFTON, Zachariah L                     W     M    4 Dec 1853
CLIFTON, William (Farming & Stilling)    CLIFTON, Rachel
             Father

CLOUD, Patrick H                         W     M    -- July 1862
CLOUD, James D                           CLOUD, Lutitia
             Father

CLUSLEOMEL (?)                           B/S   M    24 Oct 1853
CORN, John                               Rachel
             Elizabeth Corn, Wife of Owner

COBB                                     B/S   M    -- Nov 1855
PENN, Thomas                             Not Given
             Master

COBBS, Not Named                         B     F    17 May 1865
Unknown                                  COBBS, Catherine
             John R Cobbs, Former Owner

COBBS, Not Named                         B     F    1 Dec 1865
Unknown                                  COBBS, Lucinda
             John R Cobbs, Former Owner
```

```
CHILD'S NAME                              RACE  SEX    BIRTH DATE
FATHER\OWNER                              MOTHER
               INFORMANT
------------------------------------------------------------------------
COBBS, Sallie                             B     F      1 Mar 1865
Unknown                                   COBBS, Sarah
               John R Cobbs, Former Owner

COCK,David William                        W     M      23 Dec 1865
COCK, Preston                             COCK, Judith C
               Father

COCKERHAM, Isaac                          W     M      26 July 1858
COCKERHAM, Nath                           COCKERHAM, Rachael
               Father

COCKRAM, Elizabeth                        W     F      6 Oct 1865
COCKRAM, John                             COCKRAM, Matilda
               Father

COCKRAM, H D C                            W     M      29 May 1860
COCKRAM, Alex                             COCKRAM, Sarah
               Father

COCKRAM, Iowa                             W     F      2 Oct 1861
COCKRAM, Andrew                           COCKRAM, Texas
               Mother

COCKRAM, Jackson                          W     M      10 Feb 1859
COCKRAM, Nathaniel                        COCKRAM, Ruth
               Father

COCKRAM, Lucinda F                        W     F      30 Sept 1855
COCKRAM, John                             COCKRAM, Mahala
               Father

COCKRAM, Martha (Born Franklin Co)        W     F      29 Apr 1860
COCKRAM, Charles                          COCKRAM, Ruth
               Father

COCKRAM, Mary A                           W     F      18 Apr 1858
COCKRAM, A                                COCKRAM, Sarah A
               Father

COCKRAM, Mary Ann                         W     F      10 Aug 1861
COCKRAM, Isham                            COCKRAM, Elizabeth
               Father

COCKRAM, Mary E                           W     F      26 Jan 1854
COCKRAM, John                             COCKRAM, Malinda
               Father

COCKRAM, Mary E                           W     F      22 Apr 1857
COCKRAM, John                             COCKRAM, Mahaly
               Father
```

```
CHILD'S NAME                            RACE  SEX     BIRTH DATE
FATHER\OWNER                            MOTHER
            INFORMANT
-----------------------------------------------------------------------
COCKRAM, Nancy A                        W     F      19 Apr 1859
COCKRAM, J B                            COCKRAM, Hahala
            Father

COCKRAM, Not Named                      W     M      17 Dec 1861
COCKRAM, Peter                          COCKRAM, Mahala
            Mother

COCKRAM, Not Named                      W     M      -- July 1861
Illegitimate                            COCKRAM, Adaline
            Wm. Leroy Arrington, Neighbor

COCKRAM, Ruf A W                        W     M       4 Dec 1859
COCKRAM, Isham                          COCKRAM, Elizabeth
            Father

COCKRAM, Samuel                         W     M      24 June 1857
COCKRAM, Nathan                         COCKRAM, Rachel
            Father

COCKRAM, Sarah J                        W     F      22 Nov 1860
COCKRAM, John B                         COCKRAM, Mahala
            Father

COCKRAM, Sarah L                        W     F      12 Dec 1857
COCKRAM, Richard                        COCKRAM, Judith
            Father

COCKRAM, William J                      W     M      24 May 1860
COCKRAM, Richard                        COCKRAM, Judith
            Father

COCKRAM, William J                      W     M      22 May 1860
COCKRAM, Nathan                         COCKRAM, Rachael
            Father

COCKRAN, Not Named                      W     F       4 Aug 1862
COCKRAN, J B                            COCKRAN, Martha
            Father

COCKRAN, S A                            W     M      19 Sept 1862
COCKRAN, Alex                           COCKRAN, Sarah
            Father

COLEMAN, Malessa A                      W     F      29 June 1855
Legitimate - None Given                 COLEMAN, Sarah E
            Mother

COLLINS, Calvin J                       W     M      10 May 1855
COLLINS, Drury T                        COLLINS, Mary A
            Mother
```

36

```
CHILD'S NAME                              RACE  SEX    BIRTH DATE
FATHER\OWNER                              MOTHER
               INFORMANT
------------------------------------------------------------------------
COLLINS, John W                           W     M      8 Apr 1853
COLLINS, James M                          COLLINS, Anniss
               Father

COLLINS, Joseph                           W     M      7 May 1857
COLLINS, John                             COLLINS, Milly
               Father

COLLINS, Martha A                         W     F      26 July 1861
COLLINS, Absolum                          COLLINS, Mary J
               Father

COLLINS, Mary R                           W     F      6 Mar 1860
COLLINS, Jack                             COLLINS, Permelia
               Father

COLLINS, Not Named                        W     M      1 June 1853
COLLINS, Drury T                          COLLINS, Mary A
               Father

COLLINS, Not Named                        W     M      11 Apr 1855
COLLINS, Jackson                          COLLINS, Milly
               Father

COLLINS, Not Named                        W     M      26 Feb 1858
COLLINS, Jackson                          COLLINS, Milly
               Father

COLLINS, Not Named                        W     F      11 June 1854
COLLINS, Drury T                          COLLINS, Mary Ann
               Father

COLLINS, Thomas                           W     M      10 Sept 1854
COLLINS, Solomon                          COLLINS, Nancy
               Father

COLLINS, Thomas                           W     M      13 Apr 1859
COLLINS, James                            COLLINS, Ann
               Father

COLLINS, William T                        W     M      19 July 1862
COLLINS, J J                              COLLINS, Mary E
               Mother

COLLY, Phillip                            W     M      13 Jan 1854
COLLY, William                            COLLY, Sarah
               Father

COLMMA                                    B/S   F      -- Apr 1857
ADAMS, N P                                Sarah
               Master
```

37

```
CHILD'S NAME                          RACE  SEX    BIRTH DATE
FATHER\OWNER                          MOTHER
            INFORMANT
-------------------------------------------------------------------
COMBS, Susan                          W     F    20 Jan 1854
COMBS, Zadock                         COMBS, Susan
            Father

CONEBA                                B/S   M    -- July 1858
LANGHORNE, J S                        Page
            Master

CONNER                                B/S   F    20 Mar 1859
NOWLIN, S F                           Cortny
            Owner

CONNER, Daniel G                      W     M     7 Apr 1860
CONNER, James                         CONNER, Melitia
            Father

CONNER, Daniel V                      W     M    29 Aug 1865
CONNER, John                          CONNER, Abigail
            Father

CONNER, Exony                         W     F     4 Aug 1862
CONNER, Jonathan                      CONNER, Rosina
            Father

CONNER, Francis L                     W     M     7 Nov 1858
CONNER, William                       CONNER, Mary E
            Father

CONNER, Isaac A                       W     M    23 Apr 1860
CONNER, John                          CONNER, Abagal
            Father

CONNER, Jefferson                     W     M    15 Oct 1855
CONNER, Daniel                        CONNER, Anna
            Father

CONNER, Jno W                         W     M    26 July 1858
CONNER, James                         CONNER, Matilda
            Father

CONNER, Joshua W                      W     M     8 Nov 1860
CONNER, Leonard D                     CONNER, Maye
            Father

CONNER, Josiah                        W     M     3 June 1858
CONNER, Daniel                        CONNER, Ann
            Mother

CONNER, Judith R                      W     F     2 Feb 1854
CONNER, David                         CONNER, Susan
            Father
```

38

```
CHILD'S NAME                              RACE  SEX    BIRTH DATE
FATHER\OWNER                              MOTHER
               INFORMANT
------------------------------------------------------------------------
CONNER, Nancy A                           W     F     4 Nov 1865
CONNER, William                           CONNER, Elizabeth
               Father

CONNER, Nancy E                           W     F     1 Mar 1858
CONNER, G R                               CONNER, Nancy A
               Father

CONNER, Not Named                         W     F     27 Oct 1859
CONNER, G R                               CONNER, N A
               Father

CONNER, Not Named                         W     F     20 Aug 1861
CONNER, James Jr                          CONNER, Matilda
               Father

CONNER, Not Named (Twin)                  W     M     29 Mar 1865
CONNER, James                             CONNER, Matilda
               Father

CONNER, Not Named (Twin)                  W     M     29 Mar 1865
CONNER, James                             CONNER, Matilda
               Father

CONNER, Peter B                           W     M     3 July 1860
CONNER, Peter                             CONNER, Nancy J
               Father

CONNER, S A                               W     M     27 Sept 1858
CONNER, W B                               CONNER, Elizabeth
               Father

CONNER, S A                               W     F     25 Sept 1859
CONNER, William B                         CONNER, Elizabeth
               Father

CONWAY, Jane                              W     F     10 Nov 1860
CONWAY, Peyton                            CONWAY, Jane
               Father

CORETTS, Diel                            W     M     14 Jan 1862
CORETTS, Nicholas (Brick Layer)          CORETTS, Mary A
               Mother

CORN, Judith E                           W     F     11 Nov 1860
CORN, Peter                              CORN, Nancy C
               Father

CORN, Sarah E                            W     F     15 July 1855
CORN, Richard                            CORN, Naoma
               Father
```

```
CHILD'S NAME                              RACE  SEX    BIRTH DATE
FATHER\OWNER                              MOTHER
              INFORMANT
-----------------------------------------------------------------------
CORN, Sarah E                             W     F    11 Aug 1862
CORN, Joshua                              CORN, Matilda
              Father

COX, C C Y                                W     M     1 Dec 1859
COX, John                                 COX, Margaret
              Father

COX, Enoch P                              W     M    25 Mar 1855
COX, Preston                              COX, Judith C
              Father

COX, James A                              W     M    15 July 1857
COX, James                                COX, Jane
              Father

COX, Jerusha                              W     F     6 Oct 1858
COX, Jno                                  COX, Mary Jane
              Father

COX, John W (Born Henry Co)               W     M    31 Nar 1860
COX, George W                             COX, Nancy M
              Father

COX, Lucy                                 W     F    29 Sept 1858
COX, P                                    COX, Judith C
              Father

COX, Martha Joyce                         W     F    19 Sept 1854
COX, G W                                  COX, Nancy M
              Father

CRADDOCK, German                          W     M    28 Dec 1854
CRADDOCK, James                           CRADDOCK, Adelpha
              Father

CRADDOCK, John                            W     M    -- Nov 1854
CRADDOCK, Thomas                          CRADDOCK, Lucinda
              Father

CRADDOCK, Louisa                          W     F    26 Feb 1859
CRADDOCK, James                           CRADDOCK, Delphia
              Father

CRADDOCK, Martin                          W     M    26 Jan 1855
CRADDOCK, James                           CRADDOCK, Delphy
              Father

CRADDOCK, Matilda J                       W     F    -- Oct 1855
CRADDOCK, Ezechiel                        CRADDOCK, Lucy
              Father


                           40
```

```
CHILD'S NAME                                    RACE  SEX    BIRTH DATE
FATHER\OWNER                                    MOTHER
            INFORMANT
------------------------------------------------------------------------
CRADDOCK, Not Named                             W     M     8 July 1853
CRADDOCK, James                                 CRADDOCK, Louise
            Father

CRADDOCK, Peter L                               W     M     25 July 1855
CRADDOCK, James                                 CRADDOCK, Louisa
            Father

CRADDOCK, Susan R                               W     F     28 May 1861
CRADDOCK, James                                 CRADDOCK, Lucinda
            Father

CRAIG, Charles W                                W     M     3 Aug 1854
CRAIG, Columbus D                               CRAIG, Emily Ann
            Father

CRAIG, John A W                                 W     M     15 Dec 1853
CRAIG, Green                                    CRAIG, Lucinda Jane
            Father

CRAIG, Martha E                                 W     F     6 Dec 1865
CRAIG, Peter                                    CRAIG, Sally A
            Father

CRAIG, Not Named                                W     F     -- Apr 1855
CRAIG, John M (Carpenter)                       CRAIG, Eliza
            Father

CRAWFORD, Not Named                             W     M     11 Nov 1865
CRAWFORD, William                               CRAWFORD, Susan
            Father

CREASY                                          B/S   F     3 Feb 1857
WILSON, Not Given                               Sophie
            Jesse Giles, Master

CREG, Nancy E                                   W     F     27 Jan 1861
CREG, Peter                                     CREG, Sarah A
            Nancy Wood, Grandmother

CRITIA                                          B/S   F     1 June 1853
WILSON, Samuel P                                Nelly
            Luvenia Shelton, Wife of Overseer

CRITZ, Callie                                   W     F     26 Nov 1860
CRITZ, J P                                      CRITZ, Martha
            Father

CRITZ, Charlott                                 W     F     -- Dec 1857
CRITZ, B                                        CRITZ, Sally
            Father
```

```
CHILD'S NAME                            RACE  SEX    BIRTH DATE
FATHER\OWNER                            MOTHER
              INFORMANT
---------------------------------------------------------------------
CRITZ, Joseph T                         W     M    24 Feb 1860
CRITZ, William                          CRITZ, Catherine E
              Father

CRITZ, Marietta                         W     F    15 Oct 1854
CRITZ, Haman B                          CRITZ, Lavinia
              Father

CRITZ, Marietta                         W     F     5 Sept 1855
CRITZ, Haman                            CRITZ, Luvenia
              Father

CRITZ, Nancy                            W     F    25 Mar 1854
CRITZ, William                          CRITZ, Susan
              Father

CRITZ, Not Named                        W     M    18 Sept 1855
CRITZ, William Jr                       CRITZ, Susan
              Father

CRITZ, Not Named                        W     M    25 Nov 1859
CRITZ, Haman                            CRITZ, Luvenia
              Father

CRITZ, Not Named                        W     M    20 May 1862
CRITZ, William D (Wheelwright)          CRITZ, Christina
              Father

CRITZ, Not Named                        B     F    -- Aug 1865
Unknown                                 CRITZ, Mary
              Gabriel Critz, Former Owner

CRITZ, William A                        W     M    27 Jan 1853
CRITZ, Haman B                          CRITZ, Luvenia
              Father

CRUISE, David (Twin)                    W     M    19 Oct 1860
CRUISE, Peter (Blacksmith)              CRUISE, Elizabeth
              Father

CRUISE, Isaac M                         W     M    18 June 1858
CRUISE, David                           CRUISE, Sinai
              Father

CRUISE, J D                             W     M     5 July 1853
CRUISE, James                           CRUISE, Mary Ann
              Mother

CRUISE, M T                             W     M    24 Apr 1860
CRUISE, David                           CRUISE, Senai
              Father
```

```
CHILD'S NAME                           RACE  SEX      BIRTH DATE
FATHER\OWNER                           MOTHER
                  INFORMANT
-----------------------------------------------------------------------
CRUISE, Marth A                        W     F     4 Apr 1860
CRUISE, James                          CRUISE, Mary A
                  Father

CRUISE, Mary E                         W     F     15 May 1855
CRUISE, James                          CRUISE, Mary A
                  Father

CRUISE, Nancy C                        W     F     -- Sept 1857
CRUISE, Peter                          CRUISE, Elizabeth
                  Father

CRUISE, Nancy E                        W     F     24 Dec 1855
CRUISE, Petter (Blacksmith)            CRUISE, Elizabeth
                  Father

CRUISE, Not Named                      W     M     25 Aug 1857
CRUISE, James                          CRUISE, Mary A
                  Father

CRUISE, Peter                          W     M     12 Feb 1854
CRUISE, David                          CRUISE, Lena
                  Father

CRUISE, Redman                         W     M     25 June 1855
CRUISE, Redman (Blacksmith)            CRUISE, Mary A
                  Father

CRUISE, Reeny                          W     F     3 July 1862
CRUISE, David                          CRUISE, Zina
                  Father

CRUISE, Solomon (Twin)                 W     M     19 Oct 1860
CRUISE, Peter (Blacksmith)             CRUISE, Elizabeth
                  Father

CRUM, Mary E                           W     F     22 Sept 1853
CRUM, William H                        CRUM, Matilda
                  Father

CULLERS, Augusta J                     W     F     15 Mar 1859
CULLERS, J W                           CULLERS, Margaret
                  Father

DALTON, A J                            W     M     10 Feb 1860
DALTON, A J                            DALTON, Sallie
                  Father

DALTON, Almenta                        W     F     15 July 1853
DALTON, Frederick                      DALTON, Martha
                  Father
```

```
CHILD'S NAME                          RACE  SEX    BIRTH DATE
FATHER\OWNER                          MOTHER
              INFORMANT
-----------------------------------------------------------------------
DALTON, Amanda C                        W     F     4 Oct 1855
DALTON, Andrew J                        DALTON, Sally
              Father

DALTON, Avaline                         W     F    29 Apr 1859
DALTON, William                         DALTON, Jane
              Father

DALTON, Elizabeth                       W     F    19 Nov 1858
DALTON, Jackson                         DALTON, Sally
              Father

DALTON, Emberzetta                      W     F    10 Mar 1858
DALTON, J W                             DALTON, Emily
              Father

DALTON, George Washington               W     M     4 July 1759
DALTON, Fred                            DALTON, Martha
              Father

DALTON, Haman                           W     M     8 Dec 1862
DALTON, H  C (Trader)                   DALTON, Sarah
              Mother

DALTON, John Tyler                      W     M     7 Jan 1854
DALTON, Hamen C                         DALTON, Sarah
              Father

DALTON, Joseph Bishop                   W     M    10 May 1860
DALTON, F                               DALTON, Martha
              Father

DALTON, Lezier Frances                  W     F    11 May 1855
DALTON, Frederick                       DALTON, Martha
              Father

DALTON, Mary V                          W     F    12 Dec 1857
DALTON, William                         DALTON, Jane
              Father

DALTON, Mirabo T                        W     M    28 Dec 1862
DALTON, A  J                            DALTON, Sarah
              Father

DALTON, Nancy E                         W     F     4 Oct 1855
DALTON, Andrew J                        DALTON, Sally
              Father

DALTON, Nicholas                        W     M    25 Dec 1853
DALTON, Nicholas                        DALTON, Matilda
              Father
```

```
CHILD'S NAME                               RACE  SEX    BIRTH DATE
FATHER\OWNER                               MOTHER
                INFORMANT
-------------------------------------------------------------------
DALTON, Not Named                          W     M    10 Mar 1860
DALTON, William                            DALTON, Emily
            Samuel Gilbert, Grandfather

DALTON, Not Named                          W     M    27 Apr 1864
DALTON, Joseph R                           DALTON, Nancy
            Father

DALTON, Not Named                          W     F    20 Feb 1864
DALTON, A  J                               DALTON, Sarah
            Father

DALTON, Not Named                          W     M    10 Mar 1865
DALTON, J  W                               DALTON, Sallie
            Father

DALTON, Sarah                              W     F    15 Jan 1865
DALTON, A  J                               DALTON, Sarah
            Father

DALTON, William                            W     M    1 Sept 1860
DLATON, Coleman                            DALTON, Susan
            Father

DANIEL, Elizabeth M                        W     F    10 Dec 1854
DANIEL, James M                            DANIEL E J
            Father

DANIEL, Jeremiah H                         W     M    9 Jan 1857
DANIEL, James                              DANIEL, Elizabeth
            Father

DAVID                                      B/S   M    18 May 1853
CONNER, Ewell J                            Jane
            Owner

DAVID                                      B/S   M    1 Feb 1857
WILSON, Not Given                          Milly
            Jesse Giles, Master

DAVID                                      B/S   M    10 June 1860
ZEGLER, C                                  Matilda
            Master

DAVID                                      B/S   M    3 July 1862
DeHART, Tamar                              Betty
            Mistress

DAVIS, Arminda E                           W     F    14 Aug 1861
DAVIS, Samuel W                            DAVIS, Mary E
            Father
```

45

| CHILD'S NAME | RACE | SEX | BIRTH DATE |
| FATHER\OWNER | | MOTHER | |
INFORMANT			
DAVIS, Huleete	W	F	10 Apr 1860
DAVID, Charles E		DAVIS, Bettie	
Father			
DAVIS, Martha	W	F	20 Aug 1855
DAVIS, Samuel W (Shoemaker)		DAVIS, Mary C	
Father			
DAVIS, Not Named	W	F	4 June 1859
DAVIS, Charles		DAVIS, Ann	
Father			
DAVIS, Not Named	B	F	15 Nov 1865
Unknown		DAVIS, Ann	
A Davis, Neighbor			
DAVIS, Not Named	B	M	1 Oct 1865
Unknown		DAVIS, Mary	
A Davis, Neighbor			
DEAL, Martha A S	W	F	11 July 1862
DEAL, Gabriel		DEAL, Martha	
Father			
DEAL, Mary	W	F	18 Dec 1862
DEAL, William		DEAL, Mary	
Mother			
DEAL, Mary E	W	F	29 Apr 1857
DEAL, Gabriel		DEAL, Martha	
Father			
DEAL, Rhoda	W	F	27 June 1855
DEAL, William		DEAL, Mary	
Father			
DEAL, Sarah R	W	F	7 July 1859
DEAL, Gabriel		DEAL, Martha	
Father			
DEAL, William T	W	M	7 Nov 1860
DEAL, William		DEAL, Mary	
Father			
DEAN, Lydia Adaline	W	F	1 Aug 1854
Not Given		DEAN, Mary	
H H Dean, Grandfather			
DEAN, Margaret V	W	F	28 July 1854
DEAN, James D		DEAN, Easter	
Father			

```
CHILD'S NAME                                    RACE  SEX     BIRTH DATE
FATHER\OWNER                                    MOTHER
              INFORMANT
-----------------------------------------------------------------------
DeHART, Abigail                                 W     F    25 Mar 1861
DeHART, James A                                 DeHART, Lucinda
              Father

DeHART, Averett C                               W     M    11 May 1855
DeHART, Robert                                  DeHART, Elizabeth
              Father

DeHART, C P                                     W     M    29 Mar 1858
DeHART, J H (Clerk)                             DeHART, Mintoria
              Father

DeHART, Charles T                               W     M    26 Mar 1862
DeHART, Thomas                                  DeHART, Lavinia
              Father

DeHART, Elilia                                  W     F     5 Nov 1857
DeHART, Thomas                                  DeHART, Luvenia (?)
              Father

DeHART, Ewell L                                 W     M    22 May 1857
DeHART, Robert                                  DeHART, Elizabeth
              Father

DeHART, George C                                W     M    25 Aug 1862
DeHART, John C (Mechanic)                       DeHART, Milly
              Father

DeHART, J Dallas                                W     M    15 Sept 1862
DeHART, William                                 DeHART, Luisa
              James Dillion, Grandfather

DeHART, James M                                 W     M     8 June 1860
DeHART, Jesse H (Mechanic)                      DeHART, Mintoria
              Father

DeHART, Jefferson D                             W     M    16 June 1862
DeHART, John T                                  DeHART, Mary
              Father

DeHART, Louisa E                                W     F    13 Sept 1855
DeHART, Jesse H (Cabinetmaker)                  DeHART, Mintora
              Father

DeHART, Lucinda E                               W     F    10 June 1857
DeHART, John                                    DeHART, Amanda J
              Father

DeHART, Martha E                                W     F     9 May 1854
DeHART, Gabriel                                 DeHART, Martha
              Father
```

47

```
CHILD'S NAME                              RACE  SEX     BIRTH DATE
FATHER\OWNER                              MOTHER
             INFORMANT
-----------------------------------------------------------------------
DeHART, Martha E                          W     F    19 Mar 1860
DeHART, Paul                              DeHART, Viola J
             Father

DeHART, Mary A                            W     F    10 Aug 1860
DeHART, Robert                            DeHART, Maria
             Father

DeHART, Mary E                            W     F     4 Nov 1858
DeHART, James A                           DeHART, Lucinda
             Father

DeHART, Mary P                            W     F    10 Octo 1860
DeHART, Jno                               DeHART, Nancy
             Father

DeHART, Nancy A                           W     F    25 Aug 1857
DeHART, J W                               DeHART, Rebecca
             Father

DeHART, Nancy S                           W     F    12 May 1858
DeHART, J W                               DeHART, Amanda J
             Father

DeHART, Nathaniel C                       W     M    14 July 1857
DeHART, Gabriel                           DeHART, Martha
             Father

DeHART, Not Named                         W     M    10 May 1859
DeHART, Robert                            DeHART, Elizabeth
             Father

DeHART, Not Named                         W     M    10 Dec 1860
Illegitimate                             DeHART, Sarah
             Gabriel DeHart, Grandfather

DeHART, Not Named                         W     F    15 Jan 1865
Not Given                                 DeHART, Emizette
             Mother

DeHART, Oney                              W     F    15 June 1854
DeHART,William                            DeHART, Exona T
             Father

DeHart, Paul G                            W     M    26 Sept 1859
DeHART, Thomas                            DeHART, Luvenia
             Father

DeHART, Rosabell                          W     F    28 Feb 1854
DeHART, Robert                            DeHART, Elizabeth
             Father
```

```
CHILD'S NAME                                RACE  SEX    BIRTH DATE
FATHER\OWNER                                MOTHER
              INFORMANT
------------------------------------------------------------------------
DeHART, Samuel J                            W    M    15 Jan 1854
DeHART, John                                DeHART, Sarah
              Father

DeHART, Sarah E                             W    F     8 Mar 1859
DeHART, John                                DeHART, Sarah
              Father

DeHART, Thomas                              W    M    29 Oct 1862
DeHART, Paul                                DeHART, Viola J
              Mother

DeHART, Thomas N                            W    M    24 Nov 1857
DeHART, Stephen                             DeHART, Judith
              Father

DeHEART, Catherine                          W    F     4 May 1853
Not Given                                   DeHEART, Elizabeth
              Oney DeHeart, Grandmother

DeHEART, L C                                W    F    23 Mar 1853
DeHEART, J D                                DeHEART, Rebecca
              Father

DeHEART, Thomas M                           W    M    25 Aug 1853
DeHEART, Stephen                            DeHEART, Susannah
              Father

DELPHY ANN                                  B/S  F    23 Nov 1855
SOYARS, James                               Charity
              Master

DEMASIUS                                    B/S  F    17 Mar 1854
BURNETT, Jeremiah                           Harriett
              Owner

DESKINS, Lucy J                             B    F    15 Aug 1865
DESKINS, Willis                             DESKINS, Louisa
              T B Woolwine, Former Master

DEUDDAH                                     B/S  F    24 Sept 1855
VIA, James D                                Druscilla
              Master

DICK                                        B/S  M     5 May 1853
BROWN, Abram                                Not Given
              Owner

DICKERSON, James L                          W    M    21 Sept 1860
DICKERSON, William                          DICKERSON, Elizabeth
              Father

                             49
```

```
CHILD'S NAME                        RACE  SEX    BIRTH DATE
FATHER\OWNER                        MOTHER
               INFORMANT
---------------------------------------------------------------------
DICKERSON, Lucinda J V              W     F      5 Oct 1861
DICKERSON, Leonard                  DICKERSON, Lucinda
               Father

DICKERSON, Not Named                W     F      13 Nov 1858
DICKERSON, Lon                      DICKERSON, Lucinda
               Father

DILLION, Elizabeth A                W     F      1 Dec 1855
DILLION, Carrington J               DILLION, Elizabeth
               Father

DILLION, Ira P                      W     M      3 July 1855
DILLION, James                      DILLION, Lucy
               Father

DILLION, Isaac P                    W     M      26 Mar 1853
DILLION, C J (Micl ?)               DILLION, Elizabeth
               Father

DILLION, James M                    W     M      7 Apr 1858
DILLION, James                      DILLION, Lucy
               Father

DILLION, John S                     W     M      13 Jan 1865
DILLION, Peter (Brickmason)         DILLION, Mary
               Father

DILLION, Joshua J B                 W     M      -- Aug 1855
DILLION, Peter M (Brickmason)       DILLION, Lucinda
               Mother

DILLION, M  N                       B     M      16 Sept 1865
DILLION, William                    DILLION, Martha
               Father

DILLION, M E V                      W     F      8 July 1865
DILLION, Abram                      DILLION, Martha J
               Father

DILLION, Nancy A                    W     F      9 June 1854
DILLION, Jesse                      DILLION, Martha
               Father

DILLION, Not Named                  W     --     16 Apr 1858
DILLION, C J (Mechanic)             DILLION, Elizabeth
               Father

DILLION, Sarah M                    W     F      11 Sept 1854
DILLION, William D                  DILLION, Ann
               Father


                         50
```

```
CHILD'S NAME                              RACE  SEX    BIRTH DATE
FATHER\OWNER                              MOTHER
            INFORMANT
-------------------------------------------------------------------
DILLION, William B                        W     M     14 May 1857
DILLION, William                          DILLION, Mary A
            Father

DIXON, Burwell                            W     M     -- Sept 1857
DIXON, John W                             DIXON, Catherine
            Father

DIXON, Martha E                           W     F     -- July 1860
DIXON, J W (Mechanic)                     DIXON, Catherine
            Father

DOCT                                      B/S   M     10 Aug 1859
MARTIN, Joseph                            Hannah
            A Satterfield, Owner

DODSON, C C                               W     M     15 Jan 1860
DODSON, F W                               DODSON, Sarah
            Father

DODSON, Elisha J                          W     M     27 June 1861
DODSON, F  W                              DODSON, Sarah
            Father

DODSON, Frances A V                       W     F     28 Aug 1854
DODSON, E J                               DODSON, Nancy M
            Mother

DODSON, Joel H                            W     M     9 Sept 1854
DODSON, Ted William                       DODSON, Sally
            Judith Dodson, Grandmother

DODSON, Louiseana R                       W     F     28 Oct 1854
DODSON, Thomas                            DODSON, Mary
            Father

DODSON, Not Named (Born Dead)             W     M     -- -- 1853
DODSON, Fred William                      DODSON, Sarah
            Father

DOOLEY, Angeline                          W     F     -- May 1853
DOOLEY, Alfred                            DOOLEY, Angeline
            Father

DOOLEY, Not Named                         W     F     -- Sept 1857
DOOLEY, Alfred                            DOOLEY, Avaline
            Father

DOSS, Ann                                 W     F     17 June 1860
DOSS, Joel                                DOSS, Rachael
            Father


                        51
```

```
CHILD'S NAME                              RACE  SEX    BIRTH DATE
FATHER\OWNER                              MOTHER
              INFORMANT
-----------------------------------------------------------------------
DOSS, Mary V                              W      F    19 May 1862
DOSS, Joel A                              DOSS, Rachel A
              Father

DUGLASS                                   B/S    M    30 Aug 1860
CRITZ, J P                                Elizabeth
              Master

DUNCAN, Henderson                         W      M    14 June 1853
None Given                                DUNCAN, Martha J
              Herman Duncan, Grandfather

DUNCAN, John H                            W      M    24 Jan 1853
DUNCAN, William (Blacksmith)              DUNCAN, Purlina
              Father

DUNCAN, Stacey M                          W      F    10 Mar 1854
DUNCAN, Richard                           DUNCAN, Catherine
              Father

DURHAM, Alfred T                          W      M    30 May 1862
DURHAM, A  M                              DURHAM, Sarah
              Father

DURHAM, Mareannah                         W      F    15 Aug 1855
DURHAM, William (Blacksmith)              DURHAM, Pauline
              Father

DURHAM, Mary F                            W      F     9 Dec 1853
DURHAM, James N                           DURHAM, Eliza
              Father

EANES, Joshua H                           W      M    12 Dec 1862
EANES, George W                           EANES, Mary P
              Father

EANES, Louisa A                           W      F    25 Oct 1855
EANES, Raleigh (Blacksmith)               EANES, Nancy
              Father

EANES, Not Named                          W      F     6 Sept 1854
EANES, Joseph                             EANES, Martha E
              Father

EANES, Not Named                          W      M    17 Oct 1854
EANES, Silas W                            EAMES, Nancy L
              Father

EANES, Sarah A F                          W      F    -- Apr 1854
EANES, George (Miller)                    EANES, May P
              Catherine Spencer, Neighbor
```

```
CHILD'S NAME                          RACE  SEX     BIRTH DATE
FATHER\OWNER                          MOTHER
            INFORMANT
------------------------------------------------------------------------
EANS, R L                             W     M    30 Oct 1858
EANS, G W                             EANS, Mary P
            Father

EARLY                                 B/S   M    -- Mar 1861
REYNOLDS, H  W                        Eliza
            Owner

EAST, Almera                          W     F    18 Apr 1853
EAST, William A                       EAST, Elizabeth
            Father

EAST, John                            W     M    -- Feb 1859
EAST, William                         EAST, Elizabeth
            Father

EAST, Richard                         W     M     1 Apr 1855
EAST, William                         EAST, Elizabeth
            Father

EATON, John (Twin)                    W     M     1 Apr 1862
EATON, A  A                           EATON, Margaret
            Father

EATON, Kelly (Twin)                   W     M     1 Apr 1862
EATON, A  A                           EATON, Margaret
            Father

ED                                    B/S   M    10 June 1859
REYNOLDS, H W                         Milly
            Owner

ED                                    B/S   M     2 Aug 1860
FLIPPIN, Jno L                        Mary
            Master

EDENS, Mentora  E                     W     F     4 Apr 1859
EDENS, Calab                          EDENS, Bashaba
            Father

EDES, Henry Awise                     W     M    15 May 1855
EDES, Winston                         EDES, Ellen
            Father

EDES, Susan C                         W     F    29 Sept 1853
EDES, Winston                         EDES, Elender
            Father

EDIE                                  B/S   F     6 Mar 1859
SCALES, Mrs                           Elizabeth
            Owner
```

```
CHILD'S NAME                          RACE  SEX    BIRTH DATE
FATHER\OWNER                          MOTHER
              INFORMANT
-----------------------------------------------------------------------
EDINS, Not Named                      W     F    29 Dec 1855
EDINS, Andres J                       EDINS, Liatira
              Father

EDINS, Susan E                        W     F    20 July 1853
EDINS, Claiborne                      EDINS, Bushaley
              Father

EDINS, Vilky Texas                    W     F    29 Dec 1854
EDINS, Claiborne                      EDINS, Bashaba
              Father

EDINS, William C                      W     M    -- May 1857
EDINS, H H                            EDINS, Charity
              Father

EDITH                                 B/S   F    5 June 1859
VIA, C A                              Harriette
              James C Moir, Guardian

EDMUND                                B/S   M    1 Aug 1854
PENN, Mrs Susan                       Not Given
              Mistress

EDMUND                                B/S   M    -- Mar 1857
WILSON, Not Given                     Martha
              Jesse Giles, Master

EDMUND                                B/S   M    26 Nov 1859_
WILSON, Samuel                        Sophia
              Jesse Giles, Overseer

EDWARD                                B/S   M    -- May 1854
CONNER, G R                           Amanda
              Owner

EDWARDS, America                      W     F    -- June 1859
EDWARDS, George Z                     EDWARDS, Sarah
              Father

EDWARDS, James Franklin               W     M    22 Feb 1854
EDWARDS, George Z                     EDWARDS, Sally
              Father

EDWARDS, Jefferson Davis              W     M    20 Dec 1861
EDWARDS, George Z                     EDWARDS, Sally
              Father

EDWARDS, Josephine C                  W     F    20 June 1857
EDWARDS, Joseph H                     EDWARDS, Martha S
              Father
```

54

```
CHILD'S NAME                           RACE  SEX    BIRTH DATE
FATHER\OWNER                           MOTHER
              INFORMANT
-----------------------------------------------------------------------
EDWARDS, Mary E                        W     F    6 Mar 1854
EDWARDS, Levi                          EDWARDS, Charity
              Father

EDWARDS, Nancy Allice                  W     F    17 Nov 1854
EDWARDS, Joseph H                      EDWARDS, Martha S
              Father

EDWARDS, Not Named                     W     M    10 Mar 1859
EDWARDS, George Z                      EDWARDS, Sally
              Father

EDWARDS, Rhoda S                       W     F    23 Apr 1854
EDWARDS, A V                           EDWARDS, Ruthe E
              Father

EDWARDS, Susannah                      W     F    8 Apr 1854
EDWARDS, Isaac                         EDWARDS, Nancy
              Father

EFFEON                                 B/S   F    -- Feb 1854?
HAIRSTON, S W                          Matilda
              Master

ELDRIDGE                               B/S   M    10 July 1855
REYNOLDS, Thomas                       Mariah
              Owner

ELENDER                                B/S   F    24 Apr 1861
CANNADAY, William                      Mary
              Master

ELGIN, Not Named                       W     M    12 May 1858
ELGIN, Alfred                          ELGIN, America
              Father

ELGIN, Sarah E                         W     F    -- July 1853
ELGIN, Alfred                          ELGIN, America M
              Father

ELGIN, William A                       W     M    3 Jan 1862
ELGIN, Alfred                          ELGIN, America M
              Father

ELIS, George W                         W     M    28 July 1860
ELIS, Winston                          ELIS, Ellen
              fATHER

ELIZA                                  B/S   F    5 Feb 1853
PRUNTY, John                           Mary
              Owner
```

55

CHILD'S NAME FATHER\OWNER INFORMANT	RACE SEX MOTHER	BIRTH DATE
ELIZA PENN, Clark Owner	B/S F Not Given	10 May 1854
ELIZA CLARK, A B Master	B/S F Judy	-- June 1857
ELIZA SOYARS, James Master	B/S F Charity	4 June 1859
ELIZA TAYLOR, James A E B Turner, Master	B/S F Sydney	-- Aug 1860
ELIZA ANN SMITH, Sarah Mistress	B/S F Not Given	19 Apr 1854
ELIZABETH PENN, Thomas J Owner	B/S F Not Given	-- July 1855
ELIZABETH PARKER, Smith Master	B/S F Mary Jane	17 Apr 1857
ELIZABETH HAIRSTON, S W Master	B/S F Edia	-- Mar 1858
ELIZABETH HUGHES, Mat Master	B/S F Hannah	5 June 1860
ELIZABETH COCKRAM, John B William Canaday, Master	B/S F Edia	21 Sept 1860
ELIZABETH (Twin) ROBERTSON, James R Master	B/S F Ruth	20 May 1850
ELIZABETH A WOOLWINE, Thomas B Master	B/S F Frances	2 Feb 1859
ELLEN CLARK, Robert M Owner	B/S F Martha	27 Sept 1853

CHILD'S NAME FATHER\OWNER INFORMANT	RACE	SEX	BIRTH DATE MOTHER
ELLEN FRANCE, Joseph Owner	B/S Sally	F	6 Sept 1854
ELLEN STAPLES, A, Deceased Claiborne Mills, Overseer	B/S America	F	-- -- 1855
ELLEN STUART, Mrs E Owner	B/S Lucy	F	10 Nov 1858
ELLEN LANGHORNE, James S Master	B/S Lucy	F	30 June 1862
ELLEN A WOOLWINE, Thomas B Master	B/S Sarah	F	-- June 1860
ELLICK WILSON, Samuel P Jesse M Giles, Overseer	B/S Molly	M	-- Oct 1855
ELUSIA CONNER, John Master	B/S Jenny	F	3 Aug 1861
EMALINE CRITZ, William Owner	B/S Eliza	F	6 May 1859
EMANDA PRUNTY, John Master	B/S Dinah	F	2 June 1855
EMBERSON, Nancy P EMBERSON, Jabez Father	W EMBERSON, Ruth	F	15 July 1857
EMER PENN, Jackson Master	B/S Patty	F	-- June 1862
EMILY REYNOLDS, Harden W Owner	B/S Celia	F	1 Mar 1855
EMILY SMITH, Sarah Mistress	B/S Susan	F	-- Dec 1857

```
CHILD'S NAME                              RACE  SEX    BIRTH DATE
FATHER\OWNER                              MOTHER
             INFORMANT
-------------------------------------------------------------------------
EMILY                                     W/S   F    20 Feb 1857
PENN, Jefferson                           Susan
             Master

EMILY JANE                                B/S   F    11 Jan 1859
ZEGLER, Richard                           Janie
             Owner

EMMA                                      B/S   F     1 Aug 1854
PENN, Mrs Susan                           Not Given
             Mistress

EMMERSON, John W                          W     M     6 Feb 1862
EMMERSON, Wade A                          EMMERSON, Esther
             Father

EMMERSON, Louisa                          W     F    27 Aug 1860
EMMERSON, J T                             EMMERSON, Ruth
             Father

EMMERSON, Mary                            W     F    27 Oct 1854
EMMERSON, Jabez                           EMMERSON, Ruth
             Father

EMMERSON, Susan C                         W     F     4 June 1858
EMMERSON, W A                             EMMERSON, Esther J
             Father

EPHY                                      B/S   F    -- May 1859
ANGLIN, Philip                            Susan
             owner

EPPERSON, Albert J                        W     M    17 Aug 1855
EPPERSON, John W                          EPPERSON, Rhoda
             Father

EPPERSON, James N                         W     M    18 Oct 1862
EPPERSON, Nick                            EPPERSON, E  J
             James Barnard, Grandfather

EPPERSON, Jane                            W     F    20 Sept 1860
EPPERSON, Nicholas                        EPPERSON, Jane
             Father

EPPERSON, Not Named                       W     M    15 Dec 1853
EPPERSON, John                            EPPERSON, Rhoda T
             Father

ERVIN, Not Named                          B     F     9 July 1865
ERVIN, Winston                            ERVIN, Catherine
             H D Carter, Neighbor


                          58
```

CHILD'S NAME FATHER\OWNER INFORMANT	RACE SEX BIRTH DATE MOTHER
FAIN, Davis A FAIN, William Father	W M 21 July 1854 FAIN, Temperance
FAIN, Not Named FAIN, Henry Father	W M -- -- 1855 FAIN, Nancy
FAIN, Not Named FAIN, Henry Father	W F 10 Oct 1860_ FAIN, Nancy
FALKNER HYLTON, Gabriel Master	B/S M 16 Sept 1854 Lettica
FANNIE SCALES, Ab Owner	B/S F 25 Apr 1859 Lelny
FANNIE KING, B L Owner	B/S F 15 Oct 1859 Maritha
FANNY PENN, Mrs Susan Mistress	B/S F 1 Aug 1854 Not Given
FANNY PENN, George W Master	B/S F -- Sept 1862 Fanny
FANNY STAPLES, William Master	B/S F -- Jan 1862 Ann
FARIS, Augustin W FARIS, Archibald Father	W M 5 Oct 1853 FARIS, Mary
FARIS, Francis FARIS, King H Father	W F 31 Jan 1853 FARIS, Malinda F
FARIS, Louisa FARIS, William Father	W F 1 Oct 1859 FARIS, Temperance
FARMER, Mary E FARMER, Allen Father	W F 29 May 1853 FARMER, Elizabeth

```
CHILD'S NAME                             RACE  SEX    BIRTH DATE
FATHER\OWNER                             MOTHER
          INFORMANT
------------------------------------------------------------------------
FERGUSON, Charles T (Born Franklin Co)    W    M    -- Nov 1860
FERGUSON, S H                            FERGUSON, Catherine
          Father

FERGUSON, James W                         W    M    14 Apr 1855
FERGUSON, Caleb H                        FERGUSON, Frances
          Father

FERGUSON, L B T                           W    M    14 Sept 1858
FERGUSON, James P                        FERGUSON, Ruth
          Father

FERGUSON, Martha R                        W    F    12 Aug 1862
FERGUSON, James P                        FERGUSON, Ruth
          Father

FERGUSON, Mary A D F                      W    F    27 Apr 1854
FERGUSON, James                          FERGUSON, Ruth
          Mother

FERGUSON, Rebecca                         W    F     2 July 1865
FERGUSON, James P (Miller)               FERGUSON, Ruth
          Father

FERGUSON, William C                       W    M    11 May 1865
FERGUSON, C  H                           FERGUSON, Frances
          Father

FINNEY, John J                            W    M    26 Oct 1857
FINNEY, Marshall                         FINNEY, Mary
          Father

FINNEY, Louise R                          W    F     6 July 1853
FINNEY, Peter                            FINNEY, Sarah
          Father

FINNEY, Nancy V                           W    F     4 Nov 1859
FINNEY, P H                              FINNEY, P H
          Father

FINNEY, Peter W                           W    M    19 Mar 1857
FINNEY, Peter                            FINNEY, Sarah
          Father

FINNEY, Sarah E                           W    F     1 July 1855
FINNEY, Peter                            FINNEY, Sarah
          Father

FINNEY, William                           W    M     8 Nov 1862
FINNEY, William                          FINNEY, Ruth
          Father
```

```
CHILD'S NAME                                    RACE  SEX    BIRTH DATE
FATHER\OWNER                                    MOTHER
             INFORMANT
-----------------------------------------------------------------------
FITZGERALD, William Montague                    W     M    5 Sept 1860
FITZGERALD, James                               FITZGERALD, Mary A
             Father

FLEMING, Jane                                   W     F    1 Apr 1857
FLEMING, William                                FLEMING, Eliza Ann
             Father

FLEMING, Not Named                              W     F     -- June 1859
FLEMING, William                                FLEMING, Eliza
             Father

FLEMING, Susan M                                W     F    7 June 1855
FLEMING, William H                              FLEMING, Eliza
             Father

FLIPPIN, John A                                 W     M    11 May 1853
FLIPPIN, Raleigh W                              FLIPPIN, Earsley
             Father

FLIPPIN, Mildred E                              W     F    28 Oct 1855
FLIPPIN, R W                                    FLIPPIN, Ursula
             Father

FLORA                                           B/S   F    19 Sept 1855
LANGHORNE, James S                              Not Given
             Master

FLORA                                           B/S   F    8 May 1860
SMYTH, D W                                      Ruth
             Master

FLORA                                           B/S   F     -- June 1862
PENN, George W                                  Ann
             Master

FLORA                                           B/S   F    1 June 1854
PENN, Mrs Susan                                 Not Given
             Mistress

FLORENCE                                        B/S   F    16 May 1853
SCALES, Absalom                                 Ester
             Caroline Scales, Wife of Owner

FLOYD, Mary A                                   W     F    10 Sept 1861
FLOYD; B H                                      FLOYD, Jane
             Father

FOLEY, Ellen M                                  W     F     -- July 1854
FOLEY, Bailey                                   FOLEY, Kizzeah
             Mother
```

```
CHILD'S NAME                         RACE  SEX    BIRTH DATE
FATHER\OWNER                         MOTHER
               INFORMANT
---------------------------------------------------------------------
FOLEY, Ellusea                       W     F    25 Nov 1859
FOLEY, Stephen                       FOLEY, Nancy J
               Father

FOLEY, Elvira B                      W     F    -- June 1858
FOLEY, Stephen                       FOLEY, Nancy J Wood
               Father

FOLEY, G W                           W     M    -- -- 1853
FOLEY, James A                       FOLEY, Lalitia
               Foley

FOLEY, James L                       W     M    26 Mar 1853
FOLEY, Andrew J                      FOLEY, Lucinda
               Father

FOLEY, James P                       W     M    9 Mar 1859
FOLEY, James M                       FOLEY, Lucinda
               Father

FOLEY, Jeremiah                      W     M    6 Feb 1862
FOLEY, A  J                          FOLEY, Nancy J
               Father

FOLEY, Judith A                      W     F    11 May 1857
FOLEY, James A                       FOLEY, Letia
               Father

FOLEY, Judith E                      W     F    6 July 1854
FOLEY, Samuel J                      FOLEY, Avaline
               Father

FOLEY, Liber P                       W     M    31 Dec 1860
FOLEY, James M                       FOLEY, Lucinda
               Father

FOLEY, Louisa E                      W     F    1 Mar 1857
FOLEY, James                         FOLEY, Lucinda
               Father

FOLEY, Lucinda                       W     F    11 Mar 1858
FOLEY, Jackson                       FOLEY, Lucinda
               Father

FOLEY, Luella                        W     F    8 June 1862
FOLEY, Samuel J                      FOLEY, Emnera
               Father

FOLEY, Not Named                     W     M    -- Dec 1855
FOLEY, A J                           FOLEY, Lucinda
               Father
```

```
CHILD'S NAME                              RACE  SEX     BIRTH DATE
FATHER\OWNER                              MOTHER
            INFORMANT
-----------------------------------------------------------------------
FOLEY, Not Named                          W     M    -- Oct 1857
FOLEY, Samuel                             FOLEY, Avaline
            Father

FOLEY, Not Named                          W     M    7 Jan 1859
FOLEY, S J                                FOLEY, Emily E
            Father

FOLEY, Okanah L                           W     F    8 Dec 1865
FOLEY, James M                            FOLEY, Lucinda
            Father

FOLEY, P C                                W     M    11 Apr 1860
FOLEY, James H                            FOLEY, Letitia
            Father

FOLEY, Sarah E                            W     F    9 Sept 1855
FOLEY, James                              FOLEY, Lucinda
            Father

FOLEY, William R                          B     M    -- June 1859
Illegitimate                              FOLEY, Jane
            Mother

FOREST, Not Named                         W     M    21 Oct 1858
FOREST, James                             FOREST, Mary Ann
            Father

FOREST, Sandy F                           W     M    -- Apr 1857
FOREST, Joseph                            FOREST, Mary
            Father

FORTIN                                    B/S   M    -- Oct 1855
HYLTON, George W                          Susan
            Owner

FOSTER, James                             W     M    30 Sept 1860
FOSTER, A                                 FOSTER, Jane
            Father

FOSTER, L G                               W     F    -- --- 1862
Illegitimate                              FOSTER, Mary
            Mary Stanley, Grandmother

FOSTER, Susan                             W     F    -- Sept 1857
FOSTER, Abram                             FOSTER, Jane
            Father

FOSTER, William M                         W     M    26 Apr 1853
FOSTER, Russell A                         FOSTER, Lucinda J
            Father
```

63

CHILD'S NAME FATHER\OWNER	RACE	SEX	BIRTH DATE
INFORMANT	MOTHER		

CHILD'S NAME FATHER\OWNER INFORMANT	RACE	SEX	BIRTH DATE / MOTHER
FRANCES PENN, Thomas J Owner	B/S	F	15 July 1853 Mariah
FRANCES STUART, Mrs Elizabeth L Owner	B/S	F	25 June 1854 Catherine
FRANCES PENN, Jackson Owner	B/S	F	4 Oct 1854 Margaret
FRANCES PENN, Thomas Master	B/S	F	4 Oct 1855 Not Given
FRANCES PENN, Jefferson Master	B/S	F	-- Oct 1857 Eliza
FRANCES, Joseph FRANCES, William M Father	W	M	10 Feb 1864 FRANCES, Susan
FRANCESA CRITZ, Gabriel Owner	B/S	F	10 Mar 1859 Dinah
FRANCIS PENN, Thomas Master	B/S	F	-- Mar 1854 Not Given
FRANCIS, John F FRANCIS, William M Father	W	M	10 Mar 1858 FRANCIS, Susan
FRANK ANGLIN, Phillip Owner	B/S	M	12 Dec 1854 P Sukey
FRANK PENN, Susan Owner	B/S	M	-- Dec 1859 Polly
FRANK REYNOLDS, H W Owner	B/S	M	6 Aug 1859 Kittie
FRANK FLIPPIN, Jno L Master	B/S	M	14 Feb 1860 Juda

```
CHILD'S NAME                          RACE  SEX     BIRTH DATE
FATHER\OWNER                          MOTHER
            INFORMANT
--------------------------------------------------------------------
FRANK                                 B/S   M    -- May 1857
PENN, Jefferson                       Lynda
            Master

FRANK PIERCE                          B/S   M    11 Apr 1853
PENN, Clark                           Betty
            Master

FRANKLIN, Julia M E                   W     F     18 Nov 1854_
FRANKLIN, M D L                       FRANKLIN, Martha A
            Father

FRANKLIN, Mary A                      W     F     11 Aug 1853
FRANKLIN, D F                         FRANKLIN, Martha A Taylor
            Mother

FRANS, Sarah                          B     F     25 July 1865
FRANS, Alfred                         FRANS, Louisa
            Jos. Frans, Former Master

FRASHURE, Virginia M                  W     F     8 Feb 1862
FRASHURE, James W (Carpenter)         FRASHURE, Sabrina
            Mother

FRAYSER, John M  B                    W     M     28 Aug 1862
FRAYSER, R  B (Lawyer)                FRAYSER, Louisa M
            Father

FREEMAN, Not Named                    W     F     15 Apr 1862
FREEMAN, A  J                         FREEMAN, Evina
            Father

FREEMAN, William                      W     M     10 July 1860
FREEMAN, Jesse                        FREEMAN, Sallie
            Father

FRY, James T                          W     M     11 Apr 1860
FRY, Henry                            FRY, Elizabeth
            fATHER

FRY, Martha                           W     F     17 May 1853
FRY, William                          FRY, Patty
            Father

FRY, Not Named                        W     M     13 Oct 1854
FRY, John (Blacksmith)                FRY, Celia
            Father

FRY, Not Named                        W     F     16 Apr 1855
FRY, William                          FRY, Polly
            Father
```

CHILD'S NAME FATHER\OWNER INFORMANT	RACE SEX BIRTH DATE MOTHER
FRY, Thomas FRY, William Father	W M 8 Apr 1857 FRY, Polly
FULCHER, Catherine F FULCHER, John Father	W F 25 Jan 1861 FULCHER, Sallie A
FULCHER, Elbert FULCHER, Ed Father	W M 25 Mar 1859 FULCHER, Catherine
FULCHER, Emily F FULCHER, Hardin Father	W F -- July 1862 FULCHER, Luvenia
FULCHER, George E FULCHER, Edward Jr Father	W M 23 Dec 1861 FULCHER, Emerie C
FULCHER, George L W FULCHER, Harden Father	W M -- Aug 1855 FULCHER, Luvenia
FULCHER, Henry FULCHER, John Father	W M -- Dec 1857 FULCHER, Sarah
FULCHER, James A FULCHER, Gabriel F Father	W M 22 Sept 1855 FULCHER, Sarah A E
FULCHER, Mary E FULCHER, Gabriel Father	W F 5 June 1860 FULCHER, Sarah E
FULCHER, Mary Lincoln FULCHER, John Father	W F 4 May 1864 FULCHER, Sarah A
FULCHER, Not Named FULCHER, Philip Father	W F 31 Aug 1854 FULCHER, June
FULCHER, Sarah G FULCHER, John Father	W F 10 Nov 1855 FULCHER, Sarah A
FULCHER, Susan FULCHER, S Father	W F 10 Oct 1859 FULCHER, Sarah

```
CHILD'S NAME                              RACE  SEX    BIRTH DATE
FATHER\OWNER                              MOTHER
            INFORMANT
-----------------------------------------------------------------------
FULCHER, Thomas G                         W    M    23 Dec 1864
FULCHER, Edmond Jr                        FULCHER, Emily C
            Father

FULCHER, Thomas Jefferson                 W    M     1 July 1857
FULCHER, Hardin                           FULCHER, Mary
            Father

FULCHER, Victoria A                       W    F     5 July 1853
FULCHER, Hardin (Carpenter)               FULCHER, Luvenia
            Father

GABRIEL                                   B/S  M    28 Nov 1854
CLARK, Thomas M                           Not Given
            Master

GABRIEL                                   B/S  M    13 Jan 1859
HYLTON, G                                 Sally
            Owner

GALEN                                     B/S  M    16 Jan 1860
HYLTON, G                                 Percilla
            Master

GARDNER, Luvenia                          W    F    27 Feb 1859
GARDNER, Isaac                            GARDNER, Luvenia
            Father

GARDNER, Not Named                        W    M    10 Sept 1853
GARDNER, Isaac                            GARDNER, Lavenia
            Father

GATES, Charles                            W    M     3 Aug 1859
GATES, William                            GATES, Selpha
            Father

GATES, Elis V                             W    M     7 Nov 1865
GATES, R  D                               GATES, Mary A
            Father

GATES, Francis                            W    M     2 Oct 1859
GATES, John W                             GATES, Inamona
            Father

GATES, Lucy A (Born Franklin Co)          W    F    13 May 1855
GATES, William B                          GATES, Zelpha
            Father

GATES, William                            B    M    29 Mar 1865
Unknown                                   GATES, Ceily
            John Gates, Neighbor
```

```
CHILD'S NAME                                RACE  SEX    BIRTH DATE
FATHER\OWNER                                MOTHER
              INFORMANT
------------------------------------------------------------------------

GATEWOOD, George W                          W     M    -- Sept 1860
GATEWOOD, William                           GATEWOOD, Julia
              Father

GATEWOOD, Robert                            W     M    1 Apr 1857
GATEWOOD, M                                 GATEWOOD, Jane
              Father

GEORGE                                      B/S   M    -- -- 1853
HAIRSTON, S W                               Not Given
              Owner

GEORGE                                      B/S   M    9 Jan 1854
ADAMS, Joshua                               Lucy
              Owner

GEORGE                                      B/S   M    -- June 1855
TURNER, Elkanah B                           Not Given
              Master

GEORGE                                      B/S   M    -- July 1857
PENDLETON, John                             Linda
              John Lackey, Master

GEORGE                                      B/S   M    1 June 1860
KING, George                                Mary
              Master

GEORGE                                      B/S   M    1 Mar 1862
TATUM, John G                               Caroline
              Master

GEORGE                                      B/S   M    13 Dec 1862
PENN, Peter L                               Sally Ann
              Master

GEORGE                                      B/S   M    -- -- 1854
HAIRSTON, Samuel W                          Edy
              Owner

GEORGE                                      B/S   M    -- Aug 1859
PARKER, Smith                               Mary Jane
              Master

GEORGE                                      B/S   M    10 Dec 1862
MOIR, James C                               Kitty
              Master

GERMAN                                      B/S   M    1 June 1857
JARROTT, Adda L                             Nancy
              Master


                              68
```

```
CHILD'S NAME                          RACE  SEX    BIRTH DATE
FATHER\OWNER                          MOTHER
            INFORMANT
------------------------------------------------------------------------
GIDEON                                B/S    M    10 Jan 1862
TURNER, John                          Susan
            Master

GIGGIN                                B/S    M    1 May 1859
TURNER, C                             Susan
            Master

GILBERT, Henry D                      W      M    10 July 1865
Not Given                             GILBERT, Malinda
            Mother

GILBERT, James Monroe                 W      M    12 Nov 1853
GILBERT, George W                     GILBERT, Milly A
            Father

GILBERT, James W                      W      M    24 Nov 1853
GILBERT, John R                       GILBERT, Valinchea Rogers
            Father

GILBERT, Lucinda F                    W      F    27 Aug 1861
GILBERT, John                         GILBERT, Jane
            Father

GILBERT, Martha F                     W      F    28 Apr 1860
GILBERT, J F                          GILBERT, Elizabeth
            Father

GILBERT, Mary                         W      F    30 Sept 1858
GILBERT, Robert                       GILBERT, Martha Jane
            Father

GILBERT, Not Named                    W      M    18 Dec 1860
GILBERT, J R                          GILBERT, Velentia
            Father

GILBERT, Richard                      W      M    -- July 1859
GILBERT, John R                       GILBERT, Verlenetta
            Father

GILBERT, Robert M                     W      M    2 Oct 1859
GILBERT, John                         GILBERT, Jane
            Father

GILBERT, S G                          W      M    23 July 1865
GILBERT, Robert                       GILBERT, Martha J
            Father

GILBERT, Samuel G                     W      M    30 Sept 1858
GILBERT, P                            GILBERT, Malinda
            Father

                           69
```

```
CHILD'S NAME                              RACE  SEX    BIRTH DATE
FATHER\OWNER                              MOTHER
            INFORMANT
-------------------------------------------------------------------
GILBERT, Thomas F                         W     M    6 Aug 1859
GILBERT, Samuel                           GILBERT, America
            Father

GILBERT, Thomas J                         W     M    17 June 1862
GILBERT, Penn                             GILBERT, Mary
            Mother

GILL, Sarah Ann                           ?     F    2 Aug 1862
GILL, Rebecca                             Milly
            Mistress

GILLEY, Richard S                         W     M    5 July 1853
GILLEY, Fountain                          GILLEY, Jane
            Father

GILLY, Martha Susan                       W     F    15 Oct 1854
GILLY, William (Miller)                   GILLY, Luvinia
            Father

GILLY, William B                          W     M    15 July 1862
GILLY, E F                                GILLY, Jane
            Nancy Hopkins, Grandmother

GILSPIN, Martha F                         W     F    24 Aug 1862
Not Given                                 GILSPEN, Mary
            Mother

GIVIN, William R                          W     M    26 Sept 1862
GIVIN, William R                          GIVIN, Sarah A
            Phebe Hiatt, Grandmother

GOADES, John                              W     M    15 June 1864
GOADES, William                           GOADES, Letty M
            Father

GOARD, Emily F                            W     F    -- June 1855
GOARD, Jesse                              GOARD, Elizabeth
            Fathr

GOARD, John W                             W     M    27 June 1865
GOARD, William                            GOARD, Letty
            Father

GOARD, Lucinda                            W     F    13 Oct 1859
GOARD, William                            GOARD, Letty M
            Father

GOARD, Not Named                          W     F    6 Nov 1860
GOARD, William                            GOARD, Bettie
            Father
```

CHILD'S NAME FATHER\OWNER INFORMANT	RACE SEX BIRTH DATE MOTHER
GOFF, Not Named GOFF, Charles Father	W M 10 Oct 1865 GOFF, Mary A
GOING, Assina GOING, Feul (?) Father	W F 25 Sept 1855 GOING, Cyntha
GOING, Coleman GOING, Allen Father	W M 8 Mar 1858 GOING, Patsey
GOING, Not Named GOING, Henry Father	W M 10 Nov 1857 GOING, Elizabeth
GOINGS, John H GOINGS, William H Father	W M 3 Feb 1854 GOINGS, Mary
GOINGS, Rebecca Jane GOINGS, George Father	W F 17 Dec 1854 GOINGS, Sally
GOINGS, Zachery GOINGS, Ewell Father	W M 30 Apr 1854 GOINGS, Rose
GORD, Martha J GORD, William Father	W F 1 Dec 1861 GORD, Letha
GRADY, Jestine GRADY, William Father	W F 11 Feb 1859 GRADY, Elizabeth
GRADY, Rebecca J GRADY, William Father	W F 13 Feb 1860 GRADY, Eliza Ann
GRAVES WILSON, Samuel P Jesse Giles, Overseer	B/S M 10 Aug 1853 Martha
GRAY, John James GRAY, William W Father	W M -- -- 1855 GRAY, Susan
GRAY, Not Named Unknown John F Gray, Neighbor	B M 10 Sept 1865 GRAY, Ann

```
CHILD'S NAME                          RACE SEX    BIRTH DATE
FATHER\OWNER                          MOTHER
            INFORMANT
--------------------------------------------------------------------
GRAY, Virginia                        W    F    9 Oct 1865
GRAY, John F                          GRAY, Mary A
            Father

GRAYHAM, Aaron                        W    M    13 Mar 1854
GRAYHAM, James                        GRAYHAM, Rebecca
            Father

GREEN                                 B/S  M    22 July 1853
CLARK, Thomas M                       Set
            Owner

GREEN                                 B/S  M    19 June 1853
YOUNG, William D                      Betsy
            Master

GREEN                                 B/S  M    -- May 1854
VIA, James Sr                         Alsey
            owner

GREEN                                 B/S  M    -- Mar 1855
ROSS, Daniel                          Hannah
            Master

GREEN                                 B/S  M    -- Aug 1862
PENN, Mary                            Margaret
            G W Penn for Mary, Mistress

GREEN                                 B/S  M    -- Dec 1862
WRIGHT, John N                        Agness
            Master

GREENWOOD, Alice                      W    F    21 Mar 1865
GREENWOOD, Samuel                     GREENWOOD,Queen Elizabeth
            Father

GREENWOOD, Aron Quinn                 W    M    25 Oct 1854
GREENWOOD, Redman                     GREENWOOD, Mary I
            Father

GREENWOOD, Mary Permelia              W    F    8 Jan 1860
GREENWOOD, Samuel                     GREENWOOD, Elizabeth
            Father

GREENWOOD, Susannah E                 W    F    28 May 1853
GREENWOOD, Samuel                     GREENWOOD, Roqueen E
            Father

GRIFFITH, Amanda F                    W    F    2 Apr 1859
GRIFFITH, Elijah                      GRIFFITH, Susan
            Father
```

```
CHILD'S NAME                              RACE  SEX    BIRTH DATE
FATHER\OWNER                              MOTHER
            INFORMANT
------------------------------------------------------------------------
GRIFFITH, Calub                           W     M    4 June 1861
GRIFFITH, David                           GRIFFITH, Elizabeth
            Father

GRIFFITH, Charles                         W     M    20 Dec 1865
GRIFFITH, Tyler                           GRIFFITH, Alemancy
            Mother

GRIFFITH, Columbia                        W     F    -- June 1855
GRIFFITH, David                           GRIFFITH, Elizabeth
            Father

GRIFFITH, Elijah J                        W     M    3 July 1854
GRIFFITH, John C (Mechanic)               GRIFFITH, Martha
            Father

GRIFFITH, Martha                          W     F    25 Nov 1859
GRIFFITH, David                           GRIFFITH, Elizabeth
            Father

GRIFFITH, Martha A                        W     F    21 July 1859
GRIFFITH, J C (Mechanic)                  GRIFFITH, Martha
            Father

GRIFFITH, Mary Alice                      W     F    22 Mar 1865
GRIFFITH, J H                             GRIFFITH, Nancy J
            Father

GRIFFITH, not Named                       W     M    -- June 1858
GRIFFITH, J C (Mechanic)                  GRIFFITH, Martha
            Father

GRIFFITH, Not Named (Ohio)                W     M    5 Dec 1865
GRIFFITH, Mesheck T                       GRIFFITH, Lucy J
            Father

GUINN, Lorenso Doss                       W     M    15 Sept 1853
None Given                                GUINN, Elizabeth
                  Catherine Ayers, Neighbor

GUINN, Not Named                          W     M    5 Mar 1853
GUINN, James                              GUINN, Catherine
            Father

GUINN, Sally Ann                          W     F    27 Mar 1854
GUINN, James                              GUINN, Cathrine
            Father

GUNNEL, Martha                            W     F    17 Apr 1857
GUNNEL, James                             GUNNEL, Jane
            Father
```

73

```
CHILD'S NAME                          RACE  SEX    BIRTH DATE
FATHER\OWNER                          MOTHER
              INFORMANT
-----------------------------------------------------------------------
GUNNELL, Beauregard                   W     M     9 Aug 1861
GUNNELL, James                        GUNNELL, Jane
              Father

GUNNELL, Rufus A                      W     M    23 Oct 1854
GUNNELL, James                        GUNNELL, Jane
              Father

GUNTER, Mary E                        W     F     1 July 1857
GUNTER, B L                           GUNTER, Mary E
              Father

GUNTER, Nancy H                       W     F    15 Aug 1853
GUNTER, Beverly L                     GUNTER, Mary E
              Father

GUNTER, Thomas J                      W     M     6 June 1855
GUNTER, Beverly                       GUNTER, Mary
              Father

GUSLER, G W                           W     M    26 Dec 1853
GUSLER, Daniel                        GUSLER, Elizabeth
              Father

GUSLER, James P H                     W     M    23 Jan 1860
GUSLER, John J                        GUSLER, Elizabeth
              Father

GUSLER, John W                        W     M    26 Nov 1862
GUSLER, John J                        GUSLER, Elizabeth
              Father

GWINN, Sarelia                        W     F     3 May 1854
GWINN, Aaron                          GWINN, Maria Jane
              Father

HADEN, Lucy A                         W     F     5 Oct 1862
HADEN, Jesse                          HADEN, Lucy
              Nancy Haden, Grandmother

HAGAR                                 B/S   M    17 Jan 1853
SCALES, Absalom                       Jenney
              Caroline Scales, Wife of Owner

HAGOOD, Daniel                        W     M     2 Jan 1860
HAGOOD, William R                     HAGOOD, Ruth
              Father

HAGOOD, Ruth B                        W     F    27 May 1858
HAGOOD, William R                     HAGOOD, Ruth
              Father
```

```
CHILD'S NAME                          RACE  SEX    BIRTH DATE
FATHER\OWNER                          MOTHER
              INFORMANT
------------------------------------------------------------------------
HAGOOD, Susan A                       W    F    27 May 1854
HAGOOD, William R                     HAGOOD, Ruth
              Father

HAINS, Thomas                         W    M    6 Apr 1860
HAINS, Jordan                         HAINMS, Columbia
              Father

HAIRSTON, Elizabeth                   W    F    19 Aug 1855
HAIRSTON, Samuel                      HAIRSTON, Louisa
              Father

HALE, Angelina P                      W    F    28 May 1858_
HALE, S (Mechanic)                    HALE, Emaline R
              Father

HALEY, Drewry S                       W    M    -- Dec 1865
HALEY, S  H                           HALEY, S  A
              Father

HALL, Carolina                        W    F    4 June 1854
HALL, Joseph R                        HALL, Luvenia
              Father

HALL, Delila                          W    F    9 Dec 1854
HALL, Henry                           HALL, Mary J
              Father

HALL, Elizabeth                       W    F    5 Mar 1853
HALL, Adam                            HALL, Sabrina
              Mother

HALL, H H                             W    M    10 June 1853
HALL, H H (Carpenter)                 HALL, Enona Heath
              Father

HALL, Henry H                         W    M    14 Mar 1862
HALL, W  W                            HALL, Mary A
              Mother

HALL, James A                         W    M    -- Feb 1857
HALL, Adam                            HALL, Sabrina
              Father

HALL, James J                         W    M    12 Sept 1854
HALL, David                           HALL, Jane
              Father

HALL, Jno M                           W    M    14 Sept 1859
HALL, J R                             HALL, Louisa
              Father
```

75

```
CHILD'S NAME                                    RACE  SEX    BIRTH DATE
FATHER\OWNER                                    MOTHER
               INFORMANT
--------------------------------------------------------------------
HALL, Jno W                                     W     M      20 Feb 1858
HALL, N P                                       HALL, Delila
               Father

HALL, John                                      W     M      28 Dec 1855
HALL, Henry H                                   HALL, Enony
               Father

HALL, John D                                    W     M      13 July 1854
HALL, William F                                 HALL, Sarah
               Father

HALL, Joseph                                    W     M      5 Apr 1853
HALL, John                                      HALL, Nancy
               Mother

HALL, Lucinda                                   W     F      1 Feb 1862
HALL, John C                                    HALL, Nancy
               Mother

HALL, Lucinda E                                 W     F      20 Feb 1860
HALL, N R                                       HALL, Delila
               Father

HALL, Margaret                                  W     F      31 Dec 1854
HALL, David                                     HALL, Letha
               Father

HALL, Martha E                                  W     F      18 Jan 1865
HALL, William W                                 HALL, Mary A
               Susan Whitlock, Grandmother

HALL, Mary J                                    W     F      23 Mar 1862
HALL, John R                                    HALL, Jane
               Mother

HALL, Nancy A                                   W     F      15 Feb 1859
HALL, William F                                 HALL, Sarah
               Father

HALL, Nancy J                                   W     F      28 Sept 1859
HALL, John                                      HALL, Nancy
               Father

HALL, Rosina                                    W     F      15 Feb 1865
HALL, John C                                    HALL, Nancy
               Father

HALL, Sarah A                                   W     F      29 Jan 1860
HALL, Adam                                      HALL, Sabrina
               Father
```

CHILD'S NAME FATHER\OWNER INFORMANT	RACE SEX BIRTH DATE MOTHER
HALL, T C HALL, Jasper Mother	W M 17 May 1862 HALL, Lavenia
HALL, Zadock HALL, Absalom Father	W M 29 Apr 1853 HALL, Elizabeth
HALLY, A J HALLY, Peyton Mother	W M 29 Sept 1860 HALLY, Sarah J
HANBY, Albert HANBY, John A Father	W M 5 Mar 1860 HANBY, Mary S
HANBY, Frances HANBY, D S Father	W F 16 Sept 1858 HANBY, Susan
HANBY, Gabriel HANBY, John A Father	W M -- June 1857 HANBY, Mary
HANBY, John HANBY, John A Father	W M 9 Nov 1859 HANBY, Mary
HANBY, Not Named HANBY, H Father	W M 1 Dec 1857 HANBY, Susan
HANBY, Thomas HANBY, John A (Physician) Father	W M 3 Sept 1854 HANBY, Mary L
HANBY, Virginia HANBY, H H Father	W F 16 Sept 1855 HANBY, Susan
HANCOCK HANCOCK, Peter Father	W M -- -- 1855 HANCOCK, Elizabeth
HANCOCK, Catherine HANCOCK, John Father	W F 5 Sept 1860 HANCOCK Jane
HANCOCK, Crawford HANCOCK, F (Blacksmith) Father	W M 12 Mar 1859 HANCOCK, Frances

```
CHILD'S NAME                              RACE  SEX     BIRTH DATE
FATHER\OWNER                              MOTHER
              INFORMANT
------------------------------------------------------------------------
HANCOCK, E A                              W     F     17 June 1858
HANCOCK, Green                            HANCOCK, Elizabeth G
              Father

HANCOCK, Ellen                            W     F     15 Oct 1857
HANCOCK, John W                           HANCOCK, Jane
              Father

HANCOCK, F W                              W     M     14 Mar 1862
HANCOCK, Fleming (Blacksmith)             HANCOCK, Frances
              Father

HANCOCK, Joseph A                         W     M      9 July 1854
HANCOCK, John W                           HANCOCK, Jane
              Father

HANCOCK, Joshua G                         W     M      3 Apr 1855
HANCOCK, Greenville                       HANCOCK, Elizabeth G
              Father

HANCOCK, Julia                            W     F     10 Feb 1865
HANCOCK, John T                           HANCOCK, Exony
              Fleming Hancock, Grandfather

HANCOCK, Kisiah E                         W     F     13 May 1862
HANCOCK, P S                              HANCOCK, Elizabeth
              Father

HANCOCK, Mildred D R                      W     F      9 Aug 1862
HANCOCK, Green                            HANCOCK, Elizabeth J
              Father

HANCOCK, Samuel A                         W     M     15 Apr 1853
HANCOCK, Peter S                          HANCOCK, Elizabeth
              Father

HANCOCK, Tunesia                          W     F     12 Aug 1865
HANCOCK, Fleming (Blacksmith)             HANCOCK, Francis
              Father

HANDY, Ben Franklin                       W     M      1 May 1857
HANDY, William                            HANDY, Mary Ann
              Father

HANDY, Beverage A                         W     M      1 June, 1854
HANDY, Henry J                            HANDY, Vienna Ann
              Father

HANDY, Elizabeth                          W     F     27 June 1859
HANDY, Peter                              HANDY, Matilda
              Father
```

```
CHILD'S NAME                              RACE  SEX     BIRTH DATE
FATHER\OWNER                              MOTHER
              INFORMANT
-----------------------------------------------------------------------
HANDY, Manda L V                          W     F    15 June 1853
HANDY, William H                          HANDY, Mary A
              Father

HANDY, Mary E                             W     F    20 Oct 1853
HANDY, Hardin                             HANDY, Catherine
              Father

HANDY, Matilda E                          W     F    29 Nov 1861
HANDY, William                            HANDY, Mary
              Father

HANDY, Nancy Ann                          W     F    27 Nov 1855
HANDY, Preston                            HANDY, Susan
              Father

HANDY, Not Named                          W     M     7 July 1858
HANDY, J                                  HANDY, Hannah E
              Father

HANDY, Not Named                          W     M     8 Apr 1865
HANDY, Johyn                              HANDY, Elizabeth
              Father

HANDY, Powatan J                          W     M     3 Nov 1853
HANDY, Samuel                             HANDY, Nancy
              Mother

HANDY, Sarah A                            W     F    22 Oct 1858
HANDY, L A                                HANDY, Nancy
              Father

HANDY, Sarah J                            W     F    -- Oct 1854
HANDY, John                               HANDY, Hannah
              Mother

HANDY, Sir William J                      W     M    10 Apr 1855
HANDY, William                            HANDY, Mary A
              Father

HANDY, Susan                              W     F    26 Nov 1859
HANDY, William                            HANDY, Mary
              Father

HANNAH                                    B/S   F    20 Sept 1855
JOYCE, Perrin                             Mariah
              Owner

HARDEN                                    B/S   M    14 Aug 1854
MARTIN, Joseph                            Not Given
              A Satterfield, Manager


                       79
```

```
CHILD'S NAME                             RACE  SEX    BIRTH DATE
FATHER\OWNER                             MOTHER
             INFORMANT
----------------------------------------------------------------------
HARDY, Not Named                         W     M    25 Dec 1853
HARDY, Joseph H                          HARDY, Analiza
             Father

HARRIETT                                 B/S   F    25 Sept 1853
CLARK, Alexander B                       Jude
             Master

HARRIETT                                 B/S   F    3 Sept 1855
BROWN, Nicholas                          Martha
             Owner

HARRIETT                                 B/S   F    -- Aug 1857
CLARK, Jacob                             Susan
             Owner

HARRIETT                                 B/S   F    -- Mar 1857
ANTHONY, B A                             Rebecca
             Master

HARRIETT                                 B/S   F    -- Jan 1861
CONNER, William Sr                      Zet
             Master

HARRIETT                                 B     F    10 Feb 1864
Not Given                                Susan Jane
             H W Reynolds, Former Owner

HARRIETT (Born Dead)                     B/S   F    -- Feb 1857
COBB, John                               Oney
             Master

HARRIETT (Twin)                          B/S   F    -- Sept 1862
COBB, John R                             Mary
             Master

HARRIS, Elizabeth A                      W     F    7 Feb 1859
HARRIS, Samuel                           HARRIS, Luvenia F
             Father

HARRIS, Emily                            W     F    15 Jan 1855
HARRIS, Murphy                           HARRIS, Martha
             Father

HARRIS, Ewell J W                        W     F    8 Mar 1858
HARRIS, William                          HARRIS, mary
             Father

HARRIS, James M                          W     M    3 May 1853
HARRIS, James                            HARRIS, Elizabeth M
             Mother
```

```
CHILD'S NAME                          RACE  SEX    BIRTH DATE
FATHER\OWNER                          MOTHER
              INFORMANT
-------------------------------------------------------------------
HARRIS, Jeff Lee                      W     M     17 Oct 1862
HARRIS, Wilson                        HARRIS, Nancy
              Mother

HARRIS, John                          W     M     24 Dec 1859
HARRIS, William                       HARRIS, Eliza C
              Father

HARRIS, Josiah                        W     M     31 Dec 1853
HARRIS, Samuel                        HARRIS, Sally
              Father

HARRIS, Lowell E                      W     M     20 June 1853
HARRIS, Green                         HARRIS, Rhoda
              Father

HARRIS, Lucinda A                     W     F     2 May 1855
HARRIS, William                       HARRIS, Mary E
              Father

HARRIS, Mahala T                      W     F     19 Aug 1855_
HARRIS, William                       HARRIS, Tempy J
              Father

HARRIS, Not Named                     W     M     12 Sept 1857
HARRIS, James                         HARRIS, Elizabeth
              Father

HARRIS, Oney M                        W     F     1 Apr 1859
HARRIS, Green                         HARRIS, Rhoda
              Father

HARRIS, Rufus H                       W     M     10 June 1859
HARRIS, William                       HARRIS, Catherine
              Father

HARRIS, Sarah V                       W     F     25 June 1860
HARRIS, William T                     HARRIS, Nancy
              Father

HARRIS, Sina                          W     F     -- Sept 1862
HARRIS, William J                     HARIS, Mary E
              Father

HARRISON                              B/S   M     -- May 1859
PENN, Susan                           Milly
              Owner

HARRISON                              B/S   M     10 Apr 1861
HYLTON, Valentine                     Mage
              Owner
```

```
CHILD'S NAME                           RACE  SEX     BIRTH DATE
FATHER\OWNER                           MOTHER
              INFORMANT
-------------------------------------------------------------------------
HARRISON                               B/S   M    1 Apr 1862
HYLTON, Valentine                      Mariah
              Master

HARRISS, Amanda                        W     F    1 June 1854
HARRISS, William                       HARRISS, Elizabeth
              Father

HARRISS, Caroline                      W     F    31 July 1865
HARRISS, Samuel G                      HARRISS, Mahala
              Father

HARRISS, John Quincy                   W     M    27 Dec 1854
HARRISS, Wilson F                      HARRISS, Nancy
              Father

HARRISS, Mary C                        W     F    15 July 1865
HARRISS, William                       HARRISS, Eliza
              Father

HARRISS, Matthew (Deformed)            W     M    3 July 1857
HARRISS, Samuel                        HARRISS, Luvenia F
              Father

HARRISS, Samuel C                      W     M    1 Jan 1857
HARRISS, Green                         HARRISS, Rhoda
              Father

HARRISS, Samuel G                      W     M    1 Jan 1858
HARRISS, G                             HARRISS, Rhoda
              Father

HARRISS, William W                     W     M    -- Aug 1854
HARRISS, Green                         HARRISS, Rhoda
              Father

HARSTON, Martha Grant                  B     F    11 Aug 1865
HARSTON, Dick (Wagoner)                HARSTON, Eliza
              Mother

HATCHER, Benjamin D                    W     M    -- July 1854
HATCHER, James C                       HATCHER, Lucy
              Father

HATCHER, Charles F                     W     M    2 Sept 1855
HATCHER, Richard                       HATCHER, Delila
              Father

HATCHER, Daniel J                      W     M    15 Dec 1860
HATCHER, James C                       HATCHER, Lucy
              Father


                            82
```

```
CHILD'S NAME                            RACE  SEX    BIRTH DATE
FATHER\OWNER                            MOTHER
              INFORMANT
-----------------------------------------------------------------------
HATCHER, James P                         W    M    11 May 1858
HATCHER, Richard                         HATCHER, Delila
              Father

HATCHER, Lucinda R                       W    F    28 Feb 1853
HATCHER, Richard                         HATCHER, Delila
              Father

HATCHER, Mary B                          W    F    19 July 1859
HATCHER, John B                          HATCHER, Kezeah
              Father

HATCHER, Mildred                         W    F    17 July 1857
HATCHER, James                           HATCHER, Lucy
              Father

HATCHER, Not Named                       W    M    20 Aug 1855
HATCHER, David B                         HATCHER, Margaret
              Mother

HAYNES, Joseph H                         W    M    4 June 1854
HAYNES, Luite                            HAYNES, Avaline
              Father

HAYNES, William Thomas                   W    M    3 Dec 1860
HAYNES, Robert                           HAYNES, Jennie
              Father

HAZELWOOD, James Jackson                 W    M    8 Feb 1854
HAZLEWOOD, Josiah                        HAZLEWOOD, Ruth W
              Father

HAZLEWOOD, James M                       W    M    17 May 1859
HAZLEWOOD, Josiah                        HAZLEWOOD, Ruth
              father

HAZLEWOOD, Sarah                         W    F    28 June 1859
HAZLEWOOD, Robert                        HAZLEWOOD, Nancy
              Father

HEADEN, Not Named                        W    M    22 July 1854
HEADEN, Anderson                         HEADEN, Nancy
              Father

HEARD, Adowery                           W    F    24 Feb 1860
HEARD, C                                 HEARD, Martha
              Father

HELMS, Abram                             W    M    30 June 1860
HELMS, Adam                              HELMS, Lucinda J
              Mother
```

83

```
CHILD'S NAME                            RACE  SEX    BIRTH DATE
FATHER\OWNER                            MOTHER
            INFORMANT
------------------------------------------------------------------------
HELMS, George L                         W     M    1 Oct 1858
HELMS, Thomas H                         HELMS, Sinia
            Father

HELMS, J  A                             W     F    12 Sept 1862
HELMS, Thomas                           HELMS, Eluisa J
            Mother

HELMS, Jacob                            W     M    12 Dec 1857
HELMS, Adam                             HELMS, Luvenia J
            Father

HELMS, Kezeah E                         W     F    9 Dec 1859
HELMS, T J                              HELMS, Louisa J
            Father

HENDRICK, Henry H                       W     M    1 July 1859
HENDRICK, William                       HENDRICK, Jane
            Father

HENDRICK, Lucinda C                     W     F    12 Oct 1855
HENDRICK, William                       HENDRICK, Jane
            Father

HENDRICK, Mary Ann                      W     F    15 Jan 1854
HENDRICK, William                       Not Given
            Father

HENDRICK, William Lee                   W     M    1 July 1861
HENDRICK, William                       HENDRICK, Jane
            Father

HENRIETT                                B/S   F    -- Feb 1857
KOGER, Jacob W                          Catherine
            James C Moit, Master

HENRIETTA                               B/S   F    -- Sept 1862
STAPLES, S  G                           Jane
            Master

HENRIETTA                               B/S   F    2 May 1862
TATUM, J John, Dec'd                    Leeta
            John C Tatum, on hire to Estate

HENRY                                   B/S   M    28 May 1853
SCALES, Absalom                         Mariah
            Caroline Scales, Wife of Owner

HENRY                                   B/S   M    15 June 1853
HUGHES, Jemima                          Mary
            J R Hughes, Son of Owner


                              84
```

```
CHILD'S NAME                            RACE  SEX    BIRTH DATE
FATHER\OWNER                            MOTHER
             INFORMANT
---------------------------------------------------------------------
HENRY                                   B/S   M     10 Feb 1854
WALLER, James A                         Not Given
             Owner

HENRY                                   B/S   M     3 July 1855
HATCHER, David B                        Mary
             Margaret Hatcher, Mistress

HENRY                                   B/S   M     20 Aug 1855
FLIPPIN, J L                            Mary
             Owner

HENRY                                   B/S   M     -- Sept 1858
NELSON, Sally                           Not Given
             PEDIGO, Lewis

HENSLEY, George D                       W     M     -- June 1857
HENSLEY, Alexander                      HENSLEY, Martha
             Father

HENSLEY, Henry C                        W     M     1 Mar 1855
HENSLEY, Alexander (Miller)             HENSLEY, Martha A
             Father

HENSLEY, Sarah F                        W     F     15 Oct 1853
HENSLEY, Alexander                      HENSLEY, Martha A
             Father

HENSLEY, William L                      W     M     5 May 1853
None Given                              HENSLEY, Catherine
             W M C Hensley, No Relation

HERD, Not Named                         W     F     15 Dec 1855
HERD, Claiborne                         HERD, Martha
             Father

HIATT, Elizabeth                        W     F     27 Feb 1859
HIATT, John                             HIATT, Polly
             Father

HIATT, Elizabeth                        W     F     27 Feb 1859
HIATT, Franklin                         HIATT, Kittie
             Father

HIATT, Jefferson Davis                  W     M     22 July 1861
HIATT, John                             HIATT, Polly
             Father

HIATT, Jordan Lee                       W     M     27 Feb 1859
HIATT, Ephraim                          HIATT, Lucinda
             Father
```

CHILD'S NAME FATHER\OWNER INFORMANT	RACE	SEX	BIRTH DATE MOTHER
HIATT, Martha E HIATT, Ephram Mother	W	F	5 June 1862 HIATT, Lucinda
HIATT, Mintora V HIATT, John Mother	W	F	11 July 1855 HIATT, Polly
HIATT, Not Named HIATT, F Father	W	F	1 Aug 1857 HIATT, Ritty
HIGH, Elizabeth HIGH, William H (Teaching School) Father	W	F	5 July 1853 HIGH, Mary
HILL, Augustus HILL, F F Father	W	M	27 May 1859 HILL, Susannah
HILL, Elizabeth HILL, Manning D Father	W	F	13 June 1853 HILL, Louise
HILL, Howard J HILL, P J Father	W	M	1 Sept 1861 HILL, Susan
HILL, John Robert HILL, Manning D Mother	W	M	19 Feb 1855 HILL, Louisa J
HILL, Lucinda J HILL, M D Father	W	F	30 July 1860 HILL, Lucy
HILL, Martha HILL, M D Father	W	F	20 Mar 1859 HILL, Louisa
HILL, Martha Jane HILL, Philip J Father	W	F	25 Nov 1854 HILL, Susan J
HILL, Not Named HILL, Philip Sarah Brown, Neighbor	W	F	-- Dec 1862 HILL, Susan
HINES, Samuel HINES, James Father	W	M	3 Nov 1859 HINES, Emily

```
CHILD'S NAME                          RACE  SEX    BIRTH DATE
FATHER\OWNER                          MOTHER
              INFORMANT
---------------------------------------------------------------------
HODGES, John H                        W    M    8 Mar 1858
HODGES, Robert (Ditcher)              HODGES, Ann
              Father

HODGES, Mary Ann (Very Pretty)        W    F    21 Apr 1854
HODGES, Jeremiah (Tobacconist)        HODGES, Sarah Ann
              Father

HODGES, William Lee                   W    M    21 Oct 1855
HODGES, Jeremiah                      HODGES, Sarah A
              Father

HOLLANDSWORTH, Benjamin F             W    M    5 Sept 1853
HOLLANDSWORTH, Barton                 HOLLANDSWORTH, M E
              Father

HOLLANDSWORTH, Not Named              W    F    -- Jan 1855
HOLLANDSWORTH, William                HOLLANDSWORTH, Frances
              Father

HOOKER, Daniel A                      W    M    25 Feb 1854
HOOKER, Jesse                         HOOKER, Elizabeth
              Father

HOOKER, Joel                          W    M    29 Feb 1855
HOOKER, Samuel                        HOOKER, Lucinda
              Father

HOOKER, Mary E                        W    F    25 Apr 1859_
HOOKER, Jno                           HOOKER, M D
              Father

HOOKER, Nanny E                       W    F    15 Sep 1862
HOOKER, J W                           HOOKER, M  D
              Father

HOOKER, Ruth                          W    F    -- --- 1862
HOOKER, John W                        HOOKER, Margaret D
              Father

HOPKINS, Elizabeth S                  W    F    6 Dec 1853
HOPKINS, David                        HOPKINS, Sarah S
              Father

HOPKINS, Ellen J                      W    F    17 Dec 1862
HOPKINS, Harvey D                     HOPKINS, Nancy
              Mother

HOPKINS, Fleming R  J                 W    M    17 May 1862
HOPKINS, David                        HOPKINS, Sarah L
              Father
```

```
CHILD'S NAME                        RACE  SEX    BIRTH DATE
FATHER\OWNER                        MOTHER
            INFORMANT
------------------------------------------------------------------------
HOPKINS, James A                    W     M    19 Aug 1860
HOPKINS, H D                        HOPKINS, Nancy
            Father

HOPKINS, Joshua T                   W     M    15 Nov 1853
HOPKINS, John                       HOPKINS, Henthy
            Father

HOPKINS, Lucinda M                  W     F    24 Dec 1861
HOPKINS, William T                  HOPKINS, Nancy
            Father

HOPKINS, Margaret A                 W     F    23 Apr 1854
HOPKINS, Thomas                     HOPKINS, Mary
            Father

HOPKINS, Thomas G                   W     M    26 Dec 1858
HOPKINS, Dua                        HOPKINS, Sarah L
            Father

HOPKINS, William R                  W     M    11 Oct 1853
HOPKINS, Harden                     HOPKINS, Elizabeth
            Father

HORATIO                             B/S   M    21 Nov 1862
ZENTMEYER, John N                   Ruth
            Master

HOUCHENS, Columbus F                W     M    14 Apr 1855
HOUCHENS, Abram                     HOUCHENS, Martha
            Father

HOUCHENS, Laura A                   W     F    28 June 1858
HOUCHENS, I C                       HOUCHENS, Nancy E
            Father

HOUCHINS, America R                 W     F    13 Sept 1857
HOUCHINS, A W                       HOUCHINS, Martha
            Father

HOUCHINS, E C                       W     M    19 June 1859
HOUCHINS, A W                       HOUCHINS, Martha
            Father

HOUCHINS, M L                       W     M    12 Feb 1860
HOUCHINS, I C                       HOUCHINS, Nancy
            Father

HOUCHINS, Sarah A                   W     F    5 May 1862
HOUCHINS, Abram W                   HOUCHINS, Martha
            Father
```

```
CHILD'S NAME                          RACE  SEX    BIRTH DATE
FATHER\OWNER                          MOTHER
              INFORMANT
-----------------------------------------------------------------------
HOUCHINS, William H                   W     M    27 July 1853
HOUCHENS, Abram                       HOUCHENS, Martha
              Father

HOWELL, Josiah                        W     M     8 Aug 1858
HOWELL, Thomas                        HOWELL, Virginia
              Father

HOWELL, Mary                          W     F     1 Oct 1859
HOWELL, Thomas                        HOWELL, Virginia
              Father

HOWELL, Not Named                     W     M    31 July 1854
HOWELL, M A                           HOWELL, Elizabeth
              Father

HOWELL, Not Named                     W     M    16 July 1858
HOWELL, H B                           HOWELL, Susannah
              Father

HOWELL, Susan S                       W     F    11 July 1853
HOWELL, Fountain                      HOWELL, Nancy
              Father

HOWELL, Victoria                      W     F    10 Oct 1860
HOWELL, E P                           HOWELL, Martha J Young
              Father

HOWELL, William T                     W     M    25 Apr 1862
HOWELL, Thomas                        HOWELL, Virginia
              Father

HUBBARD, A                            W     M    14 May 1854
HUBBARD, William                      HUBBARD, Celia
              Father

HUBBARD, David                        W     M    18 Sept 1855
HUBBARD, Jonathan                     HUBBARD, Nancy
              Father

HUBBARD, Eliza P                      W     F     1 Feb 1853
HUBBARD, Benjamin                     HUBBARD, Agnes
              Father

HUBBARD, Emazetta                     W     F    26 Dec 1860
HUBBARD, William                      HUBBARD, Celia
              Father

HUBBARD, Joel M (Twin)                W     M     1 Apr 1859
HUBBARD, Benjamin B                   HUBBARD, Agness
              Father
```

```
CHILD'S NAME                              RACE  SEX    BIRTH DATE
FATHER\OWNER                              MOTHER
              INFORMANT
---------------------------------------------------------------------------
HUBBARD, John                             W     M    -- Sept 1854
HUBBARD, Benjamin                         HUBBARD, Agnes
              Father

HUBBARD, Josh A (Twin)                    W     M    1 Apr 1859
HUBBARD, Benjamin B                       HUBBARD, Agness
              Father

HUBBARD, Lucy A                           W     F    -- Sept 1853
HUBBARD, Jonathan                         HUBBARD, Frances
              Father

HUBBARD, Luvenia A                        W     F    16 June 1862
HUBBARD, Benjamin B                       HUBBARD, Agness
              Mother

HUBBARD, Mary                             W     F    8 Feb 1857
HUBBARD, Benjamin                         HUBBARD, Agness
              Father

HUBBARD, Milly                            W     F    -- Apr 1860
HUBBARD, Jonathan                         HUBBARD, Frances
              Father

HUBBARD, N E                              W     M    17 Apr 1858
HUBBARD, William                          HUBBARD, Celia
              Father

HUBBARD, Victoria                         W     F    17 Oct 1858
HUBBARD, J W                              HUBBARD, Milly
              Father

HUBBARD, Zara                             W     M    20 July 1862
HUBBARD, J  W                             HUBBARD, Sarah
              Mother

HUDNAL, Joseph R                          W     M    8 Feb 1853
HUDNAL, Richard N                         HUDNAL, Catherine
              Father

HUGHES, G  W                              W     M    24 July 1865
HUGHES, John                              HUGHES, Barbara A
              Father

HUGHES, John Henry                        B     M    12 Mar 1865
Unknown                                   HUGHES, Violet
              Nancy Hughes, Former Owner

HUGHES, Mary J                            W     F    13 Apr 1853
HUGHES, James M                           HUGHES, Nancy M
              Father
```

```
CHILD'S NAME                        RACE  SEX    BIRTH DATE
FATHER\OWNER                        MOTHER
          INFORMANT
-----------------------------------------------------------------------
HUGHES, Not Named                   W     F    15 Dec 1860
HUGHES, John                        HUGHES, Martha
          Father

HUGHES, William M                   W     M    28 Feb 1860
HUGHES, William J                   HUGHES, Delila
          Father

HUGHS, Beverage A                   W     M    22 June 1855
HUGHS, William J                    HUGHS, Delila
          Father

HUGHS, Kizziah C J                  W     F    25 July 1854
HUGHS, John J                       HUGHS, Barbara A
          Father

HUGHS, Not Named                    W     F    22 Sept 1857
HUGHS, William J                    HUGHS, Delila
          Father

HUNLEY, George E  L                 W     M    24 June 1862
HUNLEY, Edward                      HUNLEY, Druscilla
          Mother

HUNLEY, Sarah                       W     F    18 May 1860
HUNLEY, George W                    HUNLEY, Lucinda
          Father

HUTCHENSON, James                   W     M    1 May 1853
HUTCHENSON, Andy                    HUTCHENSON, Martha
          Father

HYLTON, Amanda                      W     F    19 Mar 1858
HYLTON, William B                   HYLTON, Eliza A
          Father

HYLTON, Breckinridge                W     M    6 June 1857
HYLTON, Augustin                    HYLTON, Mary
          Father

HYLTON, Ed M                        W     M    23 July 1859
HYLTON, Moses                       HYLTON, Elizabeth
          Father

HYLTON, Edward J                    W     M    20 July 1853
HYLTON, Hardin                      HYLTON, Charity
          Father

HYLTON, Elizabeth                   W     F    19 Sept 1860
HYLTON, William                     HYLTON, Eliza A
          Father
```

```
CHILD'S NAME                              RACE  SEX    BIRTH DATE
FATHER\OWNER                              MOTHER
               INFORMANT
-----------------------------------------------------------------------
HYLTON, Gabriel                           W     M    30 May 1861
HYLTON, Valentine                         HYLTON, Mary A
               Father

HYLTON, George V                          W     M    28 Sept 1862
HYLTON, Gabriel                           HYLTON, Lucy A
               Father

HYLTON, Hardin J  F                       W     M    2 Sept 1862_
HYLTON, Hardin                            HYLTON, Charity
               Father

HYLTON, Henry S                           W     M    4 Sept 1858
HYLTON, Isaac                             HYLTON, Roxany
               Father

HYLTON, Isaac McDaniel                    W     M    25 Aug 1854
HYLTON, Absalom                           HYLTON, Martha
               Father

HYLTON, J W                               W     M    11 July 1858
HYLTON, J W                               HYLTON, Emeline
               Father

HYLTON, Jeremiah                          W     M    4 July 1853
HYLTON, Gabriel                           HYLTON, Lucy
               Father

HYLTON, Louisa                            W     F    23 July 1858
HYLTON, Ira                               HYLTON, Elizabeth
               Father

HYLTON, Martha                            W     F    27 May 1860
HYLTON, Gabe                              HYLTON, Lucy
               Father

HYLTON, Mary                              W     F    -- Dec 1853
HYLTON, Moses                             HYLTON, Elizabeth
               Father

HYLTON, Mary E                            W     F    13 Feb 1855
HYLTON, Henry                             HYLTON, Catherine
               Father

HYLTON, Mary L                            W     F    20 Oct 1855
HYLTON, Harden                            HYLTON, Charity
               Father

HYLTON, Nat N                             W     M    17 Apr 1858
HYLTON, N N                               HYLTON, Elizabeth
               Mother
```

CHILD'S NAME FATHER\OWNER INFORMANT	RACE SEX BIRTH DATE MOTHER
HYLTON, Not Named HYLTON, Austin 　　　　Father	W　　M　　11 Oct 1859 HYLTON, May
HYLTON, Not Named HYLTON, Hardin 　　　　Father	W　　M　　20 Nov 1859 HYLTON, Charity
HYLTON, Peter HYLTON, Henry 　　　　Father	W　　M　　4 May 1853 HYLTON, Catherine
HYLTON, Sarah A HYLTON, Hardin 　　　　Father	W　　F　　30 Apr 1857 HYLTON, Casety
HYLTON, Sarah A HYLTON, H 　　　　Father	W　　F　　30 Apr 1858 HYLTON, Charity
HYLTON, Temperance A HYLTON, Newman 　　　　Mother	W　　F　　9 Feb 1854 HYLTON, Elizabeth
HYLTON, William D HYLTON, George 　　　　Father	W　　]M　　10 Sept 1854 HYLTON, Oney
HYLTON, William J HYLTON, Isaac 　　　　Father	W　　M　　4 Mar 1860 HYLTON, Lucinda
HYLTON, William M HYLTON, Moses 　　　　Father	W　　M　　10 Aug 1862 HYLTON, Elizabeth
IDIA VIA, A C 　　　　Mistress	B/S　F　　25 Sept 1860 Pocohontas
INGRAM, Idea INGRAM, R L 　　　　Father	W　　F　　3 May 1860 INGRAM, Idea
INGRAM, Joseph P INGRAM, Richard L 　　　　Father	W　　M　　21 Aug 1857 INGRAM, Ida
INGRAM, Joshua INGRAM, Isaac 　　　　Father	W　　M　　30 Aug 1854 INGRAM, Jane

```
CHILD'S NAME                            RACE  SEX    BIRTH DATE
FATHER\OWNER                            MOTHER
             INFORMANT
-----------------------------------------------------------------------
INGRAM, Martha A                        W      F    6 Sept 1854
INGRAM, Samuel C                        INGRAM, Sarah
             Father

INGRAM, Not Named                       W      M    -- -- 1853
INGRAM, Isaac                           INGRAM, Jane
             Father

INGRAM, R L                             W      M    9 Aug 1828
INGRAM, R L                             INGRAM, Ida
             Father

IRA                                     B/S    M    -- Apr 1855
ADAMS, Abram                            Celia
             Master

ISAAC (Twin)                            B/S    M    20 May 1857
ROBERTSON, James R                     Ruth
             Master

ISABELLA                                B/S    F    -- Nov 1857
HUGHS, James                           Amanda
             Master

ISABELLA                                B/S    F    11 Jan 1859
ZEGLER, Richard                        Eliza
             Owner

ISRAEL, Mary J                          W      F    15 May 1853
ISRAEL, William                        ISRAEL, Mariah
             Richard Mills, Neighbor

IVEY, Francis                           W      F    12 Dec 1853
IVEY, Alexander (Farming & Trading)    IVEY, Avaline
             Father

IVIE, Benjamin T                        W      M    8 Nov 1855
IVIE, George G                         IVIE, Mary J
             Father

IVIE, Catherine                         W      F    14 Dec 1860
IVIE, George                           IVIE, Eliza
             Father

IZREAL                                  B/S    M    10 Oct 1862
DAVIS, B  A                             Rachel
             Master

JACK                                    B/S    M    -- May 1862
PENN, James A                          Dicy
             Master
```

```
CHILD'S NAME                          RACE  SEX    BIRTH DATE
FATHER\OWNER                          MOTHER
              INFORMANT
-------------------------------------------------------------------
JACKSON                               B/S   M    15 June 1862
MURPHY, Austis                        Nancy
              Mistress

JACKSON, Carroll M                    W     M     3 Apr 1860
JACKSON, C B                          JACKSON, Permelia
              Father

JACKSON, Germima                      W     F    19 Apr 1854
JACKSON, Carroll B                    JACKSON, Permelia
              Father

JACKSON, Not Named                    W     F    28 Feb 1858
JACKSON, C B                          JACKSON, Permelia
              Father

JACKSON, Not Named                    W     F    25 Sept 1862
JACKSON, C  B                         JACKSON, Permelia
              Father

JACOB                                 B/S   M     5 Aug 1853
STUART, Chesdle D                     Lucy
              Elizabeth Stuart, Mother of Owner

JACOB                                 B/S   M    10 Nov 1859
CLARK, Robert                         Martha
              Master

JACOB                                 B/S   M    12 Mar 1859
PARKER, Smith                         Milly
              Master

JACOB                                 B/S   M     4 Oct 1860
FOLEY, James H                        Sarah
              Joe France, Master

JAMENA                                B/S   F    20 Jan 1857
CLARK, Thomas                         Nancy
              Owner

JAMES                                 B/S   M    16 Aug 1854
KING, George W                        Not Given
              Owner

JAMES                                 B/S   M    15 June 1855
STONE, Tandy                          Not Given
              Master

JAMES                                 B/S   M    27 Apr 1857
EDWARDS, Joseph H                     Lucy
              Master
```

CHILD'S NAME	RACE	SEX	BIRTH DATE
FATHER\OWNER	MOTHER		
INFORMANT			

JAMES	B/S	M	29 Apr 1859
MORAN, Nelson	Sary		
Master			
JAMES	B/S	M	-- Mar 1860
JOYCE, R M	Pajr (?)		
James S Langhorne, Master			
JAMES	B/S	M	10 Mar 1861
MURPHY, Austrip	Nancy		
Owner			
JAMES	B/S	M	7 Nov 1861
REYNOLDS, H W	Sallie		
Owner			
JAMES	B/S	M	-- May 1862
HAIRSTON, Samuel W	Nice		
Master			
JAMES	B/S	M	-- Aug 1862
CRITZ, William D	Rhoda		
Master			
JAMES B	B/S	M	30 Sept 1858
CONNER, William	Rozett		
Master			
JAMES WESLEY	B/S	M	14 Sept 1854
PENN, Mrs Susan	Not Given		
Mistress			
JANE	B/S	F	17 June 1853
VIA, James Sr	Mary		
Owner			
JANE	B/S	F	1 Sept 1853
CONNER, William	Lucy		
Owner			
JANE	B/S	F	16 Aug 1854
MARTIN, John H	Not Given		
Owner			
JANE	B/S	F	-- July 1854
WRIGHT, John	Aggy		
Owner			
JANE	B/S	F	-- June 1855
HAIRSTON, Ruth	Margaret		
B G Walker, Overseer			

```
CHILD'S NAME                              RACE  SEX    BIRTH DATE
FATHER\OWNER                              MOTHER
            INFORMANT
-----------------------------------------------------------------------
JANET                                     B/S   F     -- Apr 1858
COCKRAM, Ed                               Phillis
            Master

JARROTT, Lucinda R (Born Henry Co)        W     F     -- July 1857
JARROTT, Robert                           JARROTT, Fernesea
            Father

JARROTT, Mary L                           W     F     10 May 1855
JARROTT, Robert                           JARROTT, Taresa
            Father

JATHINA                                   B/S   F     3 July 1853
MORAN, Nelson                             Sarah
            Owner

JEFF                                      B/S   M     15 Jan 1853
PENN, Thomas Sr                           Elizabeth
            Owner

JEFF DAVIS                                B/S   M     10 Mar 1862
PENN, Jackson                             Betsy
            Master

JEFFERSON                                 B/S   m     8 July 1854
COBB, John R                              Kizzeah
            Owner

JEFFERSON (Twin)                          B/S   M     10 July 1857
CONNER, William                           Ruth
            Mother

JEFFERSON D                               B/S   M     1 July 1861
CRITZ, James P                           Nancy
            Owner

JEFFERSON D                               B/S   M     10 May 1861
TATUM, John G                            Callie
            Owner

JEFFERSON, Florence                       W     F     29 Nov 1860
JEFFERSON, James M                        JEFFERSON, Nancy J
            Father

JEFFERSON, Mary A                         W     F     25 Sept 1854
JEFFERSON, Edward F                       JEFFERSON, Malinda
            Father

JEFFERSON, Nancy O M                      W     F     2 Jan 1859
JEFFERSON, James M                        JEFFERSON, Mary J
            Father
```

CHILD'S NAME FATHER\OWNER INFORMANT	RACE SEX BIRTH DATE MOTHER
JEFFERSON, Not Named (Born Dead) JEFFERSON, James M Father	W F 12 Mar 1855 JEFFERSON, Nancy
JEFFERSON, Richard Lee JEFFERSON, James H Father	W M 13 Apr 1854 JEFFERSON, Elizabeth
JEFFERSON, William C JEFFERSON, P G Father	W M 18 Mar 1860 JERRERSON, Louisa
JENETTA JOYCE, Hamilton Master	B/S F 5 Dec 1853 Tilda
JENKINS, America Ann JENKINS, Joel (Blacksmith) Father	W F 28 July 1860 JENKINS, Catherine
JEREMIAH ROSS, Daniel Master	B/S M 4 July 1858 Hannah
JEREMIAH CONNER, G R Ann Conner, Mistress	B/S M 12 Sept 1861 Amanda
JERRY CORN, John Elizabeth Corn, Mistress	B/S M 10 June 1855 Rachel
JESSUP, Percilla J JESSUP, E S Father	W F 12 Aug 1859 JESSUP, Delila
JETT, Eli JETT, E M (Dock) Father	W M 8 Aug 1858 JETT, Nancy
JETT, Hyberma J E JETT, E N Mother	W F 1 July 1859 JETT, Nancy
JETT, James T JETT, E M Father	W M 19 May 1862 JETT, E M
JIM GILBERT, Frederick Owner	B/S M 3 June 1853 Nilly

```
CHILD'S NAME                        RACE  SEX    BIRTH DATE
FATHER\OWNER                        MOTHER
            INFORMANT
-----------------------------------------------------------------
JIM                                 B/S   M      16 Mar 1855
BROWN, Nicholas                     Eliza
            Owner

JOE                                 B/S   M      19 Feb 1853
PENN, Thomas Sr                     Polly
            Owner

JOEL                                B/S   M      5 May 1862
SHELTON, Lewis                      Jane
            Master

JOHN                                B/S   M      2 May 1853
DeHEART, Charles                    Mariah
            Master

JOHN                                B/S   M      5 Jan 1853
PENN, Thomas J                      Suckey
            Owner

JOHN                                B/S   M      19 Feb 1854
BURNETT, Mary A                     Lucy
            Owner

JOHN                                B/S   M      -- Jan 1854
FINNEY, Joshua                      Ann
            Owner

JOHN                                B/S   M      -- May 1854
VIA, James Sr                       Charlott
            Owner

JOHN                                B/S   M      30 July 1855
WILSON, Samuel P                    Susan
            Jesse M Giles, Overseer

JOHN                                B/S   M      -- Nov 1855
PENN, Martha                        Not Given
            Mistress

JOHN                                B/S   M      -- Oct 1855
REYNOLDS, Harden W                  Druscilla
            Owner

JOHN                                B/S   M      -- May 1855
NOWLIN, James                       Mariah
            Owner

JOHN                                B/S   M      -- Feb 1857
PILSON, Richard                     Permelia
            Master
```

99

CHILD'S NAME FATHER\OWNER INFORMANT	RACE	SEX	BIRTH DATE
	MOTHER		
JOHN FINNEY, Susan Mistress	B/S Eliza	M	-- Feb 1857
JOHN TURNER, E B Master	B/S Lydney	M	-- Apr 1858
JOHN HANBY, H H Master	B/S Martha	M	14 Jan 1859
JOHN SMITH, Sallie Owner	B/S ELIZABETH	M	22 Oct 1860
JOHN PUCKETT, Robert Jackson Penn, Master	B/S Polly	M	-- Oct 1860
JOHN NOWLIN, L F Owner	B/S Puss	M	1 June 1861
JOHN PENN, Mary G W Penn for Mary, Mistress	B/S Margaret	M	-- Feb 1862
JOHN KENNERLY, Joseph (or James) Master	B/S Lucy	M	-- June 1862
JOHN D CONNER, G R Owner	B/S Amanda	M	26 Mar 1853
JOHN W PARKER, John Smith Parker, Present Owner	B/S Milly	M	-- Mar 1854
JONES ANGLIN, Philip Owner	B/S Thenia	M	10 May 1859
JONES, John A JONES, Peter D Father	W JONES, Nancy	M	17 Dec 1855
JONES, Joshua A JONES, Floyd Father	W JONES, Nancy Ann	M	3 Aug 1862

100

```
CHILD'S NAME                              RACE  SEX    BIRTH DATE
FATHER\OWNER                              MOTHER
             INFORMANT
------------------------------------------------------------------------
JONES, Lucinda E                          W     F    15 July 1860
JONES, Isaac                              JONES, Sarah
             Father

JONES, Mary                               W     F    21 Jan 1859
JONES, Peter D                            JONES, Nancy Jane
             Father

JONES, Not Named                          W     M    13 June 1854
JONES, R M                                JONES, Mary
             Father

JONES, Ruth                               W     F    20 June 1860
JONES, Peter D                            JONES, Nancy
             Father

JONES, Sarah A                            W     F    23 Oct 1857
JONES, Isaac                              JONES, Sarah
             Father

JONES, William A                          W     M    20 Sept 1853
JONES, Peter A (Unable to Labor)          JONES, Nancy
             Augustine Jones, Grandfather

JONES, William D                          W     M    21 July 1855
JONES, Isaac                              JONES, Sarah
             Father

JORDAN                                    B/S   M    1 May 1854
MURPHY, William L                         Eveline (Slave)
             Owner

JOSEPH                                    B/S   M    20 Sept 1857
PIKE, Joseph                              Jennie
             Master

JOSEPH                                    B/S   MO   30 Aug 1860
BRYANT, John T                            Charlotte
             Mary Burnett, Mistress

JOSEPH                                    B/S   M    -- Dec 1862
ZIGLAR, Christopher                       Eley
             Richard Ziglar, Young Master

JOSHUA                                    B/S   M    6 Jan 1859
REYNOLDS, H W                             Mary
             Owner

JOSIAH                                    B     M    10 July 1864
Not Given                                 Celey
             Isham Barnard, Former Owner
```

CHILD'S NAME FATHER\OWNER INFORMANT	RACE SEX BIRTH DATE MOTHER
JOYCE, Flem G JOYCE, R M Father	W M 30 May 1860 JOYCE, Mary
JOYCE, Fleming F JOYCE, R M Father	W M 2 Oct 1859 JOYCE, Mary
JOYCE, Hamilton JOYCE, Hamilton Mother	W M 16 Mar 1862 JOYCE, Elizabeth
JOYCE, John P JOYCE, L G Father	W M 7 May 1858 JOYCE, Martha J
JOYCE, Martha S JOYCE, Richard Father	W F 5 Feb 1855 JOYCE, Mary
JOYCE, Mary JOYCE, Perrin Father	W F 20 Feb 1857 JOYCE, Mary
JOYCE, Richard J JOYCE, Calvin (Miller) Father	W M 15 June 1853 JOYCE, Sarah
JOYCE, Sarah C JOYCE, Richard James Joyce, Grandfather	W F -- Oct 1862 JOYCE, Mary
JOYCE, Sarah J JOYCE, Samuel Mother	W F 12 May 1854 JOYCE, Martha J
JOYCE, Sarah T? JOYCE, Calvin Father	W F 8 Oct 1862 JOYCE, Sarah
JOYCE, Tempa Ann JOYCE, L G Father	W F 1 Apr 1862 JOYCE, Nancy A
JOYCE, Thomas JOYCE, Richard Father	W M -- May 1857 JOYCE, Mary
JOYCE, Thomas W JOYCE, H Father	W M 8 June 1860_ JOYCE, Elizabeth

```
CHILD'S NAME                             RACE  SEX   BIRTH DATE
FATHER\OWNER                             MOTHER
              INFORMANT
----------------------------------------------------------------
JOYCE, Watson                            W     M    13 Jan 1859
JOYCE, Perrin                            JOYCE, Mary
              Father

JOYCE, William A                         W     M    31 May 1862
JOYCE, P  C                              JOYCE, Mary
              Father

JUDA                                     B/S   F    6 June 1853
HAIRSTON, Samuel W                       Not Given
              Owner

JUDA                                     B/S   F    26 Jan 1859
GRIFFITH, William                        Sally
              Owner

JUDA                                     B     F    2 June 1864
Father Not Given                         Susan
              L F Nowling, Former Owner

JUDITH                                   B/S   F    18 Apr 1855
POINDEXTER, Judith                       Matilda
              James R Poindexter, Young Master

JUDITH                                   B/S   F    -- Jan 1858
HAIRSTON, S W                            Mat
              Master

JULIA                                    B/S   F    5 Aug 1853
STUART, Cheadle D                        Martha
              Elizabeth Stuart, Mother of Owner

JULIA                                    B/S   F    2 June 1854
ROBERTSON, William J                     Martha
              Owner

JULIA                                    B/S   F    15 Sept 1857
PARKER, Smith                            Mildred
              Master

JULIA                                    B/S   F    10 Aug 1858
FLIPPEN, Joseph                          Mary
              Owner

JULIA                                    B/S   F    -- July 1862
HAIRSTON, Samuel W                       Malinda
              Master

JULIA                                    B/S   F    15 Oct 1862
MOORE, Ann                               Alis
              Mistress
```

| CHILD'S NAME | RACE | SEX | BIRTH DATE |
| FATHER\OWNER | MOTHER | | |
INFORMANT			

```
CHILD'S NAME                          RACE  SEX    BIRTH DATE
FATHER\OWNER                          MOTHER
            INFORMANT
------------------------------------------------------------------------
JULIA A                               B/S    F    -- Sept 1857
HUGHS, James                          Violet
            Master

JULINA                                B/S    F    10 June 1860
RAKES, German                         Hannah
            William Spencer, Master

JULUIS                                B/S    M    30 May 1859
HUGHS, James M                        Amanda
            Owner

JUSTICE, Adaline                      W      F    29 Sept 1855
JUSTICE, John                         JUSTICE, Amy A
            Father

JUSTICE, Elizabeth                    W      F    2 Aug 1859
JUSTICE, John                         JUSTICE, Mary A
            Father

JUSTICE, Tyler                        W      M    -- -- 1853
JUSTICE, John                         JUSTICE, Mary A
            Father

KEATON                                B/S    M    -- Dec 1857
BENNETT, Mrs                          Letha
            Mistress

KEATON, Hiram M                       W      M    13 Mar 1854
KEATON, Hiram                         KEATON, Susan
            Father

KEATON, John W                        W      M    25 Oct 1854
KEATON, J                             KEATON, Perlina
            Father

KEATON, Jordan B                      W      M    20 Jan 1853
KEATON, Jordan                        KEATON, Kisesiah
            Father

KEATON, Lucinda Ruth                  W      F    26 Feb 1854
KEATON, Sampson                       KEATON, Mary
            Father

KEATON, Martha J                      W      F    30 Aug 1853
KEATON, Madison                       KEATON, Sarah A
            Father

KEATON, Martha S L                    W      F    2 May 1859
KEATON, Hiram                         KEATON, Susan
            Father
```

```
CHILD'S NAME                           RACE  SEX     BIRTH DATE
FATHER\OWNER                           MOTHER
            INFORMANT
---------------------------------------------------------------------
KEATON, Nancy Jane                      W      F    -- Aug 1855
KEATON, Madison                         KEATON, Sarah A
            Father

KEATON, Not Named                       W      M    -- Sept 1857
KEATON, Joshua                          KEATON, Avaline
            Father

KEATON, Peter D                         W      M    8 Jan 1860
KEATON, William                         KEATON, Martha A
            Father

KENNER                                  B/S    F    15 Apr 1859
CRITZ, Gabriel                          Mary
            Owner

KENNERLY, Joe                           B      F    29 Dec 1865
Unknown                                 KENNERLY, Sarah
            Joseph Kennerly, Former Owner

KENNERLY, Not Named                     B      F    1 Aug 1865
Unknown                                 KENNERLY, Clara
            Joseph Kennerly, Former Owner

KERNELIA A                              B/S    F    1 Aug 1860
MOIR, James C                           Katy
            Master

KESSIAH                                 B/S    F    27 May 1853
NOWLIN, James                           Reah N
            Owner

KESSIAH                                 B/S    F    -- Jan 1854
STAPLES, Col A                          Not Given
            Claiborne Mills, Overseer

KEZEAH                                  B/S    F    9 Jan 1859
HAIRSTON, S W                           Nancy
            Master

KING                                    B/S    M    3 Apr 1853
PENN, Clark                             Sally
            Master

KING, Not Named                         W      F    25 Sept 1860
KING, William                           KING, Malinda
            Father

KING, Not Named                         W      F    10 Nov 1864
KING, John                              KING, Eliza
            Father
```

```
CHILD'S NAME                          RACE  SEX    BIRTH DATE
FATHER\OWNER                          MOTHER
              INFORMANT
------------------------------------------------------------------------
KING, Not Named                       W      F     2 Apr 1865
KING, Henry                           KING, Matilda
              Father

KING, Roxana Emily                    W      F    18 Dec 1854
KING, Ben S                           KING, Mary Ann
              Father

KIZZIAH                               B/S    F     7 June 1854
PENN, Clark                           Not Given
              Owner

KNOWLES, Elavenia                     W      F     9 May 1862
KNOWLES, Newman W                     KNOWLES, Emarella
              Father

KNOWLES, John B                       W      M    17 Aug 1854
KNOWLES, Naaman                       KNOWLES, Avaline
              Father

KNOWLES, Not Named                    W      F    27 Dec 1854
KNOWLES, David                        KNOWLES, Elizabeth
              Father

KNOWLES, Not Named                    W      M     6 Aug 1862
KNOWLES, David                        KNOWLES, Elizabeth
              Father

KNOWLS, Not Named                     W      M    15 May 1859
KNOWLS, D R                           KNOWLS, Elizabeth
              Father

KNOWLS, Ruth E                        W      F    17 Dec 1858
KNOWLS, n W                           KNOWLS, Abrella
              Father

KNOWLS, Sarah J                       W      F     8 Mar 1853
KNOWLS, David                         KNOWLS, Elizabeth
              Father

KNOWLS, Susan                         W      F     6 June 1857
KNOWLS, David                         KNOWLS, Elizabeth
              Father

KOGER, John D                         W      M     9 Mar 1857
KOGER, Jacob W                        KOGER, Elizabeth
              Father

KOGER, John L (Twin)                  W      M     9 Dec 1854
KOGER, A T                            KOGER, Nancy
              Father
```

```
CHILD'S NAME                              RACE  SEX    BIRTH DATE
FATHER\OWNER                              MOTHER
              INFORMANT
-------------------------------------------------------------------
KOGER, Joseph K                           W     M    25 Mar 1853
KOGER, John L                             KOGER, Susan
              Joseph Koger, Grandfather

KOGER, Lucinda Ann (Twin)                 W     F     9 Dec 1854
KOGER, A T                                KOGER, Nancy
              Father

KOGER, Not Named (Twins)                  --    --    9 Dec 1853
KOGER, Augustin T                         KOGER, Nancy
              Father

LANGHORN, Frances E                       W     F    19 Dec 1854
LANGHORN, James L                         LANGHORN, Elizabeth R
              Father

LANGHORNE, Nary D                         W     F    -- Oct 1860
LANGHORNE, James S                        LANGHORNE, Elizabeth
              Father

LANGHORNE, Sarah E                        W     F     9 July 1857
LANGHORNE, James S                        LANGHORNE, Elizabeth
              Father

LATITIA                                   B/S   F    --July 1854
COBB, John R                              Carolina
              Owner

LAUREL                                    B/S   F    26 Apr 1859
SCALES, Mrs                               Avaline
              Owner

LAVINY                                    B/S   F     4 Mar 1854
ANTHONY, Benjamin A                       Rebecca
              Owner

LAW, Abram J                              W     M    31 Oct 1857
LAW, William                              LAW, Priscilla
              Father

LAW, John W                               W     M    22 June 1854
LAW, William                              LAW, Priscilla
              Father

LAW, Not Named                            W     M     8 Feb 1853
LAW, Zachariah C                          LAW, Martha A
              Father

LAWLESS, George F  M                      W     M    14 Feb 1862
LAWLESS, F  M                             LAWLESS, Zintha
              Mother

                            107
```

```
CHILD'S NAME                         RACE  SEX    BIRTH DATE
FATHER\OWNER                         MOTHER
             INFORMANT
-----------------------------------------------------------------------
LAWLESS, Matterson J  D              W     M    10 Aug 1862
LAWLESS, Thomas                      LAWLESS, Sarah A
             Father

LAWLESS, Thomas E                    W     M    19 Dec 1865
LAWLESS, G  W                        LAWLESS, Rose Anne
             Father

LAWSON, Andrew                       W     M     2 Apr 1853
LAWSON, John                         LAWSON, Kessiah
             Father

LAWSON, C  M                         W     M    22 Dec 1862
LAWSON, M  T                         LAWSON, Ruth
             Father

LAWSON, Floyd                        W     M    22 June 1854
LAWSON, Joseph                       LAWSON, Mary
             Father

LAWSON, George J                     W     M    21 May 1862
LAWSON, Lafayette                    LAWSON, Lucinda D
             Father

LAWSON, George T                     W     M     8 Apr 1858
LAWSON, M  T                         LAWSON, Ruth
             Father

LAWSON, Harden (Twin)                W     M    16 June 1859
LAWSON, A  J                         LAWSON, Malinda
             Father

LAWSON, Jacob                        W     M     9 Mar 1857
LAWSON, John                         LAWSON, Kizzeah
             Father

LAWSON, James A                      W     M    22 Oct 1862
LAWSON, Andrew J                     LAWSON, Malinda A
             Father

LAWSON, Jane E                       W     F    12 Dec 1857
LAWSON, James                        LAWSON, Jane E
             Father

LAWSON, Jno R (Twin)                 W     M    16 June 1859
LAWSON, A  J                         LAWSON, Matilda
             Father

LAWSON, John H C                     W     M    25 Aug 1853
LAWSON, James W                      LAWSON, Sally
             Father
```

```
CHILD'S NAME                           RACE  SEX    BIRTH DATE
FATHER\OWNER                           MOTHER
            INFORMANT
-------------------------------------------------------------------

LAWSON, Kezeah                          W    F    16 Nov 1860
LAWSON, John                           LAWSON, Kezeah
            Father

LAWSON, Mahala                          W    F    23 Dec 1858
LAWSON, John                           LAWSON, Keziah
            Father

LAWSON, Martha                          W    F    25 Jan 1855
LAWSON, A J                            LAWSON, Malinda
            Father

LAWSON, Martha A                        W    F    27 Feb 1859
LAWSON, Jno                            LAWSON, Mary
            Father

LAWSON, Martha A                        W    F     8 Feb 1860
LAWSON, M T                            LAWSON, Ruth
            Father

LAWSON, Not Named                       W    M     9 Dec 1853
LAWSON, William Jr                     LAWSON, Lucy
            Father

LAWSON, Not Named                       W    M    -- June 1853
LAWSON, Joseph                         LAWSON, Mary
            Father

LAWSON, Ruth                            W    F    10 Apr 1865
LAWSON, G  William                     LAWSON, Emily
            Father

LAWSON, Susan M J                       W    F    13 June 1855
LAWSON, william                        LAWSON Anna
            Father

LAYMAN, Eliza A                         W    F     1 June 1861
LAYMAN, William C                      LAYMAN, Emaline
            Father

LAYMAN, Green T                         W    M    22 Mar 1855
LAYMAN, William C                      LAYMAN, Nancy E
            Father

LAYMAN, Margaret E                      W    F    14 Dec 1853
LAYMAN, David                          LAYMAN, Sarah
            Father

LAYMAN, Margaret Ellen                  W    F    14 Feb 1854
LAYMAN, David                          LAYMAN, Sarah
            Father
```

```
CHILD'S NAME                             RACE  SEX    BIRTH DATE
FATHER\OWNER                             MOTHER
             INFORMANT
------------------------------------------------------------------------
LAYMAN, Not Named                        W      M    2 Oct 1859
LAYMAN, W C                              LAYMAN, Nancy
             Father

LAYMAN, William                          W      M    20 Dec 1865
LAYMAN, William C                        LAYMAN, Emaline
             Father

LEAK, Andrew                             W      M    4 Apr 1855
LEAK, A J                                LEAK, Jane
             Father

LEANNA                                   B/S    F    18 Jan 1861
CLARK, James                             Letha
             Owner

LEANNER                                  B/S    F    26 Nov 1854
WOOLWINE, Thomas B                       Fanny
             Owner

LEATH (Twin)                             B/S    F    5 Apr 1859
TURNER, John                             Susan
             Master

LEE                                      B/S    M    -- May 1854
COBB, John R                             Milly
             Owner

LEE                                      B/S    M    15 July 1855
MOIR, John                               Emily
             Master

LEE                                      B/S    M    16 Jan 1859
HANBY, John A                            Judy
             Master

LEE                                      B/S    M    -- June 1862
KENNERLY, Joseph (or James)              Eliza
             Master

LEE, Celia E                             W      F    26 May 1853
LEE, John                                LEE, Elizabeth A
             Father

LEE, Elizabeth                           W      F    23 May 1854
LEE, John A                              LEE, Elvira
             Father

LEE, Elizabeth                           W      F    3 Apr 1859
LEE, Jno                                 LEE, E A
             Father
```

110

```
CHILD'S NAME                              RACE  SEX    BIRTH DATE
FATHER\OWNER                              MOTHER
              INFORMANT
-------------------------------------------------------------------
LEE, George W                             W     M     1 Feb 1853
LEE, Jerman                               LEE, Mariah A
              Father

LEE, Isaac A                              W     M     18 Aug 1854
LEE, John                                 LEE, E A
              Mother

LEE, Not Named                            W     M     6 Dec 1855
LEE, Peter A (Merchant)                   LEE, Ann Mariah
              Father

LEE, Not Named                            W     F     21 Nov 1860
LEE, John                                 LEE, Elizabeth A
              Father

LEE, Not Named                            W     F     15 Jan 1865
LEE, John                                 LEE, Elizabeth A
              Father

LEE, Peter R (Rock Spring, VA)            W     M     23 Apr 1853
LEE, Peter A (Merchandisery)              LEE, Ann M
              Father

LEO                                       B/S   M     15 Dec 1861
CRITZ, James P                            Mary
              Owner

LEONARD                                   B/S   M     27 May 1860
HINES, Henry                              Rachael
              Master

LEWIS                                     B/S   M     24 Aug 1854
MARTIN, Joseph                            Not Given
              A Satterfield, Manager

LEWIS                                     B/S   M     -- July 1857
KOGER, John                               Letitia
              Master

LEWIS                                     B/S   M     27 July 1859
SCALES, AD                                Ruth
              Owner

LEWIS                                     B/S   M     7 Dec 1861
REYNOLDS, H  W                            Sallie
              Owner

LEWIS, Barbary E                          W     F     7 June 1853
Not Given                                 LEWIS, Elizabeth
              Joshua Knowls, Neighbor

                           111
```

```
CHILD'S NAME                              RACE  SEX    BIRTH DATE
FATHER\OWNER                              MOTHER
                INFORMANT
--------------------------------------------------------------------
LEWIS, Charles B                          W     M   25 Nov 1858
LEWIS, Charles                            LEWIS, Nancy A F
                Father

LEWIS, Edward W                           W     M   15 July 1857
LEWIS, Samuel                             LEWIS, Malinda
                Father

LEWIS, Joanna                             W     F   29 Oct 1859
LEWIS, Dean                               LEWIS, Arcria
                Father

LEWIS, John T                             W     M    6 Feb 1859
LEWIS, Samuel                             LEWIS, Malinda
                Father

LEWIS, Mary A                             W     F   19 Dec 1857
Not Given                                 LEWIS, Malinda
                Mother

LEWIS, William R                          W     M   17 Apr 1862
LEWIS, Samuel                             LEWIS, Malinda
                Father

LIDLO                                     B/S   ?    1 Mar 1862
TATUM, William F                          Nancy
                Master

LIGHT, Andrew J                           W     M   30 Apr 1862
LIGHT, John                               LIGHT, Lucinda
                Father

LIGHT, Austin Hill                        W     M   12 Apr 1865
LIGHT, James                              LIGHT, Lucinda
                Father

LIGHT, Eliza Jane                         W     F   15 Mar 1854
LIGHT, James                              LIGHT, Lucinda
                Father

LIGHT, Emaline                            W     F    2 Apr 1859
LIGHT, John                               LIGHT, Lucinda
                Father

LIGHT, Samuel W                           W     M   10 May 1854
LIGHT, John G                             LIGHT, Lucinda J
                Father

LIGHT, T Lacky                            W     M   14 May 1865
LIGHT, John                               LIGHT, Lucinda
                Father
```

```
CHILD'S NAME                              RACE  SEX     BIRTH DATE
FATHER\OWNER                              MOTHER
             INFORMANT
-----------------------------------------------------------------------
LILLIAN                                   B     F    7 June 1864
Father Not Given                          Puss
             Edward Tatum, Former Owner

LILLY, P  E (Born Raleigh)                W     M    9 Apr 1862
LILLY, John                               LILLY, Mary
             Father

LINVILLE                                  B/S   M    28 Dec 1854
STAPLES, Col A                            Slave Mahala
             Sally Shelton, Overseer's Wife

LOTT                                      B/S   M    -- May 1857
TUGGLE, John                              Lucy
             Master

LOUISA                                    B/S   F    -- May 1854
FINNEY, Joshua                            Annie
             Owner

LOUISA                                    B/S   F    -- Aug 1857
BOWLING, Henry T                          Delphia
             Master

LOUISA                                    B/S   F    -- Jan 1858
HAIRSTON, S W                             Nancy
             Master

LOVEL, M  N                               W     F    2 Feb 1862
LOVEL, David                              LOVEL, Malinda
             Father

LOVELL, Not Named                         W     M    29 June 1860
LOVELL, David                            LOVELL, Malinda
             Father

LOVELL, William J                         W     M    14 Aug 1855
LOVELL, John                             LOVELL, Felony
             Father

LOVINGS, James                            W     M    1 Feb 1857
LOVINGS, A J                             LOVINGS, Nancy
             Father

LOVINS, Thomas J                          W     M    1 Jan 1862
LOVINS, William                          LAVINS, Mahala
             Father

LUCINDA                                   B/S   F    1 Dec 1855
PENN, Mary                                Not Given
             J A Penn, Young Master
```

CHILD'S NAME FATHER\OWNER INFORMANT	RACE SEX BIRTH DATE MOTHER
LUCINDA CRITZ, William Owner	B/S F 3 Aug 1859 Jane
LUCINDA PENN, T J Owner	B/S F 16 May 1861 Susan
LUCINDA SPENCER, M S Master	B/S F 22 Nov 1862 America
LUCINDA TERRY, R A Master	B/S F 1 Oct 1862 Grady Ann
LUCRETIA WILSON, Samuel P Jesse M Giles, Overseer	W F 28 May 1855 Polly
LUCY VAUGHN, Wilson T Owner	B/S F 22 May 1853 Rhoda
LUCY HAIRSTON, Samuel Father	B/S F 29 Jan 1855 HAIRSTON, Louisa
LUCY HAIRSTON, S W Master	B/S F -- June 1858 Ann
LUCY CLARK, R M Owner	B/S F 26 Nov 1861 Adaline
LUCY CRITZ, William Owner	B/S F 2 Mar 1861 Martha
LUCY PENN, Jackson Master	B/S F -- Apr 1862 Lucinda
LUCY STAPLES, William Ann Staples, Mistress	B/S F 9 Sept 1862 Easther
LUCY COCKRAN, Edward Master	B/S F 9 Nov 1862 Phillis

CHILD'S NAME FATHER\OWNER INFORMANT	RACE	SEX	BIRTH DATE MOTHER
LUCY LANGHORNE, James S Master	B/S	F	3 Feb 1862 Susan
LUCY ANN MARTIN, John Master	B/S	F	10 May 1855 Not Given
LUCY B REYNOLDS, H W Master	B/S	F	-- Sept 1857 Nancy
LUVENIA STONE, Tandy Master	B/S	F	6 July 1855 Not Given
LYAIRE ADAMS, Joshua Master	B/S	F	19 Jan 1855 Isabel
LYON, C G LYON, James Father	W	M	9 Mar 1853 LYON, Sarah
LYON, Columbus G LYON, Elijah Father	W	M	3 July 1859 LYON, Milly
LYON, Elizabeth LYON, Elijah Mother	W	F	8 Apr 1862 LYON, Milly
LYON, Exony E LYON, Silas T Father	W	F	27 Dec 1865 LYON, Caroline
LYON, J T LYON, James D Father	W	M	16 Jan 1859 LYON, Sarah
LYON, James R LYON, James Father	W	M	19 Apr 1862 LYON, Sarah
LYON, Sarah M LYON, William Jr William Lyon, Grandfather	W	F	-- Dec 1862 LYON, Elvisa
MABE, Gilmer MABE, Samuel Father	W	M	12 Jan 1859 MABE, Avaline

CHILD'S NAME FATHER\OWNER	INFORMANT	RACE SEX BIRTH DATE MOTHER
MABE, John MABE, Joseph	Father	W M 15 July 1855 MABE, Naoma
MABE, John W MABE, Jesse	Father	W M 27 May 1857 MABE, Elizabeth
MABE, Lee T MABE, Joseph	Father	W M 10 Sept 1853 MABE, Oney
MABE, Samuel H MABE, Samuel	Father	W M 10 Mar 1864 MABE, Susan
MADISON STAPLES, W R	Master	• B/S M -- Sept 1857 Jane
MAHALA HAIRSTON, S W	Master	B/S F -- Dec 1860 Nancy
MAIZE, Elizabeth D MAIZE, Thomas G (Res NC)	Drury S Mays (No Relation Given)	W F 5 Dec 1854 MAIZE, Louisa
MAJOR PENN, George W	Owner	B/S M 10 Mar 1853 Ann
MAJOR REYNOLDS, James	Milly Reynolds, Owner	B/S M -- Feb 1854 Tamsey
MALINDA KOGER, John Sr	Owner	B/S F 5 Oct 1853 Martha
MALINDA TUGGLE, John	Owner	B/S F -- May 1853 Milly
MALINDA SMITH, H M	Master	B/S F 24 July 1860 Winnie
MALINDA ANGLIN, Philip	Master	B/S F 1 July 1861 Sally

116

CHILD'S NAME FATHER\OWNER	RACE	SEX	BIRTH DATE
INFORMANT	MOTHER		
MANASSA J B TURNER, Crawford	B/S	M	10 Aug 1862
Master	Mary		
MANERVA HAIRSTON, S W	B/S	F	-- Sept 1859
Master	Avaline		
MARCUS PENN, John E	B/S	M	8 June 1855
Susan L Penn, Mistress	Martha		
MARCUS WALLER PENN, John	B/S	M	9 June 1855
William M Ayers, Employer	Martha		
MARGARET KOGER, John Sr	B/S	F	4 May 1853
Owner	Set		
MARGARET KOGER, Henry	B/S	F	12 Aug 1854
Owner	Tillis		
MARGARET PRUNTY, John	B/S	F	5 Jan 1855
Master	Hannah		
MARIAH HAIRSTON, W W	B/S	F	-- -- 1853
Owner	Not Given		
MARIAH WILSON, Samuel P	B/S	F	20 Feb 1855
Jesse M Giles, Overseer	Sally		
MARIAH ZEGLER, Richard	B/S	F	-- Jan 1859
Owner	Luvenia		
MARIAH Father Not Given	B	F	11 July 1864
Sallie Smith, Former Owner	Judy		
MARIAH (Twin) VIA, C A	B/S	F	31 Aug 1862
J C Moir, for Mistress	Mary		
MARSHALL, Charlotte MARSHALL, William	W	F	30 Nov 1857
Father	MARSHALL, Charlotte		

117

```
CHILD'S NAME                              RACE  SEX    BIRTH DATE
FATHER\OWNER                              MOTHER
            INFORMANT
-----------------------------------------------------------------------
MARSHALL, Elizabeth E                     W    F     31 Nov 1854
MARSHALL, Robert                          MARSHALL, Cathrine
            Father

MARSHALL, Jefferson Davis                 W    M     5 July 1861
MARSHALL, William                         MARSHALL, Lucy
            Father

MARSHALL, Rufus M                         W    M     2 Nov 1859
MARSHALL, Robert                          MARSHALL, Catherine
            Father

MARSHALL, Williamson                      W    M     3 Jan 1854
MARSHALL, William                         MARSHALL, Charlotte
            Father

MARTHA                                    B/S  F     12 Apr 1855
VIA, James D                              Pocohontas
            Master

MARTHA                                    B/S  F     23 Nov 1855
SPENCER, William                          Lavina
            Owner

MARTHA                                    B/S  F     -- Dec 1859
REYNOLDS, Ellen                           Mariah
            Owner

MARTHA                                    B/S  F     1 Feb 1861
WILSON, Samuel P                          Martha
            Jesse M Giles, Overseer

MARTHA                                    B/S  F     10 Oct 1862
PARKER, Smith                             Mary Jane
            Master

MARTHA JANE                               B/S  F     20 Aug 1862
LACKEY, John                              Malinda
            Master

MARTIN                                    B/S  M     24 June 1853
FLIPPIN, Joseph T                         Maning
            Master

MARTIN                                    B    M     13 Dec 1864
Not Given                                 Susan
            Jane Clark, Former Owner

MARTIN                                    B/S  M     -- Oct 1858
ADAMS, J                                  Sarah
            Master
```

118

```
CHILD'S NAME                          RACE  SEX    BIRTH DATE
FATHER\OWNER                          MOTHER
            INFORMANT
-----------------------------------------------------------------------
MARTIN VAN BUREN                      B/S   M    1 Aug 1855
PENN, Susan L                         Jane
            Mistress

MARTIN, A  H                          W     M    8 Nov 1861
MARTIN, A  H                          MARTIN, Dollie
            Father

MARTIN, Archelas                      W     M    29 Mar 1853
MARTIN, John                          MARTIN, Eletha
            Father

MARTIN, Charles                       W     M    10 Aug 1865
MARTIN, A  W                          MARTIN, Ruth
            Father

MARTIN, Charles T                     W     M    12 May 1857
MARTIN, Charles T                     MARTIN, Agnes
            Father

MARTIN, Daniel                        W     M    18 Feb 1859
MARTIN, Isaac                         MARTIN, Rhoda
            Father

MARTIN, Delila                        W     F    8 Sept 1865
MARTIN, William B                     MARTIN, Martha A
            Father

MARTIN, Elizabeth                     W     F    2 June 1861
MARTIN, John                          MARTIN, Elizabeth
            Father

MARTIN, Elizabeth V                   W     F    9 Mar 1853
MARTIN, B  J                          MARTIN, Sarah A
            Father

MARTIN, Elvira                        W     F    9 Sept 1854
MARTIN, James                         MARTIN, Mary
            Father

MARTIN, Elvira                        W     F    10 May 1854
MARTIN, Stokley                       MARTIN, Mahala
            Father

MARTIN, Enona                         W     F    6 May 1853
MARTIN, James P                       MARTIN, Ruth
            Father

MARTIN, Flem (Born Franklin Co)       W     M    8 June 1858
MARTIN, J  J                          MARTIN, Susan
            Father
```

```
CHILD'S NAME                          RACE  SEX    BIRTH DATE
FATHER\OWNER                          MOTHER
              INFORMANT
--------------------------------------------------------------------------
MARTIN, George Robert                 W     M     2 Sept 1859
MARTIN, A W D                         MARTIN, Ruth
              Father

MARTIN, George W                      W     M     13 Aug 1857
MARTIN, R T                           MARTIN, Jane
              Father

MARTIN, Henry                         W     M     22 Apr 1855
MARTIN, John                          MARTIN, Elizabeth
              Father

MARTIN, Henry P                       W     M     10 Aug 1862
MARTIN, William                       MARTIN, Ann
              Father

MARTIN, Isabella                      W     F     12 Apr 1859
MARTIN, Lewis                         MARTIN, Martha
              Father

MARTIN, James L                       W     M     25 Nov 1862
MARTIN, James P                       MARTIN, Martha
              Father

MARTIN, Jancy J                       W     F     -- Apr 1860
MARTIN, Daniel                        MARTIN, America
              Father

MARTIN, John                          W     M     1 Apr 1855
MARTIN, Joshua T                      MARTIN, Martha
              Father

MARTIN, Joshua J                      W     M     26 May 1862
MARTIN, James                         MARTIN, Mary
              Father

MARTIN, Julian E                      W     F     26 Nov 1862
MARTIN, Edward                        MARTIN, Sarah
              Father

MARTIN, Luvenia J                     W     F     9 Mar 1855
MARTIN, James J                       MARTIN, Lethae
              Father

MARTIN, M T                           W     M     4 Apr 1859
MARTIN, William,                      MARTIN, Martha A
              Father

MARTIN, Madison (Born Dead)           W     M     7 May 1855
MARTIN, Isaac                         MARTIN, Rode
              Father


                          120
```

```
CHILD'S NAME                          RACE  SEX    BIRTH DATE
FATHER\OWNER                          MOTHER
              INFORMANT
------------------------------------------------------------------
MARTIN, Mary                          W     F    -- Sept 1857
MARTIN, Isaac                         MARTIN, Rhoda
              Father

MARTIN, Mary E                        W     F    1 Nov 1862
MARTIN, Samuel                        MARTIN, Elizabeth
              Mother

MARTIN, Mary J                        W     F    17 Nov 1853
MARTIN, Isaac                         MARTIN, Rhoda
              Father

MARTIN, Mary J                        W     F    22 Oct 1860
MARTIN, John B                        MARTIN, Elizabeth E
              Father

MARTIN, Mary T                        W     F    31 July 1855
MARTIN, John H                        MARTIN, Martha W
              Father

MARTIN, Not Named                     W     F    24 Dec 1854
MARTIN, William                       MARTIN, Martha
              Father

MARTIN, Not Named                     W     M    26 Oct 1854
MARTIN, James P                       MARTIN, Ruth
              Father

MARTIN, Not Named                     W     M    8 July 1854
MARTIN, Nelson                        MARTIN, Matilda
              Father

MARTIN, Not Named                     W     M    -- Sept 1859
MARTIN, C T                           MARTIN, Agness
              Father

MARTIN, Not Named                     W     F    3 June 1860
MARTIN, A H                           MARTIN, Sallie
              Father

MARTIN, Not Named                     W     M    24 May 1860
MARTIN, James                         MARTIN, Mary
              Father

MARTIN, Not Named                     W     M    22 Aug 1860
MARTIN, S                             MARTIN, Martha
              Father

MARTIN, Not Named                     W     M    21 Nov 1862
MARTIN, John B                        MARTIN, Elizabeth
              Mother

                          121
```

```
CHILD'S NAME                              RACE  SEX     BIRTH DATE
FATHER\OWNER                              MOTHER
             INFORMANT
---------------------------------------------------------------------
MARTIN, Not Named                         W     M    16 July 1862
MARTIN, Daniel                            MARTIN, America
             Mother

MARTIN, Not Named (Hole in one ear)       W     M    23 Sept 1855
MARTIN, John                              MARTIN, Letha
             Father

MARTIN, Rosannah                          W     F    10 Oct 1859
MARTIN, Charles                           MARTIN, Frances
             Father

MARTIN, Sarah                             W     F     3 May 1859
MARTIN, James                             MARTIN, Mary
             Father

MARTIN, Sarah (Born Dead)                 W     F     4 Nov 1855
MARTIN, William                           MARTIN, Nancy
             Father

MARTIN, Sarah E                           W     F    15 July 1859
MARTIN, J J                               MARTIN, Leatha
             Father

MARTIN, Sarah J                           W     F     9 Jan 1862
MARTIN, A  R                              MARTIN, Eluisa
             Father

MARTIN, Washington R                      W     M    12 July 1862
MARTIN, A  W                              MARTIN, Ruth
             Father

MARTIN, Wesley                            W     M    10 May 1853
MARTIN, Nelson                            MARTIN, Matilda
             Mother

MARTIN, William                           W     M    17 Mar 1857
MARTIN, William                           MARTIN, Martha
             Father

MARTIN, William T                         W     M     6 Dec 1858
MARTIN, Jno B                             MARTIN, Ellen E
             Father

MARTIN, William Wingfield                 W     M    25 Nov 1854
MARTIN, Benjamin J                        MARTIN, Sarah Ann
             Father

MARY                                      B/S   F    25 Sept 1853
FLIPPIN, Joseph T                         Jude
             Master
```

```
CHILD'S NAME                               RACE  SEX    BIRTH DATE
FATHER\OWNER                               MOTHER
              INFORMANT
----------------------------------------------------------------------
MARY                                       B/S    F    5 Oct 1853
WILSON, Samuel P                           Sally
              Jesse Giles, Overseer

MARY                                       B/S    F    28 July 1853
HATCHER, David B                           Not Given
              Owner

MARY                                       B/S    F    15 July 1853
PENN, Thomas J                             Mary
              Owner

MARY                                       B/S    F    30 Jan 1854
CLARK, Jacob S                             Rebecca
              Owner

MARY                                       B/S    F    20 Sept 1858
MILLS, Richard                             Carolina
              Owner

MARY                                       B/S    F    -- May 1859
PENN, Susan                                Virginia
              Owner

MARY                                       B/S    F    27 Dec 1860
HUGHES, Mat                                Violete
              Master

MARY                                       B/S    F    15 Dec 1860
NOWLIN, S F                                Mary
              Master

MARY                                       B/S    F    -- Sept 1860
TAYLOR, Jame A                             Sarah
              E B Turner, Master

MARY                                       B/S    F    9 Mar 1862
HYLTON, Gabriel                            Letty
              Master

MARY                                       B/S    F    24 Mar 1862
SPENCER, W  B                              Hannah
              Master

MARY ELIZA                                 B/S    F    -- Nov 1855
SCALES, Absalom                            Not Given
              Master

MARY FRANCES                               B/S    F    15 Aug 1862
PARKER, Smith                              Milly
              Master
```

```
CHILD'S NAME                          RACE  SEX    BIRTH DATE
FATHER\OWNER                          MOTHER
            INFORMANT
------------------------------------------------------------------

MASSEY James W                        W     M    -- -- 1853
MASSEY, Ancil                         MASSEY, Elizabeth
            Father

MASSEY, John A                        W     M    13 Nov 1862
Illegitimate                          MASSEY, Martha
            Elizabeth Massey, Grandmother

MASSEY, Mary E                        W     F    30 Mar 1860
Illegitimate                          MASSEY, Elizabeth M
            Mother

MASSEY, Not Named                     W     M    24 June 1865
MASSEY, James M                       MASSEY, Frances
            Mother

MAT                                   B/S   M    4 Apr 1855
PENN, William L                       Eliza
            Susan L Penn, Mistress

MAT                                   B/S   M    16 Dec 1860
CRITZ, J P                            Susan
            Master

MATHERLY, Not Named                   W     M    8 Aug 1853
MATHERLY, John                        MATHERLY, Martha
            Father

MATILDA                               B/S   F    -- Oct 1854
HAGOOD, Anderson                      Eliza
            Elizabeth Hagood, Owner

MATILDA                               B/S   F    21 Mar 1858
FRANCIS, William M                    Martha
            Owner

MATTHEW (Twin)                        B/S   M    10 July 1857
CONNER, William                       Ruth
            Master

MAY                                   B/S   F    15 Sept 1854
MARTIN, John                          Not Given
            Owner

MAY                                   B/S   F    20 Sept 1855
FRANCE, Joseph                        Sally
            Master

MAYSEE, James M                       W     M    30 June 1862
MAYSE, James                          MAYSE, Deby
            Mother
```

124

```
CHILD'S NAME                              RACE  SEX    BIRTH DATE
FATHER\OWNER                              MOTHER
            INFORMANT
------------------------------------------------------------------------
McALEXANDER, Anderson                     W     M     17 Apr 1855
McALEXANDER, William                      McALEXANDER, Susannah
            Father

McALEXANDER, Era                          W     F     11 Apr 1858
McALEXANDER, William                      McALEXANDER, Susan
            Father

McALEXANDER, J (Born Floyd Co)            w     f     21 May 1858
McALEXANDER, Lester                       McALEXANDER, Elizabeth M
            Father

McALEXANDER, Meshack (Twin)               W     M     13 May 1865
McALEXANDER, William                      McALEXANDER, Susannah
            Father

McALEXANDER, Not Named                    W     M     28 Sept 1857
McALEXANDER, Samuel                       McALEXANDER, Byer
            Father

McALEXANDER, Shadrack (Twin)              W     M     13 May 1865
McALEXANDER, William                      McALEXANDER, Susannah
            Father

McALEXANDER, Susannah                     W     F     15 Mar 1862
McALEXANDER, William                      McALEXANDER, Susannah
            Father

McALEXANDER, William                      W     M     20 May 1859
McALEXANDER, William                      McALEXANDER, Susan
            Father

McARHUR, Perry                            W     M     12 Apr 1861
McARTHUR, Perry                           McARTHUR, Elizabeth
            Father

McARTHUR, Elizabeth                       W     F     8 Oct 1865
McARTHUR, Perry                           McARTHUR, Elizabeth
            Father

McARTHUR, John C                          W     M     22 Apr 1860
McARTHUR, Perry                           McARTHUR, Elizabeth
            Father

McARTHUR, Milton                          W     M     4 Aug 1853
McARTHUR, Perry                           McARTHUR, Elizabeth
            Father

McARTHUR, Sarah F                         W     F     17 June 1855
McARTHUR, Perry                           McARTHUR, Elizabeth
            Father
```

```
CHILD'S NAME                                 RACE  SEX    BIRTH DATE
FATHER\OWNER                                 MOTHER
              INFORMANT
-----------------------------------------------------------------------
McARTHUR, William Burwell                    W    M    11 Feb 1859
McARTHUR, Pery                               McARTHUR, Elizabeth
              Father

McBRADY, Not Named                           W    F    10 Sept 1862
McBRADY, M W                                 McBRADY, Sarah
              Father

McCANDLESS, Susan                            W    F    16 Feb 1860
McCANDLESS, A W                              McCANDLESS, Mary
              Father

McGEHEE, Lucy E                              W    F    21 Sept 1855
McGHEE, William                              McGHEE, Martha
              Father

McGEHEE, Thomas C                            W    M    -- May 1857
McGEHEE, William                             McGEHEE, Martha A
              Father

McGHEE, Judith                               W    F    7 May 1859
McGHEE, William                              McGHEE, Martha
              Father

McGHEE, Richard D                            W    M    19 Jan 1862
McGHEE, William (Mechanic)                   McGHEE, Martha A
              Mother

McMILLION, Harden Reynolds                   W    M    30 June 1854
McMILLION, Joseph (Carp,BSmith,Marksman)     McMILLION, Nancy
              Father

McMILLION, Tabitha                           W    F    15 Mar 1854
McMILLION, G                                 McMILLION, Sally
              Father

McPEAK, Martha F                             W    F    21 Sept 1865
McPEAK, Bluford                              McPEAK, Sarah
              Father

McPEAK, Not Named                            W    F    -- Jan 1864
McPEAK, B                                    McPEAK, Sarah
              Father

MEADOWS, Charles H                           W    M    5 Oct 1853
MEADOWS, Major                               MEADOWS, Amanda
              Father

MECCA JANE                                   B/S  F    1 Nov 1855
POTTER, William                              Mecca
              Owner
```

```
CHILD'S NAME                             RACE  SEX    BIRTH DATE
FATHER\OWNER                             MOTHER
          INFORMANT
--------------------------------------------------------------------------
MEREDITH, Elizabeth                      W     F     20 May 1865
MEREDITH, Bradley                        MEREDITH, Polly
          Father

MEREDITH, John S                         W     M      9 Dec 1862
MEREDITH, Bradley                        MEREDITH, Polly
          Father

MEREDITH, Rozella                        W     F     12 May 1860
MEREDITH, Bradley                        MEREDITH, Mary
          Father

MERRIX, Sarah A                          W     F      1 Oct 1855
MERRIX, Dodson                           MERRIX, Mary
          Father

MIDKIFF, Alamenta                        W     F     27 May 1855
MIDKIFF, Joseph                          MIDKIFF, Lavenia
          Father

MIDKIFF, Aubern D                        W     M      7 Dec 1855
MIDKIFF, Jeremiah                        MIDKIFF, Elizabeth
          Father

MIDKIFF, John L H                        W     M     26 June 1860
MIDKIFF, John                            MIDKIFF, Luvenia
          Father

MIDKIFF, Martha L                        W     F     28 June 1859
MIDKIFF, Green                           MIDKIFF, mary J
          Father

MIDKIFF, Mary L                          W     F      6 Feb 1862
MIDKIFF, Joseph                          MIDKIFF, Luvenia
          Father

MIDKIFF, Nancy E                         W     F     28 Apr 1858
MIDKIFF, Jno                             MIDKIFF, Luvenia
          Father

MIFFLIN, Adalade Susannah                W     F      1 Aug 1854
MIFFLIN, Dr William (Physician & Farmer) MIFFLIN, Lydia
          Father

MILES                                    B/S   M     15 Mar 1853
WILSON, Samuel P                         Suckey
          Luvenia Shelton, Wife of Overseer

MILES                                    B/S   M     20 Apr 1854
WILSON, S P                              Milly
          O H Shelton, Overseer
```

127

```
CHILD'S NAME                            RACE  SEX    BIRTH DATE
FATHER\OWNER                            MOTHER
               INFORMANT
-----------------------------------------------------------------------
MILES, Augustin                         W     M    23 Nov 1859
MILES, John C                           MILES, Sarah
               Father

MILLEY                                  B     F    10 Oct 1864
Not Given                               Alice
               H W Reynolds, Former Owner

MILLIE                                  B/S   F    6 Mar 1861
REYNOLDS, H  W                          Martha
               Owner

MILLS, Elizabeth                        W     F    5 Aug 1860
MILLS, William                          MILLS, Sallie
               Father

MILLS, James                            W     M    1 Oct 1857
MILLS, William                          MILLS, Sally
               Father

MILLS, John F                           W     M    28 Dec 1853
MILLS, Richard                          MILLS, Judith
               Father

MILLS, Not Named                        B     F    7 May 1865
Unknown                                 MILLS, Caroline
               Richard Mills, Former Owner

MILLY                                   B/S   F    25 June 1853
TURNER, C                               Sook
               Owner

MILLY                                   B/S   F    7  Apr 1859
ADAMS, James                            Fannie
               Master

MILLY                                   B/S   F    5 Jan 1860
ROBERTSON, J R                          Ruth
               Master

MILLY                                   B/S   F    26 Nov 1860
CORN, Peter                             America
               William Conner, Master

MILTON                                  B/S   M    30 Sept 1861
FOSTER, Abram                           Lucy
               Owner

MINERVA                                 B/S   F    29 June 1854
PENN, Clark                             Not Given
               Owner
```

```
CHILD'S NAME                          RACE  SEX    BIRTH DATE
FATHER\OWNER                          MOTHER
              INFORMANT
---------------------------------------------------------------------
MINTA                                 B/S   F     -- Aug 1862
PENN, George W                        Minta
              Master

MINTORIA                              B/S   F     -- Oct 1860
EMMERSON, J T                         Lucy
              Master

MISY                                  B/S   F     1 July 1861
ZIGLER, Chriss                        Mary
              Owner

MITCHELL, George W                    W     M     27 Mar 1854
MITCHELL, Robert                      MITCHELL, Lucinda
              Father

MITCHELL, John R                      W     M     -- June 1862
MITCHELL, Allen                       MITCHELL, Francis
              Father

MITCHELL, Not Named                   W     F     28 June 1864
MITCHELL, J  Madison                  MITCHELL, Elizabeth
              Father

MITCHELL, William A Burwell           W     M     27 June 1854
MITCHELL, Allen                       MITCHELL, Frances
              Father

MITCHRELL, Sarah V                    W     F     -- Mar 1854
MITCHELL, B F                         MITCHELL, Mamie F
              Father

MIZE, Elizabeth                       W     F     17 Aug 1860
MIZE, Sampson                         MIZE, Nancy
              Father

MIZE, Not Named                       W     M     -- -- 1853
MIZE, Sampson                         MIZE, Elizabeth
              Father

MOIR, Elamanda                        W     F     10 Apr 1855
MOIR, James C (Merchant)              MOIR, Lucy E
              Father

MOIR, John A                          W     M     21 June 1853
MOIR, James C (Merchant)              MOIR, Louisa
              Father

MOIR, Not Named                       W     F     1 Nov 1857
MOIR, John W (Merchant)               MOIR, Avaline
              Father
```

129

```
CHILD'S NAME                              RACE  SEX    BIRTH DATE
FATHER\OWNER                              MOTHER
             INFORMANT
---------------------------------------------------------------------

MOIR, Not Named                           W      M    8 Apr 1860
MORI, W W (Merchant)                      MOIR, Callie V
             Father

MOLES, Herbert L                          W      M    18 Dec 1857
MOLES, John B                             MOLES, Susan
             Father

MONROE                                    B/S    M    10 June 1860
ZEGLER, C                                 Mary
             Master

MONTGOMERY, Josiah                        W      M    20 Nov 1857
MONTGOMERY, Kelly                         MONTGOMERY, Cynthia
             Father

MONTGOMERY, Tyre                          W      M    -- -- 1855
MONTGOMERY, Kelly                         MONTGOMERY, Delphy
             Mother

MOORE, Alex                               W      M    10 Jan 1859
MOORE, Jeff                               MOORE, Carolina
             Father

MOORE, Emmett                             ?      M    22 Apr 1861
MOORE, N  S                               Eliza
             Owner

MOORE, Ira                                W      M    6 July 1858
MOORE, Abram                              MOORE, Martha
             Father

MOORE, John R                             W      M    4 Nov 1853
MOORE, Henry J                            MOORE, Caroline M
             Father

MOORE, Lee                                W      M    10 Feb 1862
MOORE, William                            MOORE, Perlina A
             Mother

MOORE, Loes V                             W      F    22 Apr 1862
MOORE, Henry J                            MOORE, Caroline
             Father

MOORE, Not Named                          W      M    1 Feb 1862
Not Given                                 MOORE, Mary
             Mother

MOORE, Webster                            W      M    1 Oct 1859
MOORE, Jeff                               MOORE, Caroline
             Father
```

```
CHILD'S NAME                          RACE  SEX    BIRTH DATE
FATHER\OWNER                          MOTHER
              INFORMANT
-----------------------------------------------------------------
MOORE, William H                       W    M    28 Jan 1855
MOORE, H J                             MOORE, Caroline
              Father

MORAN, Abram                           W    M    5 Aug 1854
MORAN, William                         MORAN, Mary
              Father

MORAN, George W C                      W    M    21 Mar 1854
MORAN, James                           MORAN, Delila
              Father

MORAN, Jathina                         W    F    12 May 1860
MORAN, Elijah                          MORAN, Caroline
              Father

MORAN, Martin L                        W    M    11 May 1853
MORAN, Elijah                          MORAN, Caroline
              Father

MORAN, Not Named                       W    F    16 Feb 1864
MORAN, John                            MORAN, Ruth
              Father

MOREFIELD, Edward J                    W    M    16 Nov 1855
MOREFIELD, Wright                      MOREFIELD, Jane
              Father

MOREFIELD, James W                     W    M    14 July 1854
MOREFIELD, Josiah                      MOREFIELD, Leathy Ann
              Father

MOREFIELD, Susan Elizabeth             W    F    8 Mar 1853
MOREFIELD, William                     MOREFIELD, Mary Ann
              Father

MORRIS, Eliza Jane                     W    F    15 Aug 1854
MORRIS, Coleman A                      MORRIS, Sukey
              Father

MORRIS, Rufus                          W    M    3 June 1859
MORRIS, C G                            MORRIS, Lahy (?)
              Father

MORRIS, Sarah E J                      W    F    15 Dec 1853
MORRIS, James M (Tobacconist)          MORRIS, Mary A
              Bradly Morris, Second Cousin

MORRIS, Susan A                        W    F    5 Aug 1861
MORRIS, Calermorran                    MORRIS, Leathia
              Father
```

```
CHILD'S NAME                          RACE  SEX    BIRTH DATE
FATHER\OWNER                          MOTHER
            INFORMANT
--------------------------------------------------------------------
MORRISON, Elizabeth                    W     F    11 Mar 1860
MORRISON, M L                          MORRISON, L D
            Father

MORRISON, Exona A                      W     F    11 May 1858
MORRISON, Jno                          MORRISON, Exony
            Father

MORRISON, John H                       W     M    25 Mar 1860_
MORRISON, John                         MORRISON, Exony
            Father

MORRISON, Juda E                       W     F     7 June 1853
MORRISON, John F                       MORRISON, Mary E
            Father

MORRISON, Mary Jane                    W     F    -- June 1859
MORRISON, M L                          MORRISON, Tempa D
            Father

MORRISON, Nancy E                      W     F     4 Sept 1860
Illegitimate                           MORRISON, Jane
            Mother

MORRISON, Nancy F                      W     F    14 Feb 1854
MORRISON, Joseph                       MORRISON, Enona
            Father

MORRISON, William Green                W     M    29 Aug 1862
MORRISON, Joseph                       MORRISON, Exony
            Father

MOSES                                  B/S   M    -- Apr 1859
WRIGHT, John N                         Agness
            M Wright, Young Master

MOSS, Robert                           W     M    11 June 1860
MOSS, Jesse                            MOSS, Easter
            Father

MOSS, Sarah E                          W     F    18 Nov 1862
MOSS, Jesse (Miller)                   MOSS, Easther
            Father

MOSS, William Thomas                   W     M    10 Apr 1858
MOSS, J P                              MOSS, Easter
            Father

NANCE                                  B/S   F    15 May 1853
HATCHER, David B                       Not Given
            Owner

                               132
```

```
CHILD'S NAME                              RACE  SEX    BIRTH DATE
FATHER\OWNER                              MOTHER
               INFORMANT
------------------------------------------------------------------------
NANCE, George W                           W     M      1 Feb 1857
NANCE, James                              NANCE, Sarah
               Father

NANCY                                     B/S   F      -- June 1853
VIA, Alexander                            Lucy
               Master

NANCY                                     B/S   F      21 June 1854
ZIGLER, Christopher                       Cenia
               R M Zigler, Young Master

NANCY                                     B/S   F      -- Nov 1857
PENN, Jefferson                           Virginia
               Master

NANCY                                     B/S   F      26 Mar 1859
ZEGLER, Richard                           Lucinda
               Owner

NANCY                                     B/S   F      2 Sept 1861
ZIGLER, Chriss                            Nancy
               Owner

NANCY                                     B/S   F      29 Apr 1862
SMITH, Hardin                             Winney
               Elizabeth Smith, Mistress

NAPIER, James M                           W     M      13 Dec 1860
NAPIER, Jno                               NAPIER, Mary J
               Father

NATHAN                                    B/S   M      2 June 1859
CRITZ, William                            Martha
               Owner

NEWMAN, Elam P                            W     M      -- July 1854
NEWMAN, Armstreet W                       NEWMAN, Frances
               Father

NEWMAN, Elizabeth                         W     F      1 Mar 1854
NEWMAN, James                             NEWMAN, Sally
               Father

NEWMAN, John A                            W     M      11 Nov 1857
NEWMAN, A W                               NEWMAN, Franky
               Father

NEWMAN, Lucinda                           W     F      11 Sept 1853
NEWMAN, John                              NEWMAN, Milly
               Father


                          133
```

CHILD'S NAME FATHER\OWNER INFORMANT	RACE SEX BIRTH DATE MOTHER
NEWMAN, Mary NEWMAN, Sam Father	W F 16 May 1860 NEWMAN, Ruth
NEWMAN, Nancy NEWMAN, Samuel Father	W F 30 Sept 1858 NEWMAN, Ruth
NEWMAN, Nancy E NEWMAN, John Mother	W F 11 Sept 1862 NEWMAN, Milly
NEWMAN, Not Named NEWMAN, Joseph Father	W M -- Nov 1857 NEWMAN, Ruth
NEWMAN, Not Named NEWMAN, Samuel Father	W M 3 Mar 1864 NEWMAN, Ruth
NEWMAN, Sarah E NEWMAN, John Father	W F 5 Dec 1855 NEWMAN, Pauline
NEWMAN, Sarah L NEWMAN, Samuel Father	W F 20 Feb 1862 NEWMAN, Ruth
NEWMAN, Vinlinchia NEWMAN, John Father	W F 2 Nov 1861 NEWMAN, Ruth
NICHOLAS ADAMS, Notley P Master	B/S M 2 July 1855 Not Given
NORAN (?) MURPHY, Susan V Mistress	B/S M 12 Mar 1862 Lucinda
NOT NAMED PENN, Jackson Master	B/S M 10 July 1853 Not Given
NOT NAMED NOWLIN, Spencer Master	B/S M 15 June 1853 Not Given
NOT NAMED DALTON, Nancy James Dalton, Husband of Owner	B/S M 20 Nov 1853 Not Given

```
CHILD'S NAME                            RACE  SEX    BIRTH DATE
FATHER\OWNER                            MOTHER
            INFORMANT
------------------------------------------------------------------------
NOT NAMED                               B/S    M     30 Dec 1853
CLARK, Alexander B                      Suze
            Master

NOT NAMED                               B/S    M     1 Sept 1853
GUNTER, Elizabeth                       Not Given
            Beveraly S Gunter, Son of Owner

NOT NAMED                               B/S    --    15 Sept 1853
FALKNER, William                        Not Given
            Owner

NOT NAMED                               B/S    F     1 Aug 1853
MARTIN, John                            Not Given
            Owner

NOT NAMED                               B/S    F     15 Dec 1853
MARTIN, Joseph                          Not Given
            Anthony Satterfield, Overseer

NOT NAMED                               B/S    M     10 Mar 1853
ADAMS, Joshua Sr                        Not Given
            Master

NOT NAMED                               B/S    M     6 Nov 1853
WALLER, Edmund                          Not Given
            Master

NOT NAMED                               B/S    M     20 Sept 1853
JOYCE, Perrin                           Caroline
            Master

NOT NAMED                               B/S    M     21 Sept 1853
JOYCE, Perrin                           Reah
            Master

NOT NAMED                               B/S    M     10 May 1853
WILSON, Samuel P                        Edy
            Jesse Giles, Overseer

NOT NAMED                               B/S    M     5 May 1853
WILSON, Samuel P                        Polly
            Benjamin G Walker, Overseer

NOT NAMED                               B/S    M     1 May 1853
WILSON, Samuel P                        Dorcas
            Benjamin G Walker, Overseer

NOT NAMED                               B/S    M     5 May 1853
REED, Nathan                            Lucy
            Master
```

```
CHILD'S NAME                             RACE  SEX    BIRTH DATE
FATHER\OWNER                             MOTHER
            INFORMANT
------------------------------------------------------------------------
NOT NAMED                                B/S   F     9 Dec 1853
STAPLES, John C Heirs                    Avaline
            John Staples, One of the Heirs

NOT NAMED                                B/S   F     4 July 1853
HAGOOD, Anderson                         Caroline
            Owner

NOT NAMED                                B/S   M     1 June 1853
STONE, Tandy                             Luvenia
            Owner

NOT NAMED                                B/S   F     -- -- 1853
ROSS, Louiza                             Not Given
            S W Tensley, Neighbor

NOT NAMED                                B/S   F     -- Feb 1853
AKERS, Elizabeth                         Till
            Owner

NOT NAMED                                B/S   F     1 Dec 1854
STAPLES, A                               None Given
            William Falkner, Overseer

NOT NAMED                                B/S   M     1 Apr 1854
TATUM, Edward                            Slave Mary
            Owner

NOT NAMED                                B/S   F     -- Feb 1854
STAPLES, W C                             Not Given
            Capt James A Penn, Master

NOT NAMED                                B/S   F     -- Oct 1854
STAPLES, W C                             Not Given
            Capt James A Penn, Master

NOT NAMED                                B/S   F     -- -- ----
JOYCE, Hamilton                          Not Given
            Owner

NOT NAMED                                B/S   M     20 Oct 1854
KENNERLY, Joseph                         Not Given
            Owner

NOT NAMED                                B/S   M     21 Sept 1854
KENNERLY, Joseph                         Not Given
            Owner

NOT NAMED                                B/S   M     -- Aug 1854
ZIGLER, Christopher                      Jane
            R M Ziglar, Young Master

                            136
```

```
CHILD'S NAME                            RACE  SEX   BIRTH DATE
FATHER\OWNER                            MOTHER
              INFORMANT
---------------------------------------------------------------------
NOT NAMED                               B/S   F    -- June 1854
WILSON, Samuel P                        Bethia
              Jesse Giles, Manager

NOT NAMED                               B/S   M    -- July 1854
WILSON, Samuel P                        Eady
              Jesse Giles, Manager

NOT NAMED                               B/S   M    1 Aug 1854
WILSON, Samuel P                        Deannah
              Jesse Giles, Manager

NOT NAMED                               B/S   F    2 Oct 1854
WILSON, Samuel P                        Rachael
              Jesse Giles, Manager

NOT NAMED                               B/S   F    -- Dec 1854
WILSON, Samuel P                        Sally
              Jesse Giles, Manager

NOT NAMED                               B/S   M    -- Dec 1854
WILSON, S P                             Not Given
              B G Walker

NOT NAMED                               B/S   F    16 Nov 1854
CONNER, William                         America
              Owner

NOT NAMED                               B/S   F    15 Dec 1854
PENN, Jackson                           Esther
              Owner

NOT NAMED                               B/S   M    -- Apr 1855
PENN, George                            Not Given
              Master

NOT NAMED                               B/S   M    -- July 1855
BOWLING, Gabriel                        Not Given
              Master

NOT NAMED                               B/S   F    5 Sept 1855
MOORE, Ann                              Ally
              Mistress

NOT NAMED                               B/S   F    24 Nov 1855
WALLER, James A                         Margaret
              Owner

NOT NAMED                               B/S   F    -- Dec 1855
MILLS, Richard                          Caroline
              Owner


                        137
```

```
CHILD'S NAME                              RACE SEX   BIRTH DATE
FATHER\OWNER                              MOTHER
              INFORMANT
-----------------------------------------------------------------
NOT NAMED                                 B/S   F    -- Nov 1855
STAPLES, Abram                            Susan
              William Falkner, Overseer

NOT NAMED                                 B/S   M    28 Oct 1855
KING, George W                            Mary
              Owner

NOT NAMED                                 B/S   F    -- Sept 1855
GRAY, William W                           Manan
              Master

NOT NAMED                                 B/S   F    -- Sept 1855
STAPLES, William C                        Jane
              James H Clark, Who Hired Her

NOT NAMED                                 B/S   F    -- Dec 1855
CLARK, Jacob                              Paulina
              Owner

NOT NAMED                                 B/S   M    3 Aug 1855
HUGHS, Thomas                             Mary
              William H Ayers, Employer

NOT NAMED                                 B/S   M    -- Oct 1855
STAPLES, William C                        Ann
              Owner

NOT NAMED                                 B/S   M    -- Dec 1855
HANBY, D S                                Milly
              Owner

NOT NAMED                                 B/S   M    -- -- 1857
GUNTER, Elizabeth                         June
              B L Gunter, Master

NOT NAMED                                 B/S   M    1 Mar 1857
McCABE, William                           Emily
              Owner

NOT NAMED                                 B/S   F    17 Apr 1857
WOODALL, Joseph                           Edy
              Master

NOT NAMED                                 B/S   F    -- Nov 1857
WILSON, Not Given                         Milly
              Jesse Giles, Master

NOT NAMED                                 B/S   F    -- Nov 1857
WILSON, Not Given                         Polly
              Jesse Giles, Master
```

CHILD'S NAME FATHER\OWNER		RACE SEX	BIRTH DATE
	INFORMANT	MOTHER	

CHILD'S NAME / FATHER\OWNER	INFORMANT	RACE SEX	MOTHER	BIRTH DATE
NOT NAMED ATHEY, James	Master	B/S F	Mary	25 Feb 1857
not named ATHEY, James	Master	B/S M	Sarah	-- July 1857
NOT NAMED REYNOLDS, H W	Master	B/S F	Jane	-- Sept 1857
NOT NAMED REYNOLDS, H W	Master	B/S F	Susan	-- Sept 1857
NOT NAMED REYNOLDS, H W	Master	B/S M	Martha	-- Sept 1857
NOT NAMED REYNOLDS, H W	Master	B/S M	Mary	-- Sept 1857
NOT NAMED REYNOLDS, H W	Master	B/S M	Susan	-- Sept 1857
NOT NAMED REYNOLDS, H W	Master	B/S F	Malinda	-- Sept 1857
NOT NAMED CLARK, Thomas	Owner	B/S F	Nancy	-- Aug 1857
NOT NAMED CLARK, Jacob	Owner	B/S F	Martha	-- Aug 1857
NOT NAMED COBB, John	Master	B/S --	Milly	-- Dec 1857
NOT NAMED ADAMS, Abram	Master	B/S F	Manda	28 Aug 1857
NOT NAMED HAIRSTON, S W	Master	B/S M	Caty	-- Dec 1858

```
CHILD'S NAME                              RACE  SEX    BIRTH DATE
FATHER\OWNER                              MOTHER
                  INFORMANT
--------------------------------------------------------------------
NOT NAMED                                 B/S    M    6 Dec 1858
PENN, G W                                 Margarite
                  Thomas Penn, Master

NOT NAMED                                 B/S    M    -- Nov 1858
THOMAS, W T                               Moll
                  Master

NOT NAMED                                 B/S    M    7 Sept 1858
HATCHER, m                                Martha
                  Thomas Hatcher, Owner

NOT NAMED                                 B/S    F    -- -- 1859
WILSON, Samuel                            Martha
                  Jesse Giles, Overseer

NOT NAMED                                 B/S    F    6 July 1859
PENN, James A                             Chicy
                  Owner

NOT NAMED                                 B/S    F    -- June 1859
PENN, James A                             Sarah
                  Owner

NOT NAMED                                 B/S    F    -- Apr 1859
WALKER, John                              Deannah
                  Master

NOT NAMED                                 B/S    F    -- Feb 1859
HANBY, D S                                Amelia
                  Owner

NOT NAMED                                 B/S    F    -- Dec 1859
PENN, Susan                               Sally
                  Owner

NOT NAMED                                 B/S    F    7 Mar 1859
GRAY, Mrs                                 Maria
                  owner

NOT NAMED                                 B/S    F    22 Sept 1859
NOWLIN, S F                               Mary
                  Owner

NOT NAMED                                 B/S    F    4 June 1859
DAVIS, Charles                            Bettie
                  Owner

NOT NAMED                                 B/S    M    10 Feb 1859
WILSON, Samuel P                          Martha
                  Jesse Giles, Overseer
```

CHILD'S NAME FATHER\OWNER INFORMANT	RACE	SEX	BIRTH DATE
	MOTHER		
NOT NAMED WILSON, Samuel P Jesse Giles, Overseer	B/S Milly	M	10 Feb 1859
NOT NAMED WILSON, Samuel P Jesse Giles, Overseer	B/S Sally	M	10 Feb 1859
NOT NAMED WILSON, Samuel P Jesse Giles, Overseer	B/S Edie	F	10 Feb 1859
NOT NAMED WILSON, Samuel P Jesse Giles, Overseer	B/S Sally	F	10 Feb 1859
NOT NAMED BROWN, Nicholas Owner	B/S Emily	F	20 Dec 1859
NOT NAMED BROWN, Nicholas Owner	B/S Martha	F	20 Dec 1859
NOT NAMED REYNOLDS, H W Owner	B/S Harriett	M	10 June 1859
NOT NAMED REYNOLDS, H W Owner	B/S Priscilla	M	10 June 1859
Not Named TATUM, William F owner	B/S Emma	M	10 Dec 1859
NOT NAMED ANTHONY, B A Master	B/S Rebecca	M	-- Mar 1859
NOT NAMED DeHART, A Master	B/S Elizabeth	F	9 Oct 1859
NOT NAMED JOYCE, James Master	B/S Oney	M	-- May 1859
NOT NAMED PENN, Jack Master	B/S Esther	M	-- Dec 1859

```
CHILD'S NAME                              RACE  SEX    BIRTH DATE
FATHER\OWNER                              MOTHER
                INFORMANT
----------------------------------------------------------------------
NOT NAMED                                 B/S   F    -- Nov 1859
PENN, Jack                                Lucinda
                Master

NOT NAMED                                 B/S   F    -- Nov 1859
PENN, Jack                                Eliza
                Master

NOT NAMED                                 B/S   M    -- Aug 1859
TURNER, E B                               Sarah
                Master

NOT NAMED                                 B/S   M    -- Oct 1859
VlA, C A                                  Druscilla
                James C Moir, Guardian

NOT NAMED                                 B/S   F    15 Dec 1860
JOYCE, H                                  Juda
                Master

NOT NAMED                                 B/S   F    15 Dec 1860
JOYCE, H                                  Martha
                Master

NOT NAMED                                 B/S   F    10 Nov 1860
STAPLES, Mary                             Martha
                Anthony Satterfield, Master

NOT NAMED                                 B/S   F    10 Apr 1860
HYLTON, Val                               Ruth
                Master

NOT NAMED                                 B/S   F    1 Oct 1860
HYLTON, A                                 Mary
                Master

NOT NAMED                                 B/S   F    7 May 1860
PENN, Susan                               Keziah
                Mistress

NOT NAMED                                 B/S   F    11 Dec 1860
PENN, Polly                               Sally
                Owner

NOT NAMED                                 B/S   F    10 Mar 1860
MURPHY, William L                         Lucinda
                Master

NOT NAMED                                 B/S   F    13 Feb 1860
MURPHY, William L                         Luvenia
                Master
```

CHILD'S NAME FATHER\OWNER	INFORMANT	RACE SEX MOTHER	BIRTH DATE
NOT NAMED COBB, J R	Master	B/S F Mary	10 June 1860
NOT NAMED COBB, J R	Master	B/S M Keziah	10 May 1860
NOT NAMED COBB, J R	Master	B/S F Exony	16 Apr 1860
NOT NAMED COBB, J R	Master	B/S M Susan	18 Mar 1860
NOT NAMED HAIRSTON, S W	Master	B/S M Jane	-- June 1860
NOT NAMED BROWN, Nicholas	Owner	B/S F Emily	7 Oct 1861
NOT NAMED CLARK, Thomas J	Owner	B/S M Jestin	1 Oct 1861
NOT NAMED HATCHER, Margaret	Owner	B/S M Martha	24 Mar 1861
NOT NAMED HATCHER, Margaret	Owner	B/S M Nancy	7 Nov 1861
NOT NAMED PENN, T J	Owner	B/S M Milly	10 July 1861
NOT NAMED PENN, T J	Owner	B/S M Julia	19 July 1861
NOT NAMED PENN, T J	Owner	B/S M Martha	7 July 1861
NOT NAMED REYNOLDS, H W	Owner	B/S F Susan	-- June 1861

143

CHILD'S NAME	RACE	SEX	BIRTH DATE
FATHER\OWNER	MOTHER		
INFORMANT			

CHILD'S NAME / FATHER\OWNER / INFORMANT	RACE	SEX	BIRTH DATE / MOTHER
NOT NAMED REYNOLDS, H W Owner	B/S	F	10 Apr 1861 Lucinda
NOT NAMED REYNOLDS, H W Owner	B/S	M	10 Apr 1861 Bettie
NOT NAMED REYNOLDS, H W Owner	B/S	M	15 June 1861 Sarah
NOT NAMED REYNOLDS, H W Owner	B/S	F	10 Mar 1861 Celia
NOT NAMED WILSON, Samuel P Jesse M Giles, Overseer	B/S	M	1 Apr 1861 Hannah
NOT NAMED WILSON, Samuel P Jesse M Giles, Overseer	B/S	F	-- July 1861 Bettie
NOT NAMED PENN, Peter L Master	B/S	F	-- July 1862 Catherine
NOT NAMED DAVIS, B A Master	B/S	F	27 May 1862 Not Given
NOT NAMED HANBY, D S Master	B/S	M	20 Aug 1862 Not Given
NOT NAMED KENNERLY, Joseph (or James) Master	B/S	m	-- May 1862 Clara
NOT NAMED STAPLES, S G Master	B/S	M	-- Dec 1862 Mary
NOT NAMED SAWYERS, Sarah J Master	B/S	F	1 July 1862 Hannah
NOT NAMED WEST, F B Master	B/S	F	7 Mar 1862 Mariah

144

```
CHILD'S NAME                             RACE  SEX    BIRTH DATE
FATHER\OWNER                             MOTHER
                INFORMANT
-----------------------------------------------------------------------
NOT NAMED                                B/S   M     -- Nov 1862
WILSON, S  P                             Liza
                Jesse Giles, Overseer

NOT NAMED                                B/S   F     -- Nov 1862
WILSON, S  P                             Polly
                Jesse Gilel, Overseer

NOT NAMED                                B/S   F     -- Dec 1862
WILSON, S  P                             Martha
                Jesse Giles, Overseer

NOT NAMED                                B/S   F     1 July 1862
ANTHONY, Martha                          Jane
                Mistress

NOT NAMED                                B/S   F     -- Aug 1862
PENN, Mrs M  C                           Barbary
                Mistress

NOT NAMED                                B     M     -- Mar 1864
Not Given                                Ann
                Henry Tuttle, Former Owner

NOT NAMED                                B     F     11 Sept 1864
Not Given                                Mary
                Joseph Clark, Former Owner

NOT NAMED                                B     M     12 Dec 1864
Not Given                                Dilsa
                Joseph Clark, Former Owner

NOT NAMED                                B     M     8 July 1864
Not Given                                Jane
                Jesse Giles, Former Owner

NOT NAMED                                B     F     10 May 1864
Not Given                                Sallie
                T J Penn, Former Owner

NOT NAMED                                B     F     7 June 1864
Not Given                                Susan
                T J Penn, Former Owner

NOT NAMED                                B     F     10 June 1864
Not Given                                Ruth
                James P Critz, Former Owner

NOT NAMED                                B     F     12 Jan 1864
Not Given                                Susan
                James P Critz, Former Owner


                        145
```

CHILD'S NAME FATHER\OWNER INFORMANT	RACE SEX MOTHER	BIRTH DATE
NOT NAMED Not Given James P Critz, Former Owner	B M Betsy	17 Mar 1864_
NOT NAMED Not Given James P Critz, Former Owner	B M Mary	2 June 1864
NOT NAMED STAPLES, John S Master	B/S M Ruth	9 Dec 1853
NOT NAMED (4 Slaves) REYNOLDS, Harden W Owner	B/S F Not Given	-- -- ----
NOT NAMED (Born Dead) REYNOLDS, Harden W Owner	B/S M Anny	-- Aug 1855
NOT NAMED (Born Dead) CONNER, John Master	B/S M Mary J	2 Feb 1858
NOT NAMED (Born Dead) VIA, C A J C Moir, Guardian for C A Via	B/S -- Druscilla	-- Sept 1858
NOT NAMED (Born Dead) FRANCES, Joseph Master	B/S F Sarah	15 Aug 1859
NOT NAMED (Born Dead) FLIPPIN, John T Owner	B/S M Rhoda	1 Sept 1861
NOT NAMED (Born Dead) CARTER, M D Perlina Carter, Mistress	B/S F Martha	10 Mar 1862
NOT NAMED (Twins) (Born Dead) BRIM, Joseph Owner	B/S M Not Given	1 Apr 1854
NOWLIN, Avlella NOWLIN, Charles P Father	W F NOWLIN, Nancy	-- June 1857
NOWLIN, Charles A NOWLIN, David Father	W M NOWLIN, Catherine	28 Jan 1855

```
CHILD'S NAME                                    RACE  SEX    BIRTH DATE
FATHER\OWNER                                    MOTHER
              INFORMANT
---------------------------------------------------------------------
NOWLIN, David J  D                              W      M    29 July 1862
NOWLIN, David                                   NOWLIN, Catharine
              Mother

NOWLIN, Enoch L                                 W      M    15 Oct 1860
NOWLIN, C P                                     NOWLIN, Nancy
              Father

NOWLIN, Geworge S                               W      M    10 Feb 1853
NOWLIN, C P                                     NOWLIN, Nancy
              Mother

NOWLIN, Mancy A                                 W      F    17 Apr 1855
NOWLIN, Charles P                               NOWLIN, Nancy
              Father

NOWLIN, Not Named                               W      M     8 Feb 1858
NOWLIN, D                                       NOWLIN, Catherine
              Mother

NOWLIN, Not Named                               W      M    31 Aug 1862
NOWLIN, C  C (Saddler & Tanner)                 NOWLIN, Easther
              Father

NOWLING, Not Named                              B      F     1 June 1865
Unknown                                         NOWLING, Puss
              S F Nowling, Former Owner

NUNN, George W                                  W      M     2 Apr 1861
NUNN, Major                                     NUNN, Ellen
              Father

NUNN, John J                                    W      M    15 Sept 1855
NUNN, Major                                     NUNN, Ellen
              Father

OAKLEY, Eliza Virginia                          W      F    11 Oct 1861
OAKLEY, William M                               OAKLEY, Amanda
              Father

OAKLEY, Mary Frances                            W      F     7 Jan 1855
OAKLEY, William M                               OAKLEY, Amanda
              Mother

ODILAY                                          B/S    F    23 Mar 1860
DeHART, Charles                                 Marin
              Charles Ross, Master

OLDHAM, Lucinda                                 W      F    23 Oct 1857
OLDHAM, William                                 OLDHAM, Sarah F
              Father


                          147
```

```
CHILD'S NAME                          RACE  SEX    BIRTH DATE
FATHER\OWNER                          MOTHER
            INFORMANT
------------------------------------------------------------------------
OLDHAM, Susan A                       W     F      6 Feb 1853
OLDHAM, William                       OLDHAM, Sarah F
            Father

OLIVER M                              B/S   M      7 Mar 1854
BOWLING, James M                      Matilda
            Owner

ONEAL, A P B                          W     M      22 June 1860
ONEAL, John H                         ONEAL, Aramelia
            Father

ONEAL, Combray E C                    W     F      29 June 1855
ONEAL, John H                         ONEAL, Amelia
            Father

ONEAL, Demasquis D L                  W     M      12 Dec 1857
ONEAL, John H                         ONEAL, Milly
            Father

ORANDER, George C                     W     M      22 May 1854
ORANDER, Mathew                       ORANDER, Mary Ann
            Father

ORANDER, John J                       W     M      11 Oct 1853
ORANDER, Pleasant W                   ORANDER, Barbara A
            Mother

OREGON LEE                            B/S   M      22 Nov 1862
TERRY, H  B                           Mahala
            Master

OVERBY, Allison                       W     F      -- Nov 1859
OVERBY, Thomas                        OVERBY, Ann
            Father

PACK, Andrew J                        W     M      24 Dec 1854
PACK, James                           PACK, Martha
            Father

PACK, Ann                             W     F      1 Jan 1857
PACK, James                           PACK Lucy
            Father

PACK, Elijah                          W     M      20 Sept 1855
PACK, Tyrea                           PACK, Penelope
            Father

PACK, Foulks G                        W     M      -- Apr 1855
PACK, James                           PACK, Louisa
            Father
```

```
CHILD'S NAME                              RACE  SEX     BIRTH DATE
FATHER\OWNER                              MOTHER
              INFORMANT
------------------------------------------------------------------------
PADGET, Sarah Jane                        W     F    19 Nov 1854
PADGET, Andrew J                          PADGET, Elizabeth F
              Father

PADGET, William F                         W     M     5 Jan 1853
PADGET, Andrew C                          PADGET, Elizabeth
              John Fry, No Connection

PADGETT, A J                              W     m    20 Aug 1862
PADGETT, A  C (Blacksmith)                PADGETT, Elizabeth
              James W Padgett, Uncle

PADGETT, Not Named                        W     M     1 May 1864
PADGETT, A  C (Blacksmith)                PADGETT, Elizabeth
              Father

PANNELL, William M                        W     M    10 Sept 1860
PANNELL, Jno                              PANNELL, Sallie
              Father

PARKER, Henrietta                         W     F     3 Sept 1860
PARKER, Smith                             PARKER, Elizabeth T
              Father

PARKER, Ira L                             W     M    27 Oct 1853
PARKER, William                           PARKER, Eveline
              Father

PARKER, John Y                            W     M    13 July 1859
PARKER, William                           PARKER, Sarah
              Father

PARKER, Julia Ann                         W     F     5 Dec 1853
PARKER, Henry                             PARKER, Frankey
              Mother

PARKER, Julian                            W     F     2 Feb 1854
PARKER, Henry                             PARKER, Frances
              Father

PARKER, Nancy H                           W     F    23 Nov 1859
PARKER, Lewis                             PARKER, Martha
              Father

PARKER, Not Named                         W     F    -- Jan 1857
PARKER, William                           PARKER, Sarah
              Father

PARKER, Permelia A                        W     F    27 Oct 1858
PARKER, Smith                             PARKER, Elizabeth F
              Father
```

```
CHILD'S NAME                            RACE  SEX    BIRTH DATE
FATHER\OWNER                            MOTHER
              INFORMANT
-----------------------------------------------------------------------
PARKER, Susan F                         W     F     18 May 1857
PARKER, Smith                           PARKER, Elizabeth F
              Father

PARR, Judy (Born in Poorhouse)          W     F     30 Jan 1854
LEGITIMATE                              PARR, Sally
              William Critz, Sr, Supt.

PARR, Not Named (Born in Poorhouse)     W     F     15 July 1854
LEGITIMATE                              PARR, Charlotte
              William Critz, Sr, Supt

PATRICK                                 B/S   M     -- Apr 1854
TURNER, John                           Not Given
              Owner

PATRICK                                 B/S   M     15 Apr 1855
HYLTON, Nancy                          Jane
              G Hylton, Young Master

PATRICK                                 B/S   M     1 Mar 1861
HYLTON, George W                       Rachael
              Owner

PATSY                                   B/S   F     -- May 1855
STUART, Elizabeth                      Susan
              Mistress

PAYNE                                   B/S   M     4 Mar 1855
PENN, Clark                            Bettie
              Owner

PAYNE, Howard                           W     M     11 Apr 1854
PAYNE, John B (Merchant)               PAYNE, Ellen S
              Father

PEDIGO, Ann                             W     F     15 Nov 1858
PEDIGO, A G                            PEDIGO, Lucinda
              Father

PEDIGO, Benjamin S                      W     M     17 Nov 1855
PEDIGO, Albert G                       PEDIGO, Lucinda
              Father

PEDIGO, Carla                           W     F     30 June 1853
PEDIGO, A G                            PEDIGO, Lucinda J
              Father

PEDIGO, Charles S                       W     M     4 July 1859
PEDIGO, E B                            PEDIGO, Lucy
              Father
```

```
CHILD'S NAME                          RACE  SEX    BIRTH DATE
FATHER\OWNER                          MOTHER
             INFORMANT
-----------------------------------------------------------------------
PEDIGO, Elizabeth M                    W    F    17 Sept 1853
PEDIGO, Elijah B                       PEDIGO, Lucy
             Father

PEDIGO, Emily                          W    F    19 Feb 1861
PEDIGO, E  B                           PEDIGO, Lucy
             Father

PEDIGO, Not Named                      W    M    10 Nov 1857
PEDIGO, A G                            PEDIGO, Lucinda
             Mother

PEDIGO, Rosa L                         W    F    15 Feb 1862
PEDIGO, A  G                           PEDIGO, Lucinda J
             Father

PENDLETON, Binford F                   W    M    25 Feb 1854
PENDLETON, Harden                      PENDLETON, Ruth
             Father

PENDLETON, Daniel                      W    M    13 Aug 1857
PENDLETON, Harden                      PENDLETON, Ruth
             Father

PENDLETON, Emeline E                   W    F    30 Oct 1853
PENDLETON, Ryall                       PENDLETON, Nancy
             Mother

PENDLETON, John W                      W    M    30 Mar 1857
PENDLETON, Wilson                      PENDLETON, Sarah E
             Father

PENDLETON, Lucinda A                   W    F    25 Dec 1858
PENDLETON, Wilson                      PENDLETON, Sarah A
             Father

PENDLETON, Milly                       W    F    27 Apr 1859
PENDLETON, John                        PENDLETON, Ann
             Father

PENDLETON, Not Named                   W    F    25 Mar 1857
PENDLETON, John                        PENDLETON, Anna
             Father

PENDLETON, Not Named                   W    M    17 Nov 1860
PENDLETON, W S                         PENDLETON, Sarah
             Father

PENDLETON, Ruth E                      W    F    7 Apr 1860
PENDLETON, William                     PENDLETON, Elizabeth
             Father
```

```
CHILD'S NAME                              RACE  SEX     BIRTH DATE
FATHER\OWNER                              MOTHER
               INFORMANT
-----------------------------------------------------------------------
PENDLETON, Sarah J                        W     F    19 June 1858
PENDLETON, Royall                         PENDLETON, Nancy
               Father

PENDLETON, William E                      W     M    17 June 1858
PENDLETON, Jno                            PENDLETON, Mary J
               Father

PENN, Idea                                W     F    -- June 1859
PENN, P M                                 PENN, Sarah
               Father

PENN, John L                              W     M     1 May 1853
PENN, Thomas J (Merchant)                 PENN, Lucinda C
               Father

PENN, Keziah                              B     F    30 June 1865
PENN, Marshall                            PENN, Minta
               Father

PENN, Leath                               W     F    22 Mar 1862
PENN, Peter L                             PENN, Sarah
               Father

PENN, Martin                              W     M    24 Nov 1854
PENN, Jackson                             PENN, Martha
               Father

PENN, Mary Ann                            W     F    -- Apr 1854
PENN, G W                                 PENN, Anne
               Father

PENN, Not Named                           W     M    13 July 1853
PENN, Jackson                             PENN, Martha A
               Father

PENN, Not Named                           B     F    17 Apr 1865
Unknown                                   PENN, Milly
               W S Penn, Former Owner

PENN, Stoneman                            B     F     7 June 1865
Unknown                                   PENN, Jane
               W S Penn, Former Owner

PENN, Thomas                              W     M     6 July 1859
PENN, James A                             PENN, Lucinda
               Father

PENNY                                     B/S   F    -- -- 1855
HYLTON, Nancy Jane                        Mary
               G Hylton, Young Master


                            152
```

```
CHILD'S NAME                          RACE  SEX    BIRTH DATE
FATHER\OWNER                          MOTHER
          INFORMANT
------------------------------------------------------------------------
PERIS                                 B/S   M     5 Mar 1861
SMITH, Sarah                          Matilda
          Owner

PERKINS, C Columbus                   W     M     10 Sept 1860
PERKINS, Jarrard                      PERKINS, Catherine
          Father

PERKINS, Nancy L                      W     F     27 Apr 1855
PERKINS, Jarard                       PERKINS, Catherine
          Father

PERKINS, Not Named                    W     F     22 Dec 1859
PERKINS, J                            PERKINS, Catherine
          Father

PERRY                                 B/S   M     10 Oct 1861
REYNOLDS, H  W                        Kit
          Owner

PERRY                                 B/S   M     -- May 1861
CONNER, William Sr                    Martha
          Master

PERRY                                 B/S   M     -- Nov 1862
ZIGLAR, Christopher                   Nancy
          Richard Ziglar, Young Master

PETER                                 B/S   M     29 May 1853
OVERBY, Allen T                       Jenny
          Master

PETER                                 B/S   M     11 Sept 1858
MOORE, N H                            Eliza
          Owner

PETER                                 B/S   M     -- Sept 1859
HAIRSTON, S W                         Malinda
          Master

PETER                                 B/S   M     1 Apr 1861
STAPLES, Mary                         Letha
          H Shelton, Overseer

PETER L                               B/S   M     -- Jan 1858
HAIRSTON, S W                         Esther
          Master

PHARISS, Henry William                W     M     15 Oct 1854_
PHARISS, King H (Overseer)            PHARISS, Malinda F
          Father

                           153
```

```
CHILD'S NAME                      RACE  SEX    BIRTH DATE
FATHER\OWNER                      MOTHER
              INFORMANT
--------------------------------------------------------------------
PHEBY                             B/S   F    -- June 1860
HAGOOD, William R                 Lucinda
              Master

PHILIP                            B/S   M    27 May 1853
TURNER, William                   Julina
              Owner

PHILPOTT, John L                  W     M    16 May 1857
PHILPOTT, John J                  PHILPOTT, Elizabeth
              Father

PICKERAL, Not Named               W     M    -- May 1862
PICKERAL, Thomas                  PICKERAL, Margaret
              Father

PICKERAL, Not Named (Twin)        W     M    -- May 1862
PICKERAL, Thomas                  PICKERAL, Margaret
              Father

PIKE, Abram                       W     M    15 Oct 1855
PIKE, Ben                         PIKE, Nancy
              Father

PIKE, Charles                     W     M    1 Mar 1857
PIKE, William                     PIKE, Matilda
              Father

PIKE, Gabriel                     W     M    25 Aug 1853
PIKE, Benjamin                    PIKE, Nancy
              Father

PIKE, Joseph W                    W     M    1 May 1857
PIKE, Joseph                      PIKE, Sarah
              Father

PIKE, Not Named                   W     F    28 July 1862
PIKE, Benjamin                    PIKE, Nancy
              Father

PIKE, Sarah C                     W     F    29 Aug 1853
PIKE, William                     PIKE, Vashta
              Father

PIKE, William                     W     M    5 July 1861
PIKE, John                        PIKE, Sallie
              Father

PILSON, Mary E                    W     F    13 May 1859
PILSON, William                   PILSON, S E
              Father
```

```
CHILD'S NAME                           RACE  SEX    BIRTH DATE
FATHER\OWNER                           MOTHER
              INFORMANT
------------------------------------------------------------------------
PILSON, Not Named                      W     M    10 Mar 1854
PILSON, William                        PILSON, Elizabeth
              Father

PINE                                   B/S   F    25 Dec 1862
FRANCE, Joseph                         Sally
              Master

PLASTER, Elkanah                       W     M    10 Apr 1865
PLASTERS, Jefferson                    PLASTERS, Mary J
              C Plasters, Grandfather

PLASTER, Luetsa J                      W     F    27 Oct 1862
PLASTER, Creed                         PLASTER, Rhuhama
              Jane Plaster, Grandmother

PLASTERS, Harvey L                     W     M    21 Sept 1854
PLASTERS, Mark H                       PLASTERS, Luvenia
              Father

PLASTERS, John H                       W     M    6 Apr 1854
PLASTERS, Jonas                        PLASTERS, Sally
              Mother

PLASTERS, Milton F                     W     M    7 Apr 1861
PLASTERS, Creed                        PLASTERS, Rhuhama
              Father

PLASTERS, Not Named (Born Dead)        W     F    4 Nov 1855
PLASTERS, Jonas (Milling)              PLASTERS, Sarah
              Father

PLASTERS, Thomas                       W     M    -- Dec 1857
PLASTERS, James                        PLASTERS, Sally
              Father

PLASTERS, Thomas J R                   W     M    18 Mar 1859
PLASTER, Thomas J                      PLASTERS, Mary J
              Father

PLEASANT                               B/S   M    -- Jan 1857
COBB, John                             Juley
              Master

PLEASANT                               B     M    1 Sept 1864
Not Given                              Emily
              Nicholas Brown, Former Owner

POCOHONTAS                             B/S   F    27 Apr 1862
TURNER, Crawford                       Susan
              Master


                          155
```

```
CHILD'S NAME                                    RACE  SEX    BIRTH DATE
FATHER\OWNER                                    MOTHER
            INFORMANT
-------------------------------------------------------------------------
POFF, James M (Floyd Co)                        W     M    3 June 1865
POFF, John                                      POFF, Margaret
            Father

POINDEXTER, Sarah Jane                          W     F    10 Apr 1854
POINDEXTER, James K                             POINDEXTER, Susan
            Father

POINDEXTER, Susan E                             W     F    26 June 1853
POINDEXTER, James K                             POINDEXTER, Susan J
            Father

POLINA                                          B/S   F    -- Aug 1862
CLARK, Robert M                                 Polly
            Owner

POTTER, Bishop F                                W     M    21 Aug 1854
POTTER, William C (Blacksmith)                  POTTER, Julia Ann
            Mother

POWELL                                          B/S   M    7 Jan 1861
GRAY, John F                                    Lucy
            Owner

POWELL, Billie B                                W     F    3 Mar 1861
POWELL, William                                 POWELL, Mary J
            Father

POWELL, Not Named                               W     F    6 Nov 1859
POWELL, William                                 POWELL, Susan
            Father

PRATER, Elizabeth                               W     F    5 June 1862
PRATER, John D                                  PRATER, Sarah
            Mother

PRATER, Mahala                                  W     F    13 Nov 1854
PRATER, John D                                  PRATER, Sally
            Father

PRESTON                                         B/S   M    1 Oct 1859
HUGHES, James M                                 Violet
            Owner

PRICE, Ann                                      B     F    16 Sept 1865
PRICE, Jacob                                    PRICE, Amanda
            Father

PRICE, Not Named                                W     M    19 Sept 1853
None Given                                      PRICE, Joyce
            Mother
```

CHILD'S NAME FATHER\OWNER INFORMANT	RACE SEX BIRTH DATE MOTHER
PUCKET, Juda PUCKET, Elijah Father	W F 25 Feb 1857 PUCKET, Sarah
PUCKET, Mary J PUCKET, Elijan Mother	W F 19 May 1855 PUCKET, Sarah
PUCKET, Nancy C PUCKET, Riley Father	W F 20 June 1861 PUCKET, Matilda
PUCKETT, Eli PUCKETT, Harry Father	W M 17 Dec 1865 PUCKETT, Sallie
PUCKETT, Eluisa E PUCKETT, D F Mother	W F 20 Aug 1862 PUCKETT, Elizabeth
PUCKETT, George W PUCKETT, Doct F Father	W M 26 Mar 1855 PUCKETT, Elizabeth
PUCKETT, James B PUCKETT, Robert Father	W M 26 May 1860 PUCKETT, Louisa
PUCKETT, Not Named PUCKETT, Elijah Father	W M 27 Nov 1860 PUCKETT, Sarah
PUCKETT, Not Named PUCKETT, Riley Father	W M 20 Dec 1865 PUCKETT, Matilda
PUCKETT, Rhoda PUCKETT, Riley Father	W F 24 Dec 1858 PUCKETT, Matilda
PUCKETT, Sarah PUCKETT, D F Father	W F 16 June 1860 PUCKETT, Elizabeth
PURDY, A T PRUDY, John J Father	W M 1 Feb 1859 PURDY, Peggy S
PURDY, Frances (Twin) PURDY, Braxton Father	W F 22 Aug 1861 PURDY, Mary

CHILD'S NAME FATHER\OWNER INFORMANT	RACE SEX BIRTH DATE MOTHER
PURDY, Isabella (Twin) PURDY, Braxton Father	W F 22 Aug 1861 PURDY, Mary
PURDY, John J PURDY, John J Father	W M 20 Sept 1853 PURDY, Peggy S
PURDY, Joshua PURDY, Braxton Father	W M 7 May 1857 PURDY, Mary Ann
PURDY, Martha J R PURDY, John J Father	W F 7 Feb 1862 PURDY, P T
PURDY, Martha J S PURDY, Braxton Mother	W F 7 Sept 1855 PURDY, Mary A
PURDY, Mary Allice PURDY, James Father	W F 13 Oct 1854 PURDY, Julia
PURDY, Mary F PURDY, John A Father	W F 18 Nov 1853 PURDY, Martha
PURDY, Mary Jane PURDY, Joshua Father	W F 11 Sept 1853 PURDY, Martha A
PURDY, Nancy D PURDY, John J Father	W F 31 Aug 1857 PURDY, Margaret S
RACHAEL DODSON, George C Owner	B/S F -- Nov 1855 Frances
RACHEL WILSON, Samuel P Jesse M Giles, Overseer	B/S F 1 Dec 1855 Jully
RACHEL IVY, John W Master	B/S F 4 Apr 1862 Liza
RACHEL E CONNER, Jonathan Owner	B/S F -- Apr 1853 May

158

```
CHILD'S NAME                          RACE  SEX    BIRTH DATE
FATHER\OWNER                          MOTHER
            INFORMANT
-----------------------------------------------------------------------
RADFORD, James J                      W     M    15 July 1862
RADFORD, Robert                       RADFORD, Aney
            Mother

RADFORD, Not Named                    W     M    23 Apr 1858
RADFORD, R P                          RADFORD, Aria
            Father

RADFORD, Not Named                    W     M    24 Jan 1859
RADFORD, R P                          RADFORD, Ann
            Father

RADFORD, Sparrel M                    W     M    17 Aug 1860
RADFPRD, Robert                       RADFORD, Asa
            Father

RAKES, Charles J                      W     M    11 Nov 1854
RAKES, Richard                        RAKES, Sarah
            Mother

RAKES, E J                            W     M    -- Apr 1860
RAKES, Samuel J                       RAKES, Ruth A
            Father

RAKES, Ellen M                        W     F     4 Dec 1858
RAKES, C C                            RAKES, Jula Ann
            Father

RAKES, John A                         W     M    27 Mar 1857
RAKES, Calvin J                       RAKES, Juley Ann
            Father

RAKES, Judy D A                       W     F    25 Nov 1860
RAKES, German                         RAKES, Mary
            Father

RAKES, Lewis F                        W     M    28 Sept 1858
RAKES, Jack                           RAKES, Mary A
            Father

RAKES, Lydia                          W     F    14 June 1857
RAKES, C J                            RAKES, Delila
            Father

RAKES, Martha J                       W     F    -- Jan 1859
RAKES, C J                            RAKES, Delila
            Father

RAKES, Millard T                      W     M    28 Sept 1853
RAKES, Samuel J                       RAKES, Ruth
            Mother
```

CHILD'S NAME FATHER\OWNER INFORMANT	RACE SEX BIRTH DATE MOTHER
RAKES, Nancy RAKES, Calvin J (Miller) Father	W F 24 June 1855 RAKES, Delila
RAKES, Nancy A RAKES, R R Father	W F -- July 1859 RAKES, Sarah D
RAKES, Nathaniel J RAKES, Samuel J Father	W M 4 Oct 1854 RAKES, Ruth A
RAKES, Not Named RAKES, Samuel J Father	W M -- Dec 1862 RAKES, Ruth
RAKES, Sarah RAKES, Jackson Chesley Rakes, Grandfather	W F 15 Dec 1853 RAKES, Delila
RAKES, Sarah RAKES, Jackson Father	W F 15 Jan 1854 RAKES, Delila
RAKES, Sarah E RAKES, Jerman Father	W F 8 Sept 1853 RAKES, Mary A
RAKES, Sarah E RAKES, S J Father	W F 4 Oct 1858 RAKES, Ruth A
RAKES, Thomas RAKES, C J Father	W M 20 Apr 1862 RAKES, Delila
RAKES, Thomas D RAKES, David Father	W M -- Jan 1862 RAKES, Rosena
RAKES, Turner F RAKES, A Father	W M 29 Dec 1858 RAKES, Violet A
RANGELEY, George N RANGELEY, James Father	W M 10 May 1855 RANGELEY, Harriett
RATLIFF, Delila A RATLIFF, C C Father	W F 9 Feb 1862 RATLIFF, Milly A

CHILD'S NAME FATHER\OWNER INFORMANT	RACE SEX BIRTH DATE MOTHER
RATLIFF, Elizabeth RATLIFF, C C Father	W F 19 Dec 1858 RATLIFF, Emily A
RATLIFF, Elizabeth C RATLIFF, A Father	W F 11 Aug 1858 RATLIFF, Mildred C
RATLIFF, Elizabeth C RATLIFF, Alex Father	W F 4 Nov 1860 RATLIFF, Milly C
RATLIFF, George M RATLIFF, Lewis Father	W M 17 May 1859 RATLIFF, Elizabeth
RATLIFF, John P RATLIFF, Lewis Father	W M 8 Jan 1862 RATLIFF, Elizabeth
RATLIFF, John W RATLIFF, John Father	W M 14 Mar 1855 RATLIFF, Catherine
RATLIFF, Martha Jane RATLIFF, Alexander (Constable) Father	W F 17 June 1854 RATLIFF, Milly C
REA, Mary J REA, Henry Father	W F 6 Feb 1860 REA, Martha Ann
REA, Samuel REA, Samuel Father	W M 14 Dec 1860 REA, Purlina
READ CONNER, E J Owner	B/S M -- Dec 1854 Jane
READ TERRY, Susannah J Finney, Son of Owner	B/S M -- Dec 1854 Eliza
REED ZIGLER, Christopher Richard Ziglar, Son of Owner	B/S M 10 July 1853 Elee
REED HAGOOD, Anderson Owner	B/S M 11 Jan 1853 Eliza

161

```
CHILD'S NAME                              RACE  SEX     BIRTH DATE
FATHER\OWNER                              MOTHER
             INFORMANT
---------------------------------------------------------------------
REED                                      B/S   M    11 Sept 1855
PENN, Clark                               Martha
             Owner

REED                                      B/S   M    -- Sept 1860
BARTER, James                             Harriett
             Master

REUBEN                                    B/S   M    23 Feb 1859
SCALES, Ab                                Betsey
             Owner

REYNOLDS, Alice                           W     F    13 Feb 1860
REYNOLDS, Shadrack                        REYNOLDS, Sarah
             Father

REYNOLDS, Amanda                          W     F    16 Apr 1859
REYNOLDS, A J                             REYNOLDS, Mary
             Father

REYNOLDS, Anthony T                       W     M    7 Oct 1865
REYNOLDS, William                         REYNOLDS, Rebecca
             Father

REYNOLDS, Emily                           W     F    7 Jan 1860
REYNOLDS, P M                             REYNOLDS, Mary E
             Father

REYNOLDS, Henretta                        W     F    5 Oct 1861
REYNOLDS, I B                             REYNOLDS, Sallie
             Father

REYNOLDS, James                           B     M    -- July 1865
REYNOLDS, Robert                          REYNOLDS, Dalinia
             Father

REYNOLDS, James F                         W     M    28 Aug 1859
REYNOLDS, William                         REYNOLDS, Rebecca
             Father

REYNOLDS, John G                          W     M    13 Mar 1855
REYNOLDS, Harden W                        REYNOLDS, Nancy J
             Father

REYNOLDS, Letitia F                       W     F    8 Feb 1861
REYNOLDS, William A                       REYNOLDS, Rebecca
             Father

REYNOLDS, Martha J                        W     F    19 May 1862
REYNOLDS, William M                       REYNOLDS, Martha J
             Mother
```

```
CHILD'S NAME                          RACE  SEX     BIRTH DATE
FATHER\OWNER                          MOTHER
           INFORMANT
-----------------------------------------------------------------------
REYNOLDS, Minnie S                     W    F    11 Sept 1858
REYNOLDS, J B                         REYNOLDS, Roxany
           Father

REYNOLDS, Nancy R                      W    F    1 Jan 1855
REYNOLDS, Fleming                     REYNOLDS, Tempy E
           Father

REYNOLDS, Not Named                    W    M    19 May 1865
REYNOLDS, James B                     REYNOLDS, Rozanna
           Father

REYNOLDS, Not Named                    W    M    -- July 1854
REYNOLDS, Capt James                  REYNOLDS, Rosanny
           Father

REYNOLDS, Not Named (Born Dead)        W    M    -- Nov 1860
REYNOLDS, William                     REYNOLDS, Luresseta
           Father

REYNOLDS, Richard L                    W    M    28 Mar 1859
REYNOLDS, Fleming                     REYNOLDS, Tempa
           Father

REYNOLDS, Virginia                     W    F    20 Feb 1859
REYNOLDS, William                     REYNOLDS, Rebecca
           Father

REYNOLDS, W A B                        W    M    8 June 1858
REYNOLDS, P M                         REYNOLDS, Mary E
           Father

REYNOLDS, William L                    W    M    29 Oct 1862
REYNOLDS, Fleming                     REYNOLDS, Tempia L
           Mother

RHODA                                  B/S  F    10 Oct 1859
PENN, Susan                           Lucinda
           William L Murphy, Owner

RHOOME                                 B/S  M    15 Apr 1854
MARTIN, Joseph                        Not Given
           A Satterfield, Manager

RICHARD                                B/S  M    -- Sept 1857
TURNER, Crawford                      Susan
           Master

RICHARDSON, N A                        W    M    -- Dec 1853
RICHARDSON, James W                   RICHARDSON, Sally
           Father
```

163

```
CHILD'S NAME                              RACE  SEX    BIRTH DATE
FATHER\OWNER                              MOTHER
            INFORMANT
-------------------------------------------------------------------------

RICHMAN, Sarah J                          W    F    3 Nov 1855
RICHMAN, William                          RICHMAN, Emily
            Father

RICHMOND, Daniel A                        W    M    10 June 1853
RICHMOND, James G (Miller)                RICHMOND, Elizabeth
            Father

RICKMAN, Ellen                            W    F    27 Mar 1860
RICKMAN, William                          RICKMAN, Emily
            Father

RICKMAN, Not Named                        W    M    25 Mar 1864
RICKMAN, William                          RICKMAN, Emily
            Father

RICKMAN, Robert Lee                       W    M    18 Mar 1861
RICKMAN, William                          RICKMAN, Emily
            Father

ROARK, D  Ann                             W    F    1 Sept 1861
ROARK, Elisha                             ROARK, Ann
            William Rickman, Neighbor

ROARK, Susan J                            W    F    25 Feb 1853
ROARK, Elisha                             ROARK, Arcannah
            Father

ROARK, William R                          W    M    1 Oct 1855
ROARK, Elisha                             ROARK, Alvianna
            Father

ROBERT                                    B/S  M    8 May 1855
WILSON, Samuel P                          Sally
            Jesse M Giles, Overseer

ROBERT                                    B/S  M    6 May 1859
ZIGLER, Reuben                            Rachael
            Owner

ROBERT                                    B/S  M    12 Aug 1862
STAPLES, Mary                             Liza
            Herbert Shelton, Overseer

ROBERT                                    B/S  M    -- Aug 1857
MURPHY, William                           Malinda
            Master

ROBERTSON, Albert R                       W    M    -- Sept 1862
ROBERTSON, David W                        ROBERTSON, Sarah
            Father
```

```
CHILD'S NAME                           RACE  SEX    BIRTH DATE
FATHER\OWNER                           MOTHER
             INFORMANT
-----------------------------------------------------------------------

ROBERTSON, Asa P                        W    M     10 Oct 1853
ROBERTSON, David J                      ROBERTSON, Nancy
             Father

ROBERTSON, C  M                         W    F     1 June 1865
ROBERTSON, Abram H                      ROBERTSON, Emezetta
             William Robertson, Grandfather

ROBERTSON, Daniel S                     W    M     16 Aug 1860
ROBERTSON, David                        ROBERTSON, Sallie
             Father

ROBERTSON, Elizabeth                    W    F     19 May 1857
ROBERTSON, William H                    ROBERTSON, Elizabeth
             Father

ROBERTSON, Elvira L                     W    F     13 Jan 1859
ROBERTSON, James R                      ROBERTSON, Elvira
             Father

ROBERTSON, Fleming W                    W    M     7 Nov 1865
ROBERTSON, Benjamin S                   ROBERTSON, Sarah E
             Father

ROBERTSON, Greenville                   W    M     19 Feb 1855
ROBERTSON, William                      ROBERTSON, Jane
             Father

ROBERTSON, John H                       W    M     15 Mar 1857
ROBERTSON, Joseph M                     ROBERTSON, Sarah
             Father

ROBERTSON, L  G                         W    M     16 Jan 1862
ROBERTSON, Abram                        ROBERTSON, Emberzetta
             Father

ROBERTSON, Mary E                       W    F     1 Sept 1858
ROBERTSON, David                        ROBERTSON, Sally
             Father

ROBERTSON, MARY F                       W    F     16 Sept 1858
ROBERTSON, J H                          ROBERTSon, Sarah C
             Father

ROBERTSON, Not Named                    W    M     19 Nov 1862
ROBERTSON, David J                      ROBERTSON, Nancy
             Father

ROBERTSON, Not Named (Twins)            W    M     31 Dec 1854
ROBERTSON, David                        ROBERTSON, Nancy
             Father
```

```
CHILD'S NAME                                RACE  SEX    BIRTH DATE
FATHER\OWNER                                MOTHER
            INFORMANT
-------------------------------------------------------------------------
ROBERTSON, Rufus F                          W     M     9 Mar 1853
ROBERTSON, William H                        ROBERTSON, Jane
            Father

ROGERS, Alla Minta                          W        F    15 Oct 1854
ROGERS, Clement                             ROGERS, Ruth
            Father

ROGERS, Amanda                              W        F    13 Nov 1862
ROGERS, Clemon                              ROGERS, Ruth
            Mother

ROGERS, Dan W                               W     M     1 Oct 1860
ROGERS, John                                ROGERS, Mary S
            Father

ROGERS, Floyd                               W     M     -- Feb 1862
ROGERS, Joseph                              ROGERS, Mary A
            Father

ROGERS, Hiram A                             W     M     13 Mar 1858
ROGERS, George R                            ROGERS, Luvenia
            Father

ROGERS, John                                W     M     1 June 1858
ROGERS, Clement                             ROGERS, Ruth
            Father

ROGERS, Mary E                              W        F    30 Oct 1855
ROGERS, John S                              ROGERS, Susan
            Father

ROGERS, Nancy N S                           W        F    15 Nov 1853
ROGERS, William                             ROGERS, Elizabeth
            Father

ROGERS, Not Named                           W        F    1 June 1861
ROGERS, G  W                                ROGERS, Leannah
            Father

ROGERS, Not Named                           W     M     1 Feb 1865
ROGERS, Clement                             ROGERS, Ruth
            Father

ROGERS, William H                           W     M     25 Nov 1853
ROGERS, George R                            ROGERS, Rebecca J
            Father

ROGERS, William P J                         W     M     -- June 1857
ROGERS, John L                              ROGERS, Susan
            Father
```

```
CHILD'S NAME                         RACE  SEX    BIRTH DATE
FATHER\OWNER                         MOTHER
              INFORMANT
-----------------------------------------------------------------------
ROLAND (Twin)                        B/S    M     31 Aug 1862
VIA, C  A                            Mary
              J C Moir, for Mistress

RORER, Abraham Lincoln               W      M     27 Nov 1865
RORER, William R                     RORER, Mary
              Father

RORER, Benjamin F                    W      M     1 Feb 1860
RORER, David C                       RORER, Sarah A
              Father

RORER, Cefus M                       W      M     -- Dec 1858
RORER, William                       RORER, Catherine
              Father

RORER, Daniel                        W      M     -- June 1857
RORER, William A                     RORER, Elizabeth
              Father

RORER, Henry L                       W      M     10 Dec 1854
RORER, David C                       RORER, Sally
              Father

RORER, Lucinda V                     W      F     27 Jan 1858
RORER, D C                           RORER, Sarah A
              Father

RORER, Not Named                     W      M     -- Sept 1853
RORER, John D                        RORER, Jane
              Father

RORER, Not Named (Twin)              W      F     17 Oct 1862
RORER, William R                     RORER, Mary A
              Father

RORER, Robert Lee                    W      M     18 Dec 1865
RORER, William G                     RORER, Catherine
              Father

RORER, Victoria J (Twin)             W      F     17 Oct 1862
RORER, William R                     RORER, Mary A
              Father

RORER, William G                     W      M     -- Feb 1854
RORER, Thomas D                      RORER, Amanda
              Father

RORRER, Abner J                      W      M     20 June 1862
RORRER, John H                       RORRER, Sarah
              Father


                        167
```

CHILD'S NAME FATHER\OWNER INFORMANT	RACE SEX BIRTH DATE MOTHER
RORRER, Elisha A RORRER, John H Father	W M 13 Oct 1860 RORRER, Sarah A
RORRER, Mary C RORRER, John H Father	W F 18 Feb 1855 RORRER, Jane
RORRER, Not Named RORRER, D C Father	W F 18 Feb 1859 RORRER, Sarah A
RORRER, Statira A RORRER, William A Father	W F -- Oct 1860 RORRER, Catherine
ROSA LEE PENN, Susan Mistress	B/S F -- Mar 1862 Lucinda
ROSABELL HOUCHINS, John Esther Houchins, Owner	B/S F 21 Mar 1854 Jane
ROSAMOND SCALES, Absalom Master	B/S F 10 Feb 1854 Nancy
ROSE ANN HYLTON, G W Owner	B/S F 20 Feb 1859 Mary
ROSE, Amanda C ROSE, J G P Sandefer, Neighbor	W F 19 Mar 1858 ROSE, Sarah
ROSE, Mary E ROSE, Jacob Father	W F 7 June 1860 ROSE, Sarah
ROSE, William P ROSE, Jacob Father	W M 23 May 1854 ROSE, Sarah
ROSS WILSON, Samuel P Jesse M Giles, Overseer	B/S M 1 June 1861 Millie
ROSS, Augusta R ROSS, Peyton R Father	W F 26 July 1853 ROSS, Mahala

```
CHILD'S NAME                            RACE  SEX     BIRTH DATE
FATHER\OWNER                            MOTHER
              INFORMANT
------------------------------------------------------------------------
ROSS, Charles P                         W     M    12 Aug 1862
ROSS, Charles P                         ROSS, Lucretia D
              Mother

ROSS, Elizabeth Ann                     W     F     6 July 1853
ROSS, McDaniel                          ROSS, Mary
              Father

ROSS, Isaac C                           W     M    13 Sept 1854
ROSS, Harden D                          ROSS, Martha J
              Father

ROSS, Jefferson D                       W     M    30 July 1862
ROSS, Hardin D                          ROSS, Martha J
              Father

ROSS, John J                            W     M    29 Dec 1855_
ROSS, Charles                           ROSS, Luvenia
              Father

ROSS, Joseph J                          W     M    25 Apr 1853
ROSS, David J (Blacksmith)              ROSS, Elizabeth
              Father

ROSS, Lucinda M                         W     F    23 Feb 1853
ROSS, Samuel A                          ROSS, Esther
              Father

ROSS, Mahala D                          W     F    18 Jan 1857
ROSS, Peyton R                          ROSS, Mahala
              Father

ROSS, Martha R                          W     F    16 Oct 1853
ROSS, James B                           ROSS, Leann
              Father

ROSS, Not Named                         W     F    10 Nov 1858
ROSS, H D                               ROSS, Martha J
              Father

ROSS, Not Named                         W     F    24 Jan 1859
ROSS, P R                               ROSS, Mahala E
              Father

ROSS, Not Named                         W     M    27 Nov 1862
ROSS, Samuel A                          ROSS, E  J
              Father

ROSS, Not Named (Born Dead)             W     M    -- -- 1855
ROSS, James M                           ROSS, Lucy E
              Father
```

169

CHILD'S NAME FATHER\OWNER INFORMANT	RACE SEX BIRTH DATE MOTHER
ROSS, P R T ROSS, Samuel A Father	W M 24 Feb 1858 ROSS, Esther J
ROSS, Samuel D W ROSS, S A Father	W M 31 Oct 1859 ROSS, Esther
RUFUS WILSON, Samuel P Jesse Giles, Overseer	B/S M 5 Apr 1853 Sally
RUFUS PENN, Thomas Master	B/S M -- June 1855 Hannah
RUFUS REYNOLDS, Harden W Owner	B/S M -- Nov 1855 Cathereine
RUFUS McCABE, William Owner	B/S M 1 Apr 1857 Letha
RUFUS (Uncommon Long Head) LEE, John G Mrs Lee, Mistress	B/S M 17 Apr 1855 Sally
RUTH TUGGLE, John Owner	B/S F -- -- !853 Milley
RUTH COCKRAM, Edward Owner	B/S F 2 Jan 1854 Phillis
RUTH WOODALL, Joseph Master	B/S F -- Mary 1857 Rachael
RUTH VIA, Alexander Master	B/S F 25 Oct 1857 Lycy
RUTH ADAMS, Joshua Master	B/S F 29 Nov 1861 Fanny
RUTH HUGH, J R S F Nowlin, Hirer	B/S F -- Apr 1862 Mary

```
CHILD'S NAME                          RACE  SEX    BIRTH DATE
FATHER\OWNER                          MOTHER
            INFORMANT
------------------------------------------------------------------------
RUTLEDGE, D E                         W     M    19 Mar 1860
RUTLEDGE, James (Carpenter)           RUTLEDGE, Susan
            Father

RUTLEDGE, Not Named                   W     F    18 June 1858
RUTLEDGE, James (Mechanic)            RUTLEDGE, Susan A
            J H Rutledge, Brother

SALLIE                                B     F     1 Aug 1864
Not Given                             Mary
            H W Reynolds, Former Owner

SALLIE LEE                            B     F    13 Dec 1864
Not Given                             Mary Ann
            H W Reynolds, Former Owner

SALLY                                 B/S   F    15 May 1854
LEAK, A J                             Juney
            Owner

SALLY                                 B/S   F    -- -- 1857
DANDRIDGE, William                    Sally
            Owner

SALLY                                 B/S   F     6 Aug 1859
REYNOLDS, H W                         Susan
            Owner

SALMONS, David                        W     M    15 Nov 1854
SALMONS, J J                          SALMONS, Permelia
            Father

SALMONS, David T                      W     M    21 Sept 1859
SALMONS, John                         SALMONS, Sarah
            Father

SALMONS, James H                      W     M    13 Feb 1858
SALMONS, J                            SALMONS, Nancy
            Father

SALMONS, John M                       W     M    21 Apr 1859
SALMONS, Jonathan                     SALMONS, Nancy

SALMONS, Waller E                     W     M     4 Jan 1862
SALMONS, Jonathan                     SALMONS, Nancy
            Father

SAM                                   B/S   M     7 Aug 1853
WILSON, Samuel P                      Nancy
            Jesse Giles, Overseer


                       171
```

CHILD'S NAME FATHER\OWNER	RACE SEX BIRTH DATE MOTHER
INFORMANT	

CHILD'S NAME / FATHER\OWNER / INFORMANT	RACE	SEX	BIRTH DATE	MOTHER
SAM CLARK, Thomas M Master	B/S	M	31 Mar 1854	Not Given
SAM PENN, Mrs M C Mistress	B/S	M	19 July 1862	Margaret
SAMPSON PENN, Thomas J Owner	B/S	M	-- Apr 1855	Not Given
SAMUEL HAGOOD, Gregory Owner	B/S	M	24 Dec 1853	Tilla
SAMUEL PRUNTY, John Owner	B/S	M	6 Jan 1853	Rachel
SAMUEL STAPLES, William C Owner	B/S	M	-- Sept 1855	Jane
SAMUEL CRITZ, Gabriel Owner	B/S	M	28 Sept 1855	Sally
SAMUEL ANTHONY, B A Master	BS	M	-- Dec 1858	Rebecca
SAMUEL BENNETT, Mary Owner	B/S	M	3 Apr 1862	Leeta
SAMUEL H IVIE, John Owner	B/S	M	19 Mar 1859	Eliza
SAND, George R SAND, John Father	W	M	23 Dec 1859	SAND, Catherine
SANDEFER, Lucy A SANDEFER, A M Father	W	F	25 July 1858	SANDEFER, Susan H
SANDEFER, Mathew SANDEFER, Gabriel P Father	W	M	3 Nov 1853	SANDEFER, Martha

```
CHILD'S NAME                               RACE  SEX    BIRTH DATE
FATHER\OWNER                               MOTHER
              INFORMANT
-----------------------------------------------------------------------
SANDEFER, Samuel A                         W     M     9 Feb 1862
SANDEFER, A  W                             SANDEFER, Susan
              James Barnard, Grandfather

SANDERS                                    B/S   M     14 Sept 1854
PENN, Polly                                Not Given
              Capt James A Penn, Master

SANDERS, Calvin L                          W     M     8 Aug 1855
SANDERS, Phelomel J                        SANDERS, Bethema
              Father

SANDERS, Not Named                         W     M     17 Apr 1857
SANDERS, Jack                              SANDERS, Mary
              Father

SANDERS, Not Named                         W     M     10 Aug 1859
SANDERS, Jack                              SANDERS, Sally
              Father

SAPP, Richard G                            W     M     24 June 1857
SAPP, S J                                  SAPP, Jumena
              Father

SARAH                                      B/S   F     12 Sept 1855
TURNER, William                            Not Given
              Master

SARAH                                      B/S   F     12 Aug 1861
ADAMS, Joshua                              Sarah
              Master

SARAH                                      B     F     8 Nov 1864
Father Not Given                           Susan
              James Sawyers, Former Owner

SARAH                                      B     F     -- Nov 1864
Father Not Given                           Keziah
              John R Cobbs, Former Owner

SARAH D                                    B/S   F     -- May 1857
FRANCE, Joseph                             Sarah
              Master

SATIRA                                     B/S   F     -- Jan 1857
DeHART, Charles                            Maria
              Master

SATTERFIELD, George E                      W     M     6 Feb 1854
SATTERFIELD, William                       SATTERFIELD, Charlotte
              Father
```

173

```
CHILD'S NAME                                  RACE  SEX    BIRTH DATE
FATHER\OWNER                                  MOTHER
              INFORMANT
-----------------------------------------------------------------------
SATTERFIELD, Marietta                         W     F     26 Sept 1855
SATTEREFIELD, William                         SATTERFIELD, Charlotte A
              Father

SAVANNAH                                      B/S   F     -- --- 1862
REYNOLDS, Hardin W                            Kitt
              Mary Reynolds, Young Mistress

SCALES, Alfred M                              W     M     11 June 1853
SCALES, Nathaniel H                           SCALES, Elizabeth
              Father

SCALES, Bettie Donald                         W     F     4 Feb 1854
SCALES, Absalom                               SCALES, Nancy Caroline
              Father

SCALES, Charlotte                             W     F     29 Nov 1858
SCALES, M H                                   SCALES, Elizabeth
              Father

SCALES, Elizabeth L                           W     F     16 Nov 1862
SCALES, N  H                                  SCALES, Elizabeth
              Mother

SCALES, Joseph C (Very Pretty) (Twin)         W     M     10 Feb 1855
SCALES, Nathaniel H                           SCALES, Elizabeth
              Father

SCALES, Nathaniel H (Very Pretty) (Twin)      W     M     10 Feb 1855
SCALES, Nathaniel H                           SCALES, Elizabeth
              Father

SCALES, Not Named                             W     F     4 Nov 1860
SCALES, N H                                   SCALES, Elizabeth
              Father

SCALES, Robert                                W     M     12 Jan 1857
SCALES, N H                                   SCALES, Elizabeth
              Father

SCOTT                                         B/S   M     1 Mar 1854
COBB, John R                                  Mary
              Owner

SCOTT, Daniel W                               W     M     27 June 1865
SCOTT, Daniel S                               SCOTT, Mary A
              Father

SCOTT, Jenneqlin                              W     F     1 Apr 1853
SCOTT, Daniel S (Farming & Smithing)          SCOTT, Mary A
              Father
```

```
CHILD'S NAME                          RACE  SEX    BIRTH DATE
FATHER\OWNER                          MOTHER
                  INFORMANT
------------------------------------------------------------------
SCOTT, John                           W     M    25 June 1861
SCOTT, John                           SCOTT, Alpha
                  Father

SCOTT, Martha A                       W     F     2 Oct 1855
SCOTT, Thomas D                       SCOTT, Lucinda E
                  Father

SCOTT, Mary E                         W     F     1 Jan 1859
SCOTT, G                              SCOTT, Lucy
                  Father

SCOTT, Nathaniel B                    W     M     9 Oct 1860
SCOTT, Green                          SCOTT, Lucy
                  Father

SCOTT, Not Named                      W     M     1 Aug 1857
SCOTT, Daniel S                       SCOTT, Mary Ann
                  Father

SCOTT, Pandora S                      W     F     4 Apr 1855
SCOTT, Greensville                    SCOTT, Lucy
                  Father

SCOTT, Samuel C                       W     M     5 Feb 1853
SCOTT, Wolford                        SCOTT, Samantha
                  Father

SCOTT, Sarah E                        W     F    30 Sept 1859
SCOTT, Thomas D                       SCOTT, Lucinda E
                  Father

SCOTT, Sarah J                        W     F     5 May 1859
SCOTT, D S                            SCOTT, Mary A
                  Father

SCOTT, Simon P                        W     M    -- Nov 1857
SCOTT, Thomas D                       SCOTT, Lucinda E
                  Father

SCOTT, Thomas B                       W     M    31 Mar 1855
SCOTT, Daniel S                       SCOTT, Mary A
                  Father

SCOTT, William B                      W     M    30 May 1857
SCOTT, Greenville                     SCOTT, Lucy
                  Father

SELITIA                               B/S   F    11 Nov 1853
SPENCER, William Sr                   Briney
                  Owner


                        175
```

```
CHILD'S NAME                              RACE  SEX    BIRTH DATE
FATHER\OWNER                              MOTHER
            INFORMANT
---------------------------------------------------------------------
SETH                                      B/S    M     3 Nov 1858
VIA, C A                                  Mary
            J C Moir, Guardian for C A Via

SETLIFF, Barnett                          W      M     6 Jan 1854
SETLIFF, Barnett                          SETLIFF, Martha
            Father

SHARP, William A                          W      M     6 Mar 1853
None Given                                SHARP, Charlotte
            Steven Sharp, Uncle

SHELOR, F B                               W      M     26 July 1858
SHELOR, O C                               SHELOR, Margaretta
            Father

SHELOR, Lucy E                            W      F     24 Apr 1855
SHELOR, Oliver C                          SHELOR, Margaret
            Father

SHELOR, Not Named (Born Dead)             W      M     16 Dec 1858
SHELOR, I B                               SHELOR, Eliza A
            Father

SHELOR, Sarah E                           W      F     15 July 1858
SHELOR, R T                               SHELOR, Mary
            Father

SHELOR, Susan                             W      F     16 July 1853
SHELOR, Randolph                          SHELOR, Mary
            Father

SHELOR, Thomas L                          W      M     -- Dec 1862
SHELOR, I  B                              SHELOR, Elizabeth
            John Shelor, Grandfather

SHELOR, William C S                       W      M     11 May 1854
SHELOR, I B                               SHELOR, Elizabeth A
            Father

SHELTON, Aaron C                          W      M     2 Oct 1855
SHELTON, Alexander                        SHELTON, Nancy
            Father

SHELTON, Elizabeth                        W      F     10 Nov 1860
SHELTON, Jacob                            SHELTON, Sallie
            Father

SHELTON, Elizabeth (Twin)                 W      F     8 Mar 1862
SHELTON, Henry (Blacksmith)               SHELTON, Sarah
            Father
```

```
CHILD'S NAME                              RACE  SEX    BIRTH DATE
FATHER\OWNER                              MOTHER
                    INFORMANT
-------------------------------------------------------------------------
SHELTON, Esther M                         W      F    6 Apr 1859
SHELTON, Fred                             SHELTON, Hetty
                    Father

SHELTON, Fanny T                          W      F    15 Apr 1854
SHELTON, O H (Overseer)                   SHELTON, Luvenia B
                    Father

SHELTON, Frederick H                      W      M    23 May 1853
SHELTON, Frederick                        SHELTON, Easter
                    Father

SHELTON, George                           W      M    17 July 1860
SHELTON, Lewis                            SHELTON, Jane
                    Father

SHELTON, George W                         W      M    14 June 1853
SHELTON, Capt Thomas (Saddler)            SHELTON, Elizabeth
                    Father

SHELTON, Haman C                          W      M    23 Dec 1860
SHELTON, A                                SHELTON, Nancy
                    Father

SHELTON, Joseph G                         W      M    3 Aug 1859
SHELTON, Levi                             SHELTON, Exona
                    Father

SHELTON, Marsella                         W      F    31 Aug 1857
SHELTON, Jacob                            SHELTON, Sarah
                    Father

SHELTON, Martha E                         W      F    22 Nov 1854
SHELTON, William H                        SHELTON, Mary E
                    Father

SHELTON, Mary                             W      F    6 Mar 1859
SHELTON, William                          SHELTON, Susan
                    Father

SHELTON, Mary F                           W      F    4 Mar 1860
SHELTON, William                          SHELTON, Mary E
                    Father

SHELTON, Mary S                           W      F    8 Dec 1854
SHELTON, Absalom                          SHELTON, Susan
                    Father

SHELTON, Neoma                            W      F    -- June 1859
SHELTON, Alex                             SHELTON, Nancy
                    Father
```

CHILD'S NAME FATHER\OWNER INFORMANT	RACE SEX BIRTH DATE MOTHER
SHELTON, Not Named SHELTON, Thomas N Father	W M 1 Sept 1853 SHELTON, Martha
SHELTON, Not Named SHELTON, William Mother	W M 16 Feb 1862 SHELTON, Mary E
SHELTON, Rufus K SHELTON, Gerald Father	W M 21 Aug 1854 SHELTON, Nancy
SHELTON, Sallie E SHELTON, G O Father	W F 25 May 1861 SHELTON, Martha
SHELTON, Sampson P SHELTON, Anderson Father	W M 20 June 1853 SHELTON, Mary
SHELTON, Samuel T (Twin) SHELTON, Henry (Blacksmith) Father	W M 8 Mar 1862 SHELTON, Sarah
SHELTON, Thomas SHELTON, Azariah Father	W M 7 Dec 1854 SHELTON, Jane
SHELTON, Virginia SHELTON, William Father	W F 8 June 1860 SHELTON, Susan
SHELTON, William SHELTON, William Fathr	W M 4 May 1859 SHELTON, Mary E
SHEPHERD, Nancy E SHEPHERD, Ewell Father	W F 20 June 1853 SHEPHERD, Leveny
SHOCKLEY, William A SHOCKLEY, James (Blacksmith) Father	W M 20 Oct 1862 SHOCKLEY, Ruth E
SHOUGH, Not Named Unknown Jacob Shough, Former Owner	B F 19 May 1865 SHOUGH, Permelia
SIMMONS, Not Named SIMMONS, William A Father	W M 26 Aug 1865 SIMMONS, Mary

```
CHILD'S NAME                              RACE  SEX    BIRTH DATE
FATHER\OWNER                              MOTHER
            INFORMANT
-------------------------------------------------------------------
SLAUGHTER, Beverage A                     W     M    -- Mar 1854
SLAUGHTER, John                           SLAUGHTER, Rosena
            Father

SLUSHER, Crawford T                       W     M    26 May 1854
SLUSHER, S J                              SLUSHER, Margaret
            Father

SLUSHER, Mary                             W     F    25 Oct 1865
SLUSHER, S  J                             SLUSHER, Margaret
            Father

SLUSHER, Not Named                        W     M    22 May 1861
SLUSHER, S  J                             SLUSHER, Margaret
            Father

SLUSHER, William R                        W     M    29 June 1862
SLUSHER, Sparrell J                       SLUSHER, Margaret
            Father

SMART, Emera C J                          W     F     1 Nov 1854
SMART, William C (Teamster)               SMART, Malinda
            Father

SMIITH, Sarah                             W     F     1 Aug 1861
SMITH, William                            SMITH, Leatha
            Father

SMITH, Ann                                W     F    24 July 1860
SMITH, H M                                SMITH, Elizabeth
            Father

SMITH, Crawford B                         W     M     9 Sept 1854
SMITH, Mumford                            SMITH, Catherine
            Father

SMITH, Eletha                             W     F     3 Nov 1854
SMITH, James                              SMITH, Judy
            Father

SMITH, Elizabeth                          W     F    28 Aug 1855
SMITH, John W                             SMITH, Susan
            Father

SMITH, Elizabeth                          W     F     9 Apr 1862
SMITH, Harden                             SMITH, Elizabeth
            Mother

SMITH, Exony D                            W     F    27 May 1862
SMITH, Daniel                             SMITH, Exony
            Father
```

```
CHILD'S NAME                           RACE  SEX    BIRTH DATE
FATHER\OWNER                           MOTHER
              INFORMANT
------------------------------------------------------------------------

SMITH, Fleming J                       W     M     -- -- 1853
SMITH, Daniel                          SMITH, Exoney
              Father

SMITH, Frances E                       W     F     23 Mar 1854_
SMITH, David W (Carpenter)             SMITH, Avaline
              Father

SMITH, George F (Born Franklin Co)     W     M     15 Dec 1858
SMITH, Robert                          SMITH, Martha A
              Father

SMITH, Joel B                          W     M     14 Aug 1862
SMITH, Mumford                         SMITH, Catherine
              Father

SMITH, John T                          W     M     25 Dec 1853
SMITH, A J                             SMITH, Tabitha
              Father

SMITH, Lewis                           W     M     5 July 1862
SMITH, Isaac                           SMITH, Finetta
              Lewis Smith, Grandfather

SMITH, Lucy                            W     F     22 Aug 1855
SMITH, Bartlett                        SMITH, Helen
              Father

SMITH, Lucy D                          W     F     -- -- 1853
SMITH, William B                       SMITH, Lydia Ann
              Father

SMITH, Lumma                           W     F     17 Sept 1853
SMITH, Joseph A                        SMITH, Letha
              Father

SMITH, Mary S                          W     F     24 Oct 1853
SMITH, William D                       SMITH, Elizabeth J
              Father

SMITH, Not Named                       W     M     23 Apr 1853
SMITH, John W                          SMITH, Susan
              Father

SMITH, Not Named                       W     M     15 Oct 1858
SMITH, Lewis                           SMITH, Martha
              Father

SMITH, Not Named                       B     F     1 Sept 1865
SMITH, Jerry                           SMITH, Martha
              Father
```

```
CHILD'S NAME                                RACE  SEX     BIRTH DATE
FATHER\OWNER                                MOTHER
            INFORMANT
----------------------------------------------------------------------
SMITH, Peter                                W     M    1 Sept 1853
SMITH, Lewis                                SMITH, Martha
            Father

SMITH, Robert Lee                           W     M    19 Apr 1865
SMITH, J W                                  SMITH, Susan
            Father

SMITH, Sarah A                              W     F    5 Sept 1858
SMITH, Joseph                               SMITH, Sarah
            Father

SMITH, Sherman                              B     M    13 May 1865
SMITH, Dick                                 SMITH, Polly
            Father

SMITH, Susan J                              W     F    17 Apr 1859
SMITH, Burwell                              SMITH, Mahala
            Father

SMITH, Synda P                              W     M    27 Mar 1859
SMITH, Daniel                               SMITH, Exony
            Father

SMITH, William D                            W     M    10 Sept 1859
SMITH, W D                                  SMITH, Jane
            Father

SMITH, William N                            W     M    30 Apr 1855
SMITH, Joseph N                             SMITH, Sally
            Father

SNELL, Not Named                            W     F    -- July 1854
SNELL, John F                               SNELL, Mary
            Thomas Spencer, Neighbor

Soch (?)                                    B/S   F    12 July 1853
BROWN, Nicholas                             Martha
            Master

SOTTY                                       B/S   F    15 Nov 1853
SCALES, Absalom                             Nancy
            Caroline Scales, Wife of Owner

SOUTHERN, William D                         W     M    15 Sept 1862
SOUTHERN, Ruben (Res Stokes Co)             SOUTHERN, Mahala
            Abijah McMillion, Grandfather

SOWDER, John                                W     M    28 Sept 1865
SOWDER, Emanuel                             SOWDER, Exony
            Mother
```

181

```
CHILD'S NAME                              RACE  SEX    BIRTH DATE
FATHER\OWNER                              MOTHER
              INFORMANT
--------------------------------------------------------------------------
SOWDER, Joshua                            W     M     -- Oct 1860
SOWDER, Emmerson                          SOWDER, Exony
              Father

SOWDER, Lee Estte                         W     M     11 Sept 1862
SOWDER, Emanuel                           SOWDER, Exony
              Mother

SOYARS, John L                            B     M     8 Sept 1861
SOYARS, James                             Kitty
              Owner

SOYARS, Richard                           W     M     22 Dec 1860
SOYARS, Richard                           SOYARS, Sashia
              Father

SOYARS, Thomas                            W     M     -- Aug 1855
SOYARS, Richard                           SOYARS, Locha
              Mother

SPANGLER, Conbury                         W     M     6 Oct 1854
SPANGLER, Washington                      SPANG1ER, Mary A
              Father

SPANGLER, Frank P                         W     M     26 Sept 1860
Illegitimate                             SPANGLER, Catherine
              Thomas Spangler, Grandfather

SPANGLER, Susan M                         W     F     10 June 1853
SPANGLER, Thomas                          SPANGLER, Mary
              Father

SPANGLER, Virginia                        W     F     26 May 1865
SPANGLER, George W                        SPANGLER, Malinda
              Father

SPARRELL                                  B/S   M     28 July 1859
COCKRAM, Ed                               Phillis
              Master

SPENCER                                   B/S   M     7 Mar 1854
YOUNG, William D                          Fanny
              Owner

SPENCER, Alexander G                      W     M     8 Aug 1865
SPENCER, James M                          SPENCER, Elizabeth
              Father

SPENCER, Asia J                           W     M     19 Mar 1853
SPENCER, William S                        SPENCER, Jane
              Father
```

```
CHILD'S NAME                          RACE  SEX     BIRTH DATE
FATHER\OWNER                          MOTHER
              INFORMANT
---------------------------------------------------------------------------
SPENCER, Austin                       W      M    3 Mar 1859
SPENCER, Hardin                       SPENCER, Nancy S
              Father

SPENCER, Druscilla R                  W      F    14 June 1859
SPENCER, Abr Jr                       SPENCER, Avaline
              Father

SPENCER, E                            W      F    17 Jan 1858
SPENCER, A                            SPENCER, Avaline
              Father

SPENCER, Emily R                      W      F    17 May 1853
SPENCER, Harden                       SPENCER, Nancy S
              Father

SPENCER, Fleming R                    W      M    7 June 1861
SPENCER, Levi                         SPENCER, Naomi
              Father

SPENCER, George R                     W      M    23 Jan 1857
SPENCER, Joseph T                     SPENCER, Luvny
              Father

SPENCER, Hardin D                     W      M    31 Oct 1862
SPENCER, Hardin                       SPENCER, Nancy S
              Father

SPENCER, James Thomas                 W      M    11 Nov 1862
SPENCER, A  J                         SPENCER, Adaline
              Father

SPENCER, John D                       W      M    30 Jan 1862
SPENCER, James                        SPENCER, Martha J
              Mother

SPENCER, John S                       W      M    16 Apr 1862
SPENCER, Peter                        SPENCER, Sabrina
              Father

SPENCER, Josiah J                     W      M    2 Sept 1859
SPENCER, William                      SPENCER, Jane
              Father

SPENCER, Lillian Sarah                W      F    29 Apr 1854
SPENCER, Martin S                     SPENCER, Mary
              Father

SPENCER, Lodesia                      W      F    23 July 1860
SPENCER, James Jr                     SPENCER, Rozannah
              Father
```

```
CHILD'S NAME                          RACE  SEX    BIRTH DATE
FATHER\OWNER                          MOTHER
            INFORMANT
-----------------------------------------------------------------------
SPENCER, Martha A                     W     F    11 Nov 1860
SPENCER, Abram J                      SPENCER, Adaline
            Father

SPENCER, Martha E                     W     F    18 May 1862
SPENCER, Joshua T                     SPENCER, Nancy A
            Father

SPENCER, Martin S                     W     M     3 July 1861
SPENCER, Martin S                     SPENCER, Mary
            Father

SPENCER, Mary A                       W     F     9 Sept 1865
SPENCER, Joshua T                     SPENCER, Mahala
            Father

SPENCER, Mary E                       W     F    17 July 1854
SPENCER, William L                    SPENCER, Phebe J
            Father

SPENCER, Mary F                       W     F    10 Nov 1859
SPENCER, James J                      SPENCER, Ruth E
            Father

SPENCER, Not Named                    W     F    -- -- 1853
SPENCER, Thomas                       SPENCER, Margaret
            Father

SPENCER, Not Named                    W     M     5 Aug 1854
SPENCER, Peter                        SPENCER, Saberia
            Father

SPENCER, Not Named                    W     M    20 Oct 1855
SPENCER, Levi                         SPENCER, Naoma
            Father

SPENCER, Not Named (Born Dead)        W     F    14 Dec 1854_
SPENCER, Levi                         SPENCER, Naomia E
            Father

SPENCER, Peter J                      W     M     8 Apr 1859
SPENCER, Peter                        SPENCER, Sabrina
            Father

SPENCER, R James                      W     M    28 Mar 1859
SPENCER, Hardin                       SPENCER, Nancy S
            Father

SPENCER, Thomas G.                    W     M    22 Feb 1859
SPENCER, J T                          SPENCER, Naomy
            Father
```

```
CHILD'S NAME                            RACE  SEX    BIRTH DATE
FATHER\OWNER                            MOTHER
            INFORMANT
-------------------------------------------------------------------------
SPENCER, Thomas P                       W     M     6 Sept 1860
SPENCER, A J                            SPENCER, Sarah
            Father

SPENCER, William P                      W     M    10 June 1854
SPENCER, William B                      SPENCER, Henrietta
            Mother

STANLEY, Daniel                         W     M    10 Sept 1858
STANLEY, Hiram                          STANELY, Lucy
            Father

STANLEY, William W                      W     M     7 Dec 1862
STANLEY, William                        STANLEY, Sarah
            Mother

STANLY, Anna                            W     F    28 Apr 1854
STANLY, Hiram                           STANLY, Lucy
            Father

STANLY, William                         W     M     5 July 1861
STANLY, Hiram                           STANLY, Lucy
            Father

STAPLES, Waller R                       B/S   M    -- June 1854
STAPLES, Col A                          Not Given
            Clairborne Mills, Overseer

STARKEY, John W                         W     M    10 Nov 1860
Illegitimate                            STARKEY, Arementa
            Mother

STARKEY, Mary Jane                      W     F    10 Nov 1865
Not Given                               STARKEY, Araminta
            Grandmother

STEGALL, William H                      W     M    10 Sept 1855
STEGALL, Nathaniel                      STEGALL, Martha A
            Mother

STONE, David J                          W     M     1 June 1854
STONE, James                            STONE, Mary A
            Mother

STONE, Not Named                        W     M    23 July 1857
STONE, Peyton                           STONE, Permelia
            Father

STONE, Susan M                          W     F    14 Mar 1860
STONE, S S                              STONE, Capian
            Father
```

```
CHILD'S NAME                                    RACE  SEX    BIRTH DATE
FATHER\OWNER                                    MOTHER
               INFORMANT
-----------------------------------------------------------------------
STOVALL, Henry H                                W     M    29 June 1862
STOVALL, M  C                                   STOVALL, Malinda A
               Father

STOVALL, Jno T                                  W     M    29 June 1859
STOVALL, Jno N                                  STOVALL, Permelia
               Father

STOVALL, Martha C                               W     F    -- July 1854
STOVALL, Joseph                                 STOVALL, Permelia
               Father

STOVALL, Not Named                              W     M    27 May 1855
STOVALL, M  C                                   STOVALL, Malinda A
               Father

STOVALL, Not Named                              W     M    3 May 1859
STOVALL, Mat                                    STOVALL, Malinda
               Father

STOVALL, P  R                                   W     F    7 May 1862
STOVALL, J  M                                   STOVALL, Permelia
               Father

STOW, George T                                  W     M    1 Oct 1855
STOW, Jared                                     STOW, Elizabeth
               Father

STOW, Jesse                                     W     M    24 June 1857
STOW, Jonathan                                  STOW, Zelpha
               Father

STUART, Benjamin                                B/S   M    -- -- 1855
PENN, Thomas                                    STUART, Sally
               Master

STUART, Susan                                   W     F    6 Apr 1857
STUART, John                                    STUART, Susan
               Father

SUSAN                                           B/S   F    13 Mar 1854
HOUCHINS, John                                  Margaret
               Esther Houchins, Owner

SUSAN                                           B/S   F    -- May 1857
WILSON, Not Given                               Sally
               Jesse Giles, Master

SUSAN                                           B/S   F    3 Oct 1859
WILSON, Samuel                                  Sally
               Jesse Giles, Overseer
```

```
CHILD'S NAME                              RACE  SEX     BIRTH DATE
FATHER\OWNER                              MOTHER
                 INFORMANT
---------------------------------------------------------------------
SUSAN                                     B/S    F    1 June 1860
PENN, Susan                               Jane
                 Mistress

SUSAN                                     B/S    F    7 Aug 1861
REYNOLDS, H  W                            Harriett
                 Owner

SUTLIFF, Samuel L                         W      M    27 May 1862
SUTLIFF, Barnett B                        SUTLIFF, Martha A
                 Mother

TAMER                                     B/S    F    -- July 1862
CLARK, Susan E                            Mary
            John A Hanby, Relative of Owner

TAMSY                                     B/S    F    19 Dec 1855
DeHART, Aaron                             Not Given
                 Master

TARA (Twin)                               B/S    F    -- Sept 1862
COBB, John R                              Mary
                 Master

TATE, Charity                             W      F    1 July 1857
TATE, James B                             TATE, Elizabeth
                 Father

TATE, Edward F                            W      M    25 July 1853
TATE, James B                             TATE, Rachel
                 Father

TATE, Elizabeth                           W      F    10 Feb 1859
TATE, James                               TATE, Elizabeth
                 Father

TATE, Not Named                           W      M    -- Nov 1859
TATE, James                               TATE, Elizabeth
                 Father

TATUM, Jane                               W      F    22 Apr 1864
TATUM, William                            TATUM, Mary
                 Father

TATUM, Miles                              B      M    10 June 1865
Unknown                                   TATUM, Eda
            Pryor Tatum, Neighbor

TATUM, Not Named                          W      M    10 Oct 1862
TATUM, William F                          TATUM, Mary A
                 Father


                          187
```

CHILD'S NAME FATHER\OWNER	INFORMANT	RACE	SEX	BIRTH DATE MOTHER
TATUM, Rachael Ann TATUM, Edward	Father	W	F	14 Apr 1854 TATUM, Charlotte D
TATUM, William B TATUM, William T	Father	W	M	8 Mar 1860 TATUM, Mary Ann
TATUM, William M TATUM, Thomas B	Father	W	M	29 Nov 1861 TATUM, Ruth
TAYLOR, David J TAYLOR, John W	Mother	W	M	7 Mar 1853 TAYLOR, Jane W
TAYLOR, Ellen TAYLOR, David P	Father	W	F	7 May 1853 TAYLOR, Malinda
TAYLOR, Ellen A TAYLOR, James A	Father	W	F	20 Aug 1858 TAYLOR, Seatire E
TAYLOR, Emily TAYLOR, James B	Father	W	F	-- Oct 1857 TAYLOR, Mary
TAYLOR, Harriett V TAYLOR, William	Father	W	F	28 Apr 1855 TAYLOR, Avaline
TAYLOR, Isaac W TAYLOR, William A	Father	W	M	10 June 1862 TAYLOR, Adaline
TAYLOR, Laurence TAYLOR, James B	Father	W	M	4 June 1859 TAYLOR, Mary
TAYLOR, Mary C TAYLOR, William F B (Physician)	Father	W	F	24 Dec 1865 TAYLOR, Fannie M
TAYLOR, Mildred Ann TAYLOR, William F B	Father	W	F	23 Jan 1862 TAYLOR, Fanny M
TAYLOR, Not Named TAYLOR, George W	Father	W	F	12 Apr 1853 TAYLOR, Hannah M

```
CHILD'S NAME                                RACE  SEX    BIRTH DATE
FATHER\OWNER                                MOTHER
         INFORMANT
--------------------------------------------------------------------------
TAYLOR, Not Named                           W     F    3 Nov 1860
TAYLOR, James A                             TAYLOR, Statira E
         Father

TAYLOR, Not Named                           W     M    6 July 1861
TAYLOR, James                               TAYLOR, Nancy
         Father

TAYLOR, Oney L                              W     M    26 Nov 1859
TAYLOR, William A                           TAYLOR, Avaline
         Father

TAZEWELL                                    B/S   M    8 Aug 1858
CONNER, James                               Jane
         Master

TAZEWELL H                                  B/S   M    23 Mar 1855
PILSON, Richard                             Not Given
         Master

TELIAM                                      B/S   M    24 Oct 1862
AYRES, Martha                               Charita
         Owner

TEMBY                                       B/S   F    27 Oct 1855
WILSON, Samuel P                            Martha
         Jesse M Giles, Overseer

TENIA                                       B/S   F    6 July 1859
WILSON, Samuel                              Betty
         Jesse Giles, Overseer

TENSLEY, J D A                              W     F    10 June 1853
TENSLEY, S W (Physician)                    TENSLEY, E J
         Father

TERRY, John H M L                           W     M    21 Mar 1858
TERRY, William M                            TERRY, Mary Jane
         Father

TERRY, Julian E (Born in Mercer Co)         W     F    30 Aug 1860
TERRY, N B                                  TERRY, Exony
         Father

TERRY, Mary A                               W     F    14 July 1853
TERRY, Nathan B                             TERRY, Enona
         Father

TERRY, Mary L                               W     F    5 Aug 1860
TERRY, William W                            TERRY, J T
         Father


                              189
```

```
CHILD'S NAME                                    RACE  SEX    BIRTH DATE
FATHER\OWNER                                    MOTHER
             INFORMANT
-------------------------------------------------------------------------
TERRY, Not Named                                W     M     29 Sept 1857
TERRY, Nathan B                                 TERRY, Enona
             Father

TERRY, Samuel W                                 W     M     -- Aug 1855
TERRY, Nathan B                                 TERRY, Exona
             Father

THOMAS                                          B/S   M     -- Feb 1855
PENN, Peter P                                   Cyntha
             Owner

THOMAS                                          B/S   M     -- Mar 1861
WILSON, Samuel P                                Sallie
             Jesse M Giles, Overseer

THOMAS GREEN                                    B/S   M     21 May 1860
PENDLETON, W S                                  Permelia
             Elizabeth Pilson, Mistress

THOMAS H                                        B/S   M     2 Oct 1859
CLARK, Jacob                                    Mary A
             Owner

THOMAS, Benjamin                                W     M     20 Feb 1853
THOMAS, John                                    THOMAS, Phebe
             Father

THOMAS, Charles J                               W     M     -- June 1862
THOMAS, James                                   THOMAS, Sintha
             Mother

THOMAS, Flora E                                 W     F     2 June 1857
THOMAS, Walter H                                THOMAS, Judith V
             Father

THOMAS, Frances                                 W     F     -- Mar 1860
THOMAS, D P                                     THOMAS, Amanda
             Father

THOMAS, George                                  W     M     4 Jan 1859
THOMAS, P J                                     THOMAS, Nary J
             Father

THOMAS, James E                                 W     M     15 Nov 1853
THOMAS, Samuel                                  THOMAS, Elenely
             Father

THOMAS, James E                                 W     M     29 Nov 1854
THOMAS, Samuel                                  THOMAS, Emily
             Father
```

190

```
CHILD'S NAME                                    RACE  SEX     BIRTH DATE
FATHER\OWNER                                    MOTHER
            INFORMANT
------------------------------------------------------------------------
THOMAS, James R M                               W      M    22 Sept 1858
THOMAS, Tazewell                                THOMAS, Letitia J
            Father

THOMAS, James W                                 W      M    13 Feb 1862
THOMAS, W  H                                    THOMAS, Virginia
            Father

THOMAS, Lesha                                   W      F     4 Feb 1857
THOMAS, Peter J                                 THOMAS, Mary Jane
            Father

THOMAS, Lews E  J                               W      F     4 Dec 1862
THOMAS, Tazewell                                THOMAS, Letitia
            Mother

THOMAS, Martha                                  W      F    10 Jan 1855
THOMAS, Archibald J                             THOMAS, Elizabeth
            Father

THOMAS, Martha E                                W      F    22 Dec 1854
THOMAS, Tazewell                                THOMAS, Latitia
            Father

THOMAS, Martha J                                W      F    18 Oct 1862
THOMAS, Andrew J                                THOMAS, Sarah J
            Father

THOMAS, Mary A                                  W      F    -- Mar 1854
THOMAS, James                                   THOMAS, Cynthy
            Father

THOMAS, Mary K                                  W      F     4 Apr 1859
THOMAS, W H                                     THOMAS, Virginia
            Father

THOMAS, May E                                   W      F    20 Nov 1862
THOMAS, Tyler D                                 THOMAS, Malinda M
            Father

THOMAS, Merebeau                                W      F     2 June 1860
THOMAS, Lewis                                   THOMAS, Amanda
            Father

THOMAS, Montague                                W      M    -- Dec 1857
THOMAS, David P                                 THOMAS, Amanda
            Father

THOMAS, Not Named                               W      M     4 Apr 1854
THOMAS, Peter J                                 THOMAS, Mary J
            Father
```

```
CHILD'S NAME                                  RACE  SEX      BIRTH DATE
FATHER\OWNER                                  MOTHER
             INFORMANT
-------------------------------------------------------------------------
THOMAS, Not Named                             W     M    1 Feb 1854
THOMAS, Pleasant C                            THOMAS, Frances
             Father

THOMAS, Not Named                             W     F    -- Dec 1857
THOMAS, Pleasant C                            THOMAS, Frances
             Father

THOMAS, Not Named                             W     M    5 Oct 1859
THOMAS, P C                                   THOMAS, Frances Thomas
             Father

THOMAS, S R                                   W     M    21 Aug 1854
THOMAS, A J                                   THOMAS, Elizabeth
             Father

THOMAS, Sarah Ann                             W     F    20 May 1853
THOMAS, Henry                                 THOMAS, Elizabeth
             Father

THOMAS, Sarah G                               W     F    14 Oct 1862
THOMAS, Peter J                               THOMAS, Mary J
             Mother

THOMAS, Susan                                 W     F    10 Sept 1860
THOMAS, P J                                   THOMAS, Mary J
             Father

THOMAS, William E                             W     M    25 Dec 1854
THOMAS, William H                             THOMAS, Phebe
             William H Thomas, (neighbor\uncle?)

THOMAS, William L                             W     F    25 May 1859
THOMAS, James W                               THOMAS, Nancy A
             Father

THOMPSON, Carolina                            W     F    -- Jan 1855
THOMPSON, Henry H                             THOMPSON, Nancy
             Father

THOMPSON, Columbus F                          W     M    12 May 1854
THOMPSON, Henry                               THOMPSON, Nancy
             Father

THOMPSON, James A                             W     M    13 Mar 1855
THOMPSON, Nelson                              THOMPSON, Elizabeth
             Father

THOMPSON, John A                              W     M    28 Oct 1854
THOMPSON, Austin                              THOMPSON, Polly
             Mother
```

```
CHILD'S NAME                              RACE  SEX    BIRTH DATE
FATHER\OWNER                              MOTHER
              INFORMANT
-----------------------------------------------------------------------
THOMPSON, Nancy E                         W     F     -- June 1859
THOMPSON, M S                             THOMPSON, Mary
              Father

THOMPSON, Not Named                       W     F     15 Sept 1853
THOMPSON, Mathers S                       THOMPSON, Mary
              Mother

THOMPSON, Samuel G                        W     M     11 Mar 1859
THOMPSON, Austin                          THOMPSON, Mary
              Father

THOMPSON, Samuel G                        W     M     -- Nov 1859
THOMPSON, Austin                          THOMPSON, Mary
              Father

THOMPSON, William M                       W     M     -- Sept 1855
THOMPSON, Mathew S                        THOMPSON, Mary
              Father

TILER                                     B/S   M     21 Aug 1860
ALLEN, Creed                              Malinda
              J S Adams, Master

TILER                                     B/S   M     21 Aug 1860
ALLEN, Creed                              Nalinda
              J S Adams, Master

TILLEY, James J                           W     M     10 May 1855
TILLEY, John W                            TILLEY, Jane
              Father

TILLEY, Martha J                          W     F     10 May 1855
TILLEY, John W                            TILLEY, Jane
              Father

TILLIS                                    B/S   F     -- Oct 1853
TURNER, Francis                           Not Given
              Owner

TILLY                                     B/S   F     10 July 1857
WILSON, Not Given                         Margaret
              Jesse Giles, Master

TILLY, Elizabeth                          W     F     30 Dec 1859
TILLY, John                               TILLY, May J
              Father

TILLY, Mary Ann                           W     F     15 Aug 1853
TILLY, John H                             TILLY, Jane
              Father


                          193
```

```
CHILD'S NAME                              RACE  SEX    BIRTH DATE
FATHER\OWNER                              MOTHER
                INFORMANT
-----------------------------------------------------------------------
TOOTIN (?)                                B/S   M    -- Oct 1855
HYLTON, George W                          Susan
                Master

TOWNS                                     B/S   M    26 June 1854
PENN, Clark                               Not Given
                Owner

TRENT, Abel                               W     M    -- Apr 1855
TRENT, Abel                               TRENT, Elizabeth
                Father

TRENT, George                             W     M    -- Dec 1857
TRENT, William                            TRENT, Charity
                Father

TRENT, Mary V                             W     F    2 May 1861
TRENT, Abel                               TRENT, Eliza
                Father

TRENT, Perry                              W     M    2 May 1859
TRENT, Abel                               TRENT, Eliza
                Father

TRENT, Reuben                             W     M    17 Aug 1853
TRENT, Abel                               TRENT, Eliza
                Father

TRENT, William A                          W     M    -- Dec 1857
TRENT, William                            TRENT, Malinda
                Father

TRENT, William J                          W     M    16 July 1855
TRENT, P W (Carpenter)                    TRENT, Mariah W
                Father

TUDOR, Greenville J                       W     M    14 July 1861
TUDOR, John                               TUDOR, Mary A
                Father

TUDOR, Martin M A                         W     F    23 July 1858
TUDOR, William                            TUDOR, Lucy
                Father

TUDOR, Susan Ann                          W     F    20 Mar 1855
TUDOR, John                               TUDOR, Nancy A
                Father

TUGGLE, Delila Jane                       W     F    -- Feb 1854
TUGGLE, Joel A                            TUGGLE, Ruth
                Father
```

```
CHILD'S NAME                         RACE  SEX      BIRTH DATE
FATHER\OWNER                         MOTHER
            INFORMANT
-----------------------------------------------------------------------
TUGGLE, George R                     W     M    26 Mar 1862
TUGGLE, Anderson                     TUGGLE, Francis
            Mother

TUGGLE, John W                       W     M     7 May 1855
TUGGLE, Henry                        TUGGLE, Lucy A E
            Father

TUGGLE, Not Named                    W     F     5 Dec 1854
TUGGLE, John                         TUGGLE, Mary
            Father

TUGGLE, Not Named                    W     F     3 Dec 1862
TUGGLE, John Jr                      TUGGLE, Mary
            Father

TUGGLE, Not Named                    W     F    28 Oct 1865
TUGGLE, Henry                        TUGGLE, Lucy
            Father

TUGGLE, Sarah                        W     F     4 Oct 1855
TUGGLE, Anderson                     TUGGLE, Frances
            Father

TUGGLE, Susannah                     W     F    15 Feb 1853
TUGGLE, James H                      TUGGLE, Martha J
            Mother

TUGGLE, Thomas A                     W     M    17 July 1853
Not Given                            TUGGLE, Catherine
            Mother

TUGGLE, Thomas G                     W     M     3 Nov 1859
TUGGLER, John Jr                     TUGGLE, Mary
            Father

TUGGLE, William J                    W     M     4 June 1857
TUGGLE, John                         TUGGLE, Lucy M
            Father

TUNER, Eluisa A                      W     F    15 Dec 1862
TURNER, George T                     TURNER, Mary A
            Father

TURNER, Delilia A                    W     F    30 Apr 1854
TURNER, John                         TURNER, Nancy
            Mother

TURNER, Elizabeth S                  W     F     3 Oct 1858
TURNER, S H                          TURNER, Ruth
            Father
```

CHILD'S NAME FATHER\OWNER INFORMANT	RACE SEX BIRTH DATE MOTHER
TURNER, Franklin Pierce TURNER, Greensville Father	W M 26 May 1853 TURNER, Rebecca
TURNER, George W TURNER, John B Father	W M 6 June 1853 TURNER, Mavmy (?)
TURNER, James T TURNER, William G Father	W M 26 July 1853 TURNER, Mary J
TURNER, John G TURNER, John G Father	W M 16 Apr 1857 TURNER, Nancy
TURNER, John L TURNER, Stephen H Father	W M 3 Feb 1862 TURNER, Malessa R
TURNER, Mahala TURNER, Jeremiah Father	W F 16 Jan 1862 TURNER, Martha J
TURNER, Mary A TURNER, Rufus (Sheriff) Father	W F 22 Sept 1858 TURNER, Rachael
TURNER, Nancy E TURNER, Greenwood Father	W F 19 May 1855 TURNER, Rebecca
TURNER, Not Named TURNER, Creed O Father	W F -- Apr 1857 TURNER, Martha
TURNER, Not Named TURNER, William G Father	W F 6 Oct 1860 TURNER, Mary J
TURNER, Not Named TURNER, Rufus N Turner, Uncle	W F 19 Aug 1862 TURNER, Rachel
TURNER, P F TURNER, S C Father	W M 4 Dec 1858 TURNER, Nancy W
TURNER, Robert E TURNER, Rufus Father	W M 13 Jan 1860 TURNER, Rachael

```
CHILD'S NAME                        RACE  SEX     BIRTH DATE
FATHER\OWNER                        MOTHER
            INFORMANT
--------------------------------------------------------------------
TURNER, Ruth E                      W     F    2 June 1860
TURNER, Samuel C                    TURNER, Nancy A
            Father

TURNER, Sallie Ann                  W     F    9 Sept 1860
TURNER, Lewis                       TURNER, Rebecca
            Father

TURNER, Samuel C                    W     M    4 Nov 1862
TURNER, Samuel C                    TURNER, Nancy M
            Father

TURNER, Shadrack L                  W     M    19 Jan 1857
TURNER, Jeremiah                    TURNER, Martha J
            Father

TURNER, Sitiramus E                 W     F    25 July 1854
TURNER, Stephen H                   TURNER, Ruth
            Father

TURNER, Thomas J                    W     M    8 Jan 1859
TURNER, Jere                        TURNER, Martha J
            Father

TYLER                               B/S   M    13 Dec 1855
PENN, Clark                         Luvenia
            Owner

TYLER                               B/S   M    -- Aug 1855
DODSON, George C                    Harriett
            Owner

TYLER                               B/S   M    -- Feb 1860
HAIRSTON, S W                       Idea
            Master

TYLER                               B/S   M    1 Sept 1861
HANBY, H  H                         Martha
            Owner

TYLOR                               B/S   M    -- -- 1854
LACKEY, John                        Linda
            Owner

TYLOR                               B/S   M    -- Oct 1855
REYNOLDS, Harden W                  Mary
            Owner

UNDERWOOD, Amanda Abigail           W     F    -- Aug 1853
UNDERWOOD, Joshua                   UNDERWOOD, Polly
            Father


                        197
```

```
CHILD'S NAME                                    RACE  SEX    BIRTH DATE
FATHER\OWNER                                    MOTHER
              INFORMANT
-----------------------------------------------------------------------
UNDERWOOD, Henry                                W     M     1 June 1853
UNDERWOOD, Samuel                               UNDERWOOD, Rebecca
              Father

UNDERWOOD, Sarah E                              W     F     15 Feb 1865
UNDERWOOD, I W                                  UNDERWOOD, Mary S
              Father

UNDERWOOD, William M                            W     M     23 Aug 1860
UNDERWOOD, J W                                  UNDERWOOD, Mary S
              Father

VANNER                                          B/S   F     17 Jan 1859
HANDY, H                                        Susan
              Owner

VAUGHAN, James C                                W     M     -- Aug 1853
VAUGHAN, Johnson                                VAUGHAN, Matilda
              Father

VAUGHAN, Z  H                                   W     F     23 Jan 1862
VAUGHAN, John J                                 VAUGHAN, Nancy E
              Mother

VAUGHN, Christopher G                           W     M     11 June 1854
VAUGHN, Wilson T                                VAUGHN, Susan
              Father

VAUGHN, Mary F                                  W     F     16 Mar 1854
VAUGHN, Joshua                                  VAUGHN, Caroline
              Father

VAUGHN, Susan                                   W     F     22 Oct 1854
VAUGHN, Thomas R                                VAUGHN, Mary
              Father

VAUGHN, Victoria A                              W     F     20 Sept 1858
VAUGHN, J J                                     VAUGHN, Nancy E
              Father

VIA, Clarenas                                   W     F     4 Sept 1858
VIA, J E                                        VIA, louisa V
              Father

VIA, Delila J                                   W     F     9 Sept 1859
VIA, Isaac                                      VIA, Martha
              Father

VIA, E Louisa E                                 W     F     6 Nov 1859
VIA, Isaac                                      VIA, Lucy
              Father
```

```
CHILD'S NAME                              RACE  SEX    BIRTH DATE
FATHER\OWNER                              MOTHER
              INFORMANT
------------------------------------------------------------------------
VIA, James Andrew                         W     M    9 Apr 1862
VIA, Alex                                 VIA, Martha E
              Mother

VIA, James E                              W     M    24 Aug 1862
VIA, James E                              VIA, Louise V
              Father

VIA, Jerisha E                            W     F    1 Feb 1860
VIA, E D                                  VIA, Nancy J
              Father

VIA, John M                               W     M    24 May 1860
VIA, James E                              VIA, S A
              Father

VIA, John R                               W     M    19 Sept 1853
VIA, William                              VIA, Mary
              Father

VIA, Leate                                W     F    -- Feb 1857
VIA, James E                              VIA, Louisa G
              Father

VIA, Martha S                             W     F    20 Mar 1865
VIA, James E                              VIA, Louisa
              Father

VIA, Mary E                               W     F    11 Dec 1857
VIA, E D                                  VIA, Nancy
              Father

VIA, Mary E F                             W     F    22 Feb 1858
VIA, Reuben                               VIA, Mary E
              Mother

VIA, Pensuannah                           W     F    -- May 1854
VIA, James                                VIA, Mary
              Father

VIA, Rice M                               W     M    30 Dec 1854
VIA, Elijah D                             VIA, Nancy
              Father

VIA, Rosilla                              W     F    24 Apr 1862
VIA, Elijah                               VIA, Nancy
              Mother

VIA, Sarah J                              W     F    26 Oct 1859
VIA, Reuben                               VIA, Mary E
              Father
```

```
CHILD'S NAME                              RACE  SEX    BIRTH DATE
FATHER\OWNER                              MOTHER
             INFORMANT
------------------------------------------------------------------------
VIA, Sarah J                              W     F    26 Oct 1860
VIA, Reuben                               VIA, Mary E
             Father

VIA, William A                            W     M    1 May 1859
VIA, William                              VIA, Mary
             Father

VICK                                      B/S   M    10 Nov 1859
BROWN, N                                  Martha
             Owner

VICTOR                                    B/S   M    -- Oct 1862
TATUM, Edward                             Puss
             Master

VINCY                                     B/S   F    -- -- 1854
HAIRSTON, Samuel W                        Edy
             Owner

VINIA                                     B/S   F    14 June 1859
WILSON, Samuel                            Eda
             Jesse Giles, Overseer

VIPPERMAN, James                          W     M    -- Sept 1857
VIPPERMAN, Daniel                         VIPPERMAN, Martha
             Father

VIPPERMAN, Not Named                      W     M    21 Mar 1859
VIPPERMAN, Daniel                         VIPPERMAN, Martha
             Father

VIPPERMAN, Ruth E J                       W     F    24 June 1854
VIPPERMAN, Daniel                         VIPPERMAN, Martha
             Father

VIPPERMAN, Sarah H                        W     F    15 Aug 1853
VIPPERMAN, William                        VIPPERMAN, Nancy
             Father

VIRGINIA                                  B/S   F    -- Mar 1857
WOODALL, Joseph                           Mary
             Master

VIRGINIA                                  B/S   F    -- Aug 1859
SCALES, Ab                                Emaline
             Owner

WADE, Thomas M                            W     M    28 Oct 1854
WADE, Joseph A (Shoemaker)                WADE, Catherine C
             Father
```

```
CHILD'S NAME                                     RACE  SEX    BIRTH DATE
FATHER\OWNER                                     MOTHER
              INFORMANT
-----------------------------------------------------------------------
WALKER, Denny G                                  W     M     27 May 1853
WALKER, Benjamin G                               WALKER, Mary J
              Father

WALKER, John M                                   W     M     10 June 1860
WALKER, Linville (Mechanic)                      WALKER, Permelia
              Father

WALKER, John R                                   W     M     26 Feb 1855
WALKER, John                                     WALKER, Ruth
              Father

WALKER, Martha A                                 W     F     2 Feb 1853
WALKER, Lenvell (Carpenter)                      WALKER, Permelia
              Father

WALKER, Not Named                                W     F     3 July 1858
WALKER, Linville (Mechanic)                      WALKER, Permelia
              Father

WALKER, Not Named                                W     F     22 June 1865
WALKER, Linville F (Millwright)                  WALKER, Permelia
              Father

WALKER, William A                                W     M     -- Nov 1857
WALKER, John                                     WALKER, Ruth
              Father

WALLER                                           B/S   M     -- Dec 1855
STAPLES, A, Deceased                             Julia
              Claiborne Mills, Overseer

WALLER                                           B/S   M     28 Sept 1857
PENN, Clark                                      Susan
              Master

WALLER                                           B/S   M     -- Sept 1857
STAPLES, W R                                     Susan
              Master

WALLER, Not Named                                W     F     30 Nov 1855
WALLER, James A                                  WALLER, Jane B
              Father

WALLER, Sarah M (Born Surry Co, NC)              W     F     13 Sept 1853
WALLER, James A                                  WALLER, June R
              Father

WALTER                                           B/S   M     -- Jan 1855
SCALES, Absalom                                  Not Given
              Master
```

```
CHILD'S NAME                              RACE  SEX    BIRTH DATE
FATHER\OWNER                              MOTHER
          INFORMANT
---------------------------------------------------------------------
WARF, John                                W     F     -- July 1857
WARF, R L                                 WARF, Mary
          Father

WARF, Not Named                           W     M     4 Dec 1853
WARF, Romulus S                           WARF, Mary
          Father

WARF, Not Named                           W     F     18 July 1860
WARF, R S                                 WARF, Mary
          Father

WASHBURN, Carter V                        W     M     20 July 1859
WASHBURN, Thompson                        WASHBURN, Louisa Anna
          Father

WASHBURN, Madison H                       W     M     14 Nov 1855
WASHBURN, John H                          WASHBURN, Rosannah G
          Father

WASHBURN, Martha                          W     F     1 July 1865
WASHBURN, Thompson                        WASHBURN, Lavinia
          Father

WASHBURN, Sarah Jane                      W     F     1 May 1854
WASHBURN, Thomas                          WASHBURN, Louiseana
          Father

WASHBURN, Shadrack T                      W     M     11 Mar 1853
WASHBURN, John H                          WASHBURN, Rosannah
          Father

WASHINGTON                                B/S   M     1 Mar 1854
STAPLES, A                                None Given
          William Falkner, Overseer

WASHINGTON                                B/S   M     4 Dec 1859
BRIM, Joseph                              Katy
          Master

WASHINGTON, Green                         W     M     25 July 1855
WASHINGTON, David                         WASHINGTON, Ann
          Father

WASHINGTON, Susan Rachael                 W     F     18 May 1853
WASHINGTON, David                         WASHINGTON, Ann
          Father

WASHINGTON, Z                             W     M     25 Aug 1860
WASHINGTON, David (Blacksmith)            WASHINGTON, Ann
          Father
```

```
CHILD'S NAME                                    RACE  SEX     BIRTH DATE
FATHER\OWNER                                    MOTHER
                  INFORMANT
-------------------------------------------------------------------------
WATSON, Mary J                                  W     F     24 July 1859
WATSON, A J                                     WATSON, Elizabeth
                  Father

WATSON, Nancy E                                 W     F     -- -- 1854
WATSON, John                                    WATSON, Oney
                  Father

WEBB, Elenora (Twin)                            W     F     11 Nov 1862
WEBB, Henry                                     WEBB, Susan
                  Mother

WEBB, Margaret                                  W     F     -- Jan 1854
WEBB, Henry (Miller)                            WEBB, Susan M
                  Father

WEBB, Mary A                                    W     F     -- Dec 1859
WEBB, Henry                                     WEBB, Susan M
                  Father

WEBB, Not Named                                 W     F     -- Nov 1857
WEBB, Henry (Miller)                            WEBB, Sunn (?)
                  Father

WEBB, Thorban F (Twin)                          W     M     11 Nov 1862
WEBB, Henry                                     WEBB, Susan
                  Mother

WEBSTER, Clark P                                W     M     2 Apr 1853
WEBSTER, Mathers G                              WEBSTER, Martha
                  Father

WEBSTER, Samuel A (Born Raleigh, NC)            W     M     21 Apr 1854
WEBSTER, Mathew G                               WEBSTER, Martha
                  Father

WELL, Matilda F                                 W     F     24 July 1854
WELLS, George D                                 WELLS, Elizabeth S
                  Father

WELLS, America J                                W     F     23 Oct 1862
WELLS, J R                                      WELLS, Elizabeth
                  Father

WELLS, Mary F                                   W     F     15 Dec 1853
WELLS, John S                                   WELLS, Matilda
                  Father

WELLS, Not Named                                W     M     30 Apr 1853
WELLS, George D                                 WELLS, Susan E
                  Father
```

203

CHILD'S NAME FATHER\OWNER	INFORMANT	RACE SEX BIRTH DATE MOTHER
WELLS, William WELLS, William	Father	W M 1 May 1857 WELLS, Mary
WEST, A L WEST, W G	Father	W M 14 June 1860 WEST, Elizabeth
WEST, A R WEST, W J	Father	W F 8 Sept 1858 WEST, Elizabeth
WEST, Robert WEST, William N (Bricklayer)	Father	W M -- Feb 1862 WEST, Lucy J
WHITLOCK, Ira B M WHITLOCK, Jonal	Mother	W M 4 Jan 1865 WHITLOCK, Susan
WHITLOCK, John B WHITLOCK, Jareal	Father	W M -- Oct 1862 WHITLOCK, Susan
WILLARD, Jeremiah WILLARD, Luke	Father	W M 1 Oct 1864 WILLARD, Catherine
WILLARD, Lucinda J WILLARD, James	Father	W F 30 June 1854 WILLARD, Ruth
WILLARD, Lulucia Avaline Baseborn	Pleasant Ellis, Reputed Father	W F 29 July 1854 WILLARD, Sally
WILLARD, Mary J WILLARD, Allen	Father	W F 1 Aug 1853 WILLARD, Fanny
WILLARD, Not Namd Not Given	William Critz, Overseer of Poor	W F -- Dec 1859 WILLARD, Lucy
WILLARD, Not Named Not Given	William Critz, Overseer of Poor	W F -- Dec 1859 WILLARD, Sally
WILLARD, Oney W WILLARD, James	Father	W F -- Dec 1858 WILLARD, Ruth E

CHILD'S NAME FATHER\OWNER INFORMANT	RACE SEX BIRTH DATE MOTHER
WILLARD, Ruth A WILLARD, James Father	W F -- Nov 1860 WILLARD, Ruth
WILLIA, Mary Ellen WILLIS, Green Father	W F 6 Sept 1859 WILLIS, Permelia
WILLIAM HAIRSTON, S W Owner	B/S M -- -- 1853 Not Given
WILLIAM SCALES, Absalom Master	B/S M -- Apr 1855 Not Given
WILLIAM PENN, Thomas J Owner	B/S M -- Feb 1855 Not Given
WILLIAM WILSON, Samuel P Thomas Winn, Overseer	B/S M -- July 1859 Rachael
WILLIAM HYLTON, Val Master	B/S M 6 Dec 1860 Jane
WILLIAM HYLTON, Isaac John Hubbard, Master	B/S M 30 Oct 1860 Senai
WILLIAM WILSON, Samuel P Jesse M Giles, Overseer	B/S M 1 Feb 1861 Hannah
WILLIAM FLIPPIN, John T Master	B/S M 6 Mar 1862 Lucinda
WILLIAM Father Not Given James Sawyers, Former Owner	B M 13 Oct 1864 Martha
WILLIAM Father Not Given William F Tatum, Former Owner	B M 22 Apr 1864 Em
WILLIAM B CONNER, M Milly Conner, Mistress	B/S M 3 June 1858 Virginia

```
CHILD'S NAME                            RACE  SEX    BIRTH DATE
FATHER\OWNER                            MOTHER
              INFORMANT
---------------------------------------------------------------------
WILLIAM H                               B/S    M    26 Feb 1859
SHELTON, G O                            Martha
              Owner

WILLIAM LOTTE                           B/S    M    7 Apr 1853
NOWLIN, C P                             Not Given
              Nancy Nowlin, Mistress

WILLIAM R                               B/S    M    20 June 1860
COCKRAM, John B                         Rhoda
              William Cannaday, Master

WILLIAM REUBEN                          B/S    M    26 Apr 1859
HYLTON, G W                             Rachael
              Owner

WILLIAMS, James P                       W      M    23 Apr 1862
WILLIAMS, Jacob W                       WILLIAMS, Lucinda
              Mother

WILLIAMS, John P                        W      M    5 Nov 1853
WILLIAMS, Marshall                      WILLIAMS, Deely M
              Father

WILLIAMS, Kessiah E                     W      F    18 Mar 1853
WILLIAMS, Sparrell D                    WILLIAMS, Exony
              Father

WILLIAMS, Mary E                        W      F    27 Jan 1855
WILLIAMS, Creed T                       WILLIAMS, Elizabeth
              Father

WILLIAMS, Mary J                        W      F    -- Mar 1857
WILLIAMS, Samuel                        WILLIAMS, Enona
              Father

WILLIAMS, Not Named                     W      F    14 Feb 1855
WILLIAMS, Sparrell D                    WILLIAMS, Levina
              Father

WILLIAMS, Not Named                     W      M    -- June 1857
WILLIAMS, Joshua                        WILLIAMS, Nancy
              Father

WILLIAMS, Not Named                     W      M    1 June 1859
WILLIAMS, Sparrell                      WILLIAMS, Exona
              Father

WILLIAMS, Not Named                     W      F    2 Oct 1861
WILLIAMS, S  D                          WILLIAMS, Exony
              Father
```

```
CHILD'S NAME                              RACE SEX     BIRTH DATE
FATHER\OWNER                              MOTHER
            INFORMANT
------------------------------------------------------------------------
WILLIAMS, Sally                           W    F    20 June 1854
WILLIAMS, J E (Wheelwright)               WILLIAMS, Nancy
            Father

WILLIAMS, Samuel                          W    M    18 Dec 1859
WILLIAMS, Marshall                        WILLIAMS, Amanda
            Father

WILLIAMS, Sarah Ann                       W    F    1 Oct 1853
Not Known                                 WILLIAMS, Susan
            William W Williams, Brother

WILLIAMS, William                         W    M    30 Apr 1859
WILLIAMS, Samuel                          WILLIAMS, Susan
            Father

WILLIS, Alex                              W    M    8 Aug 1854
WILLIS, G                                 WILLIS, Permelia A
            Father

WILLIS, John R                            W    M    2 May 1861
WILLIS, John                              WILLIS, Marinda
            Father

WILLIS, Martha J                          W    F    10 May 1855
WILLIS, John Jr                           WILLIS, Renda
            Father

WILLIS, Not Named                         W    M    1 July 1859
WILLIS, John                              WILLIS, Matilda
            Father

WILLIS, Thomas J                          W    M    23 Sept 1862
WILLIS, Greensville                       WILLIS, Permelia A
            Father

WILLS, Mary C                             W    F    11 June 1853
WILLS, Edward                             WILLS, Merica
            Father

WILSON, Jesse F                           W    M    6 Dec 1862
WILSON, William F                         WILSON, Francis
            Father

WILSON, Not Named                         B    F    10 Oct 1865
Unknown                                   WILSON, Polly
            Jesse Giles, Neighbor

WILSON, Not Named                         B    M    1 Sept 1865
Unknown                                   WILSON, Judy
            Jesse Giles, Neighbor
```

```
CHILD'S NAME                            RACE  SEX    BIRTH DATE
FATHER\OWNER                            MOTHER
            INFORMANT
--------------------------------------------------------------------
WIMBISH, James                          B     M     20 Feb 1865
WIMBISH, James S                        WIMBISH, Statira
            Father

WIMBISH, Jane                           W     F     14 Jan 1860
WIMBISH, Jno                            WIMBISH, Mahala
            Father

WIMBISH, Jane (Twin)                    W     F      4 Sept 1860
WIMBISH, William                        WIMBISH, Rebecca
            Father

WIMBISH, Judith V                       W     F      5 Mar 1862
WIMBISH, James B                        WIMBISH, Mahala J
            Mother

WIMBISH, Mary  E                        W     F     20 May 1854
WIMBISH, William H                      WIMBISH, Rebecca E
            Mother

WIMBISH, Mary E                         W     F     27 Jan 1859
WIMBISH, Joseph                         WIMBISH, Mahala Jane
            Father

WIMBISH, Not Named (Born Dead)          W     M      5 June 1864
WIMBISH, William                        WIMBISH, Rebecca
            Father

WIMBISH, Sennia (Twin)                  W     F      4 Sept 1860
WIMBISH, William                        WIMBISH, Rebecca
            Father

WIMBISH, Virginia                       W     F     15 Feb 1861
WIMBISH, John B                         WIMBISH, Jane
            Father

WIMMER, Isabella A                      W     F     10 Jan 1854
WIMMER, John W                          WIMMER, Ruth R
            Father

WINN, John D                            W     M     20 Feb 1857
WINN, William                           WINN, Callie M
            Father

WINN, Lucy                              W     F     10 Oct 1859
WINN, Thomas (Overseer)                 WINN, Mary
            Father

WINNIE                                  B/S   F     -- Oct 1859
HILL, F F                               Susan
            Daniel Gray, Owner
```

```
CHILD'S NAME                            RACE  SEX    BIRTH DATE
FATHER\OWNER                            MOTHER
              INFORMANT
-------------------------------------------------------------------
WITT, Hillory                           W     M    27 Dec 1854
WITT, William (Brick Mason)             WITT, Virginia N
              Father

WITT, John S                            W     M    14 May 1853
WITT, William (Brick Laying)            WITT, Virginia N
              Father

WITT, Louisa E                          W     F    -- -- 1853
WITT, A H (Mason)                       WITT, Permelia
              Father

WOOD, Allen T                           W     M    25 Jan 1864
WOOD, Martin                            WOOD, Elizabeth
              Father

WOOD, Asa F                             W     M    17 Jan 1860
WOOD, James M                           WOOD, Druscilla
              Father

WOOD, Avaline                           W     F     3 Apr 1854
WOOD, Stephen H                         WOOD, Rachel
              Father

WOOD, C  E                              W     M     9 Nov 1862
WOOD, James P                           WOOD, Margaret
              Father

WOOD, Daniel H                          W     M     3 Nov 1860
WOOD, R J                               WOOD, Judith J
              Father

WOOD, Eleney                            W     F     7 Sept 1854
Not Given                               WOOD, Nancy
              Mother

WOOD, Elizabeth                         W     F     6 July 1855
WOOD, James                             WOOD, Nancy
              Father

WOOD, Franklin                          W     M    12 June 1865
WOOD, Martin                            WOOD, Lucy
              Father

WOOD, Green A                           W     M    -- Sept 1862
WOOD, William G                         WOOD, Jinsy
              Father

WOOD, Isaac M                           W     M     8 Nov 1858
WOOD, Levi                              WOOD, Elizabeth
              Father
```

209

WOOD, J T
WOOD, Joel T
    Father

W   M   11 May 1854
WOOD, Ann

WOOD, James
WOOD, J M
    Father

W   M   10 Mar 1864
WOOD, Drusilla

WOOD, James H
WOOD, Richard
    Father

W   M   10 Mar 1854
WOOD, Elizabeth

WOOD, Jeff P
WOOD, R J
    Father

W   M   4 Nov 1858
WOOD, Judith A

WOOD, John
WOOD, Edward
    Father

W   M   -- Oct 1855
WOOD, Nancy

WOOD, John F
WOOD, Jeremiah
    Father

W   M   31 May 1862
WOOD, Eliza

WOOD, John J
WOOD, John
    Father

W   M   29 Apr 1860
WOOD, Martha

WOOD, John L
WOOD, James
    Father

W   M   -- Aug 1859
WOOD, Ruth

WOOD, John R
WOOD, Joel
    Father

W   M   1 Aug 1855
WOOD, Malinda

WOOD, John Robert
WOOD, John
    Father

W   M   12 Feb 1854
WOOD, Martha H

WOOD, Julia A
WOOD, Edward
    Father

W   F   2 Apr 1854
WOOD, Nancy

WOOD, Laurabell
WOOD, Levi
    Father

W   F   6 May 1862
WOOD, Elizabeth

WOOD, Lydia M
WOOD, A J
    Father

W   F   15 May 1858
WOOD, Elsby

```
CHILD'S NAME                              RACE  SEX    BIRTH DATE
FATHER\OWNER                              MOTHER
            INFORMANT
-----------------------------------------------------------------
WOOD, Malissa Frances                     W     F    -- May 1854
WOOD, William G                           WOOD, Jane
            Father

WOOD, Margaret J                          W     F    15 June 1855
WOOD, Alexander                           WOOD, Elizabeth
            Father

WOOD, Martha                              W     F    7 Oct 1859
WOOD, John                                WOOD, Martha
            Father

WOOD, Mary F                              W     F    5 Feb 1855
WOOD, Andrew J                            WOOD, Elizabeth
            Father

WOOD, Nancy A (Born Wyoming)              W     F    7 Feb 1860
WOOD, Alex                                WOOD, Sarah J
            Father

WOOD, Not Named                           W     M    -- June 1859
WOOD, James                               WOOD, Delila
            Father

WOOD, Peter                               W     M    6 Dec 1860
WOOD, James                               WOOD, Elizabeth
            Father

WOOD, Sarah                               W     F    -- Dec 1859
WOOD, Alex                                WOOD, Ellen Jane
            Father

WOOD, Sarah A                             W     F    2 Feb 1859
WOOD, J J                                 WOOD, Elizabeth
            Father

WOOD, Sparrell                            W     M    3 Feb 1860
WOOD, Alex                                WOOD, Elizabeth
            Father

WOOD, Step G                              W     M    -- May 1858
WOOD, S H                                 WOOD, Rachael
            Father

WOOD, Susan                               W     F    3 Mar 1859
WOOD, Alex                                WOOD, Jane
            Father

WOOD, Susan E                             W     F    24 Feb 1853
WOOD, Richard J                           WOOD, Judith J
            Father
```

```
CHILD'S NAME                              RACE  SEX    BIRTH DATE
FATHER\OWNER                              MOTHER
              INFORMANT
-------------------------------------------------------------------------
WOOD, Susan L                             W     F    -- May 1860
WOOD, S H                                 WOOD, Rachael
              Father

WOOD, Tazewell A                          W     M    31 Aug 1854
WOOD, Gabriel                             Wood, Luelly
              Father

WOOD, Thomas E                            W     M    21 Apr 1862
WOOD, Alex                                WOOD, Maria J
              Mother

WOOD, Wesley M (Born Floyd Co)            W     M    22 Feb 1860
Illegitimate                              WOOD, Sarah
              Mother

WOOD, William C                           W     M    17 Dec 1861
WOOD, James M                             WOOD, Druscilla
              Father

WOOD, William D                           W     M    27 Feb 1854
WOOD, James                               WOOD, Lavinia A
              Father

WOOD, Willy A                             W     M    29 Apr 1853
WOOD, John                                WOOD, Martha
              Father

WOODALL, Frances                          W     F    17 Apr 1857
WOODALL, Joseph                           WOODALL, Mary Ann
              Father

WOODALL, Not Named                        W     F    12 Nov 1855
WOODALL, James W (Miller)                 WOODALL, Mary A
              Father

WOODALL, Not Named                        W     F    10 Apr 1864
WOODALL, J  W                             WOODALL, Mariah
              Father

WOODS, Not Named                          W     M    25 May 1857
WOODS, Martin                             WOODS, Mary
              Father

WOODS, Not Named (Slightly Deformed)      W     M    5 Feb 1853
WOODS, Martin                             WOODS, Nancy
              William W Gray, No Connection

WOOLWINE, Hannibal C                      W     M    4 July 1854
WOOLWINE, Thomas B (Saddler)              WOOLWINE, Sally
              Father


                           212
```

```
CHILD'S NAME                               RACE  SEX    BIRTH DATE
FATHER\OWNER                               MOTHER
              INFORMANT
------------------------------------------------------------------------
WOOLWINE, Henry L (Twin)                    W     M    26 May 1860_
WOOLWINE, Thomas B (Sadler)                 WOOLWINE, Sally
              Father

WOOLWINE, William B (Twin)                  W     M    26 May 1860
WOOLWINE, Thomas B (Sadler)                 WOOLWINE, Sally
              Father

WORTH, Joseph M                             W     M    10 Dec 1865
WORTH, William E                            WORTH, Susan
              Father

WRAY, Sarah                                 W     F     3 Nov 1854
WRAY, Joseph                                WRAY, Martha
              Father

WRIGHT, Delila J                            W     F    11 Apr 1865
WRIGHT, Mashall C                           WRIGHT, Nancy E
              Father

WRIGHT, Martha E                            W     F    11 Apr 1860
WRIGHT, Josiah                              WRIGHT, Sarah L
              Father

WRIGHT, Mary                                W     F    28 Sept 1858
WRIGHT, Henry                               WRIGHT, Lucy
              Father

WRIGHT, Mary                                W     F     8 Apr 1859
WRIGHT, Martin                              WRIGHT, Mary J
              Father

WRIGHT, Nancy A D                           W     F    26 Feb 1854
WRIGHT, Josiah                              WRIGHT, Sarah L
              Father

WRIGHT, Nancy E                             W     F    16 July 1857
WRIGHT, Martin                              WRIGHT, Jane
              Father

WRIGHT, Not Named                           W     F    24 Oct 1862
WRIGHT, Columbus                            WRIGHT, Elizabeth
              Mother

WRIGHT, Sarah E J                           W     F    26 Feb 1857
WRIGHT, Josiah                              WRIGHT, Sarah S
              Father

WRIGHT, William Henry                       W     M     8 May 1860
WRIGHT, Henry                               WRIGHT, Lucy E
              Father
```

```
CHILD'S NAME                                    RACE  SEX    BIRTH DATE
FATHER\OWNER                                    MOTHER
                INFORMANT
-------------------------------------------------------------------------
YATES, Lewis                                    W     M    11 Sept 1860
YATES, John Y                                   YATES, Cally
            Father

YOUNG, America                                  W     F     6 July 1855
YOUNG, Henry                                    YOUNG, Decie
            Father

YOUNG, Florence E                               W     F    18 May 1854
YOUNG, John (Mechanic)                          YOUNG, Delphia
            Father

YOUNG, Frances                                  W     F    13 Nov 1859
YOUNG, Henry                                    YOUNG, Dicia
            Father

YOUNG, Green                                    W     M    30 Oct 1857
YOUNG, Henry                                    YOUNG, Dicey
            Father

YOUNG, Henry J                                  W     M     7 Mar 1853
YOUNG, Henry                                    YOUNG, Dessey P
            Father

YOUNG, Iredell Franklin                         W     M    16 Feb 1854
KIMBALL, John (Reputed Father - Turner)         YOUNG, Polly
            Mother

YOUNG, Lucillia                                 W     F    10 July 1860
YOUNG, Jeff                                     YOUNG, Ellen
            Father

YOUNG, Not Named                                W     F     -- Nov 1862
YOUNG, Jeff                                     YOUNG, Aling
            Bethania Young, Grandmother

YOUNG, Not Named                                W     M    14 Oct 1862
YOUNG, Henry                                    YOUNG, Disa
            Father

YOUNG, Not Named                                B     M     7 Apr 1865
YOUNG, Carter                                   YOUNG, Caroline
            Father

YOUNG, Robert Lee                               W     M    16 Sept 1865
YOUNG, C  H                                     YOUNG, Charlotte
            Father

YOUNG, William A                                W     M    20 Mar 1862
YOUNG, John C                                   YOUNG, Alamanda
            Benjamin Young, Grandfather


                        214
```

```
CHILD'S NAME                                RACE  SEX     BIRTH DATE
FATHER\OWNER                                MOTHER
            INFORMANT
----------------------------------------------------------------------
ZENTMEYER, Flora                            W     F     -- Oct 1858
ZENTMEYER, J N                              ZENTMEYER, Martha A
            G W Penn, Brother

ZIGLER, Christopher                         W     M     5 July 1853
ZIGLAR, Richard                             ZIGLAR, Catherine
          _ Father
```

SECTION II

CHILD'S NAME BIRTH DATE	FATHER	R	S	INFORMANT MOTHER
ADAMS, Charles 30 Jan 1867	ADAMS, Samuel	W	M	Neighbor ADAMS, Mary
ADAMS, Jathina A 3 Dec 1869	ADAMS, John S	W	F	Father ADAMS, Mary E
ADAMS, John A 8 Aug 1867	ADAMS, J J	W	M	Father ADAMS, Malinda
ADAMS, M M S T 15 Jan 1867	ADAMS, Joshua L	W	F	Father ADAMS, E E
ADAMS, M R R 7 July 1866	ADAMS, J J	W	F	Father ADAMS, Malinda
ADAMS, Nora 10 Jan 1867	Not Given	W	F	Neighbor ADAMS, Sophia
ADAMS, R T 11 May 1869	ADAMS, John	W	M	Father ADAMS, M J
ADAMS, Samuel Jackson 27 Jan 1867	ADAMS, William	W	M	Father ADAMS, Elizabeth Ann
ADAMS, Susan R 17 May 1866	ADAMS, William	W	F	Father ADAMS, Elizabeth
AGEE, Mary Jane W 10 Dec 1866	AGEE, W G	W	F	Mother AGEE, Jane
AGEE, W E 18 Jan 1869	AGEE, William G	W	M	Father AGEE, Jane
AKERS, Adeline 9 Oct 1867	AKERS, Elijha A	W	F	Father AKERS, Ailey J
AKERS, Alitice L 19 Sept 1869	AKERS, Samuel R	W	F	Father AKERS, Lucinda J
AKERS, L G 3 Mar 1866	AKERS, Isaac N	W	M	Mother AKERS, Nancy V
AKERS, Nancy E 5 May 1868	AKERS, W C	W	F	Father AKERS, Exony
ANDERSON, Laura Ellen (Born Stokes Co) 22 Oct 1867	ANDERSON, D W	W	F	Father ANDERSON, Rachael
ANGLIN, Rosabell 12 Apr 1867	ANGLIN, John L	W	F	Father ANGLIN, Mary

```
CHILD'S NAME                                  R  S  INFORMANT
BIRTH DATE        FATHER                             MOTHER
```

CHILD'S NAME / BIRTH DATE FATHER	R	S	INFORMANT / MOTHER
ARNOLD, Texander 13 Dec 1868 ARNOLD, Charles	B	F	Father ARNOLD, Bettie
ARRINGTON, Mintoria E 8 June 1867 ARRINGTON, Sparrell G	W	F	Father ARRINGTON, Mary E
ARRINGTON, Nancy E 24 Mar 1866 ARRINGTON, Samuel	W	F	Not Given ARRINGTON, Sarah A
ARRINGTON, Not Named (Born Dead) 25 Nov 1867 ARRINGTON, William H	W	M	Father ARRINGTON, Martha
ATKINS, David C 1 Oct 1868 ATKINS, Booker	W	M	Father ATKINS, Judith S
ATKINS, John 25 Apr 1866 ATKINS, B M	W	M	Father ATKINS, Judith S
AUSTIN, Margaret (Born Rockingham Co NC) 7 Dec 1866 AUSTIN, James R	W	F	Father AUSTIN, Nancy M
AYERS, Finetta -- Feb 1867 AYERS, W W	W	F	Father AYERS, Emily
AYERS, James M 15 July 1866 AYERS, Spencer (F M)	B	M	Not Given AYERS, Lucinda
AYERS, Thomas H 5 Sept 1868 AYERS, William H	W	M	Father AYERS, Emily
AYRES, Leonard M 23 Oct 1869 AYRES, Thomas	W	M	Father AYERS, Rachael
BAKER, L W R 20 Dec 1867 BAKER, Mat	B	F	Father BAKER, E J C
BALISLE, J H 10 June 1867 BALISLE, Lee	W	M	Father BALISLE, Nancy
BARBER, Not Named 15 July 1868 BARBER, A J	W	M	Father BARBER, Susan E
BARBOUR, James William 9 Aug 1866 BARBOUR, A J	W	M	Father BARBOUR, Susan E
BARKSDALE, Fannie 18 Dec 1869 BARKSDALE, Amos	B	F	Father BARKSDALE, Ann
BARNARD, Not Named 23 Nov 1866 BARNARD, Thomas A	W	M	Not Given BARNARD, Caroline

CHILD'S NAME BIRTH DATE	FATHER	R	S	INFORMANT MOTHER
BARNES, Bettie 18 Nov 1869	BARNES, William	W	F	Mrs Arnold, Grandmother BARNES, Sarah
BEASLEY, George R 14 Oct 1868	BEASLEY, Robert M	W	M	Father BEASLEY, mary
BEASLEY, Rebecca 18 Apr 1869	BEASLEY, Robert M	W	F	Father BEASLEY, Mary J
BEASLEY, William H 12 Dec 1866	BEASLEY, Robert M	W	M	Not Given BEASLEY, jane
BELCHER, Lura T 14 Dec 1869	BELCHER, Costley	W	F	Nancy Belcher, GMother BELCHER, Mahala
BELCHER, Martha E 21 Apr 1866	BELCHER, John	W	F	Father BELCHER, Nancy
BELCHER, Nancy S 31 Dec 1868	BELCHER, Pete	W	F	Father BELCHER, Lucy E
BELCHER, Not Named 15 Aug 1868	BELCHER, John	W	M	Father BELCHER, Nancy
BELCHER, Richard S 4 Sept 1869	BELCHER, Hardin	W	M	Father BELCHER, Louisa F
BELTON, Columbia 13 Sept 1868	Unmarried	B	F	Friend BELTON, Elizabeth
BENNETT, Adolphus 23 Sept 1868	BENNETT, John H	W	M	Grandfather BENNETT, Martha A
BENNETT, Not Named 16 Oct 1866	BENNETT, John H	W	F	Not Given BENNETT, Martha
BENTLEY, Mat Terry -- Sept 1867	BENTLEY, William	W	M	Friend BENTLEY, Martha
BIGGS, James L 21 June 1869	BIGGS, Robert W	W	M	Mother BIGGS, Nancy L
BISHOP, Henry Wade -- July 1867	BISHOP, Henry	W	M	Father BISHOP, Edna Catherine
BLACKARD, Thomas J 22 Feb 1868	BLACKARD, Aaraon (Mechanic)	W	M	Father BLACKARD, Mary J
BLACKARD, Thomas Jackson 22 Jan 1868	BLACKARD, Aaron	W	M	Father BLACKARD, Mary Jane

3

```
CHILD'S NAME                        R  S  INFORMANT
BIRTH DATE      FATHER                    MOTHER
```

CHILD'S NAME / BIRTH DATE / FATHER	R	S	INFORMANT / MOTHER
BOAZ, Elizabeth Henry 22 June 1867 BOAZ, James R	W	F	Father BOAZ, Turpehema T
BOAZ, Mary 8 Apr 1869 BOAZ, James R	W	F	Father BOAZ, T T
BONDURANT, S (Born NC) 13 Feb 1869 BONDURANT, Peter	W	M	Father BONDURANT, Emily R
BOSWELL, Not Named 15 Feb 1867 BOSWELL, John	W	M	Grandfather BOSWELL, Julia A
BOULDEN, Not Named 24 May 1869 BOULDEN, C B	W	M	Mother BOULDEN, Mary
BOWLIN, Not Named 1 June 1868 Unmarried	W	F	Neighbor BOWLIN, Bethania
BOWLIN, Susan 1 June 1868 BOWLIN, William	W	F	Mother BOWLIN, Joanna
BOWLIN, Susan M 4 Mar 1866 BOWLIN, William	W	F	Not Given BOWLIN, Joahannah Bennet
BOWLING, G W 20 Nov 1868 BOWLING, John W B	W	M	Father BOWLING, Nancy J
BOWLING, Josephine 4 May 1869 BOWLING, William	W	F	Mother BOWLING, Joanna
BOWLING, Not Named 10 June 1869 BOWLING, Gabriel	W	M	Father BOWLING, Alaminta
BOWLING, Robert Lee 12 Jan 1867 BOWLING, Gabriel	W	M	Father BOWLINA, Aleminta
BOWMAN, Byrum 2 Nov 1866 BOWMAN, Aaron	W	M	Mother BOWMAN, Margaret
BOWMAN, Golihue Martin 9 Apr 1867 BOWMAN, W D	W	M	Father BOWMAN, Margaret Jane
BOWMAN, Hiram(?) 20 Dec 1866 BOWMAN, Aaron	W	M	Father BOWMAN, Caroline
BOWMAN, Jemima 8 Apr 1868 BOWMAN, Jno A	W	F	Father BOWMAN, Nancy
BOWMAN, Jno P 15 Mar 1868 BOWMAN, William D	W	M	Father BOWMAN, Margaret

CHILD'S NAME BIRTH DATE	FATHER	R	S	INFORMANT MOTHER
BOWMAN, Jno W 26 Mar 1866	BOWMAN, Gollihue	W	M	Not Given BOWMAN, Lina
BOWMAN, Millie 14 Mar 1868	BOWMAN, Jno H	W	F	Father BOWMAN, Nellie
BOWMAN, Milton Taylor 27 Dec 1867	BOWMAN, Austin	W	M	Aunt BOWMAN, Mary
BOWMAN, Nancy 7 June 1868	BOWMAN, Jno	W	F	Father BOWMAN, Sarah A
BOWMAN, Not Named 28 Jan 1868	BOWMAN, John H	W	F	Father BOWMAN, Alena
BOWMAN, Octava A 25 July 1868	BOWMAN, James	W	F	Mother BOWMAN, Hortense E
BOWMAN, Thomas H 26 Feb 1867	BOWMAN, C G	W	M	Father BOWMAN, Susan
BOWMAN, William Thomas 16 Sept 1868	BOWMAN, Samuel G	W	M	Mother BOWMAN, Susan
BOWMAN, Willie 12 Oct 1868	Unmarried	W	M	Father (?) BOWMAN, Mary
BOYD, Arabell 20 Sept 1868	BOYD, S S	W	F	Father BOYD, Nancy A
BOYD, Cornelia G 2 Sept 1869	BOYD, William	W	F	Mother BOYD, Elmira
BOYD, Green P 3 Apr 1868	BOYD, William	W	M	Father BOYD, Almira
BOYD, John H 19 Dec 1869	BOYD, Howard	W	M	Father BOYD, Elizabeth
BOYD, Nancy E 15 Jan 1868	BOYD, Howard	W	F	Grandfather BOYD, Elizabeth
BOYD, Robert T 23 Oct 1866	BOYD, James	W	M	Not Given BOYD, Magey
BRADLEY, Martha 31 Jan 1866	BRADLEY, M W	W	F	Father BRADLEY, Sarah M
BRADLEY, Robert Lee 2 July 1868	BRADLEY, M W	W	M	Father BRADLEY, Sarah M

CHILD'S NAME BIRTH DATE	FATHER	R	S	INFORMANT MOTHER

CHILD'S NAME / BIRTH DATE	FATHER	R	S	INFORMANT / MOTHER
BRAMMER, E A 6 Jan 1867	BRAMMER, T P	W	F	Father BRAMMER, Lucinda
BRAMMER, E L A 13 Aug 1866	BRAMMER, J S	W	F	Father BRAMMER, J F
BRAMMER, George W 4 Jan 1868	BRAMMER, Jeff H	W	M	Father BRAMMER, Eliza J
BRAMMER, John G 29 Aug 1867	BRAMMER, H T	W	M	Father BRAMMER, Sally
BRAMMER, Jonathan 21 Mar 1866	BRAMMER, John (Hatter)	W	M	Father BRAMMER, Nancy J
BRAMMER, Martha S 15 Oct 1869	BRAMMER, Henry T	W	F	Father BRAMMER, Sally
BRAMMER, Mary H 19 Aug 1866	BRAMMER, Jeff H	W	F	Father BRAMMER, E J
BRAMMER, Nancy J 1 Oct 1869	BRAMMER, Jefferson H	W	F	Father BRAMMER, Eliza J
BRANCH, Emily F 8 Nov 1868	Unmarried	W	F	Brother BRANCH, Jane
BRANCH, Flournoy 17 Feb 1867	BRANCH, Joshua	W	M	Father BRANCH, Luvenia
BRANCH, Oney 20 Nov 1869	BRANCH, Joshua	W	F	Father BRANCH, Luvena
BRIM, Jinney 17 Jan 1869	BRIM, Joseph	B	F	Father BRIM, Jane
BRIM, Robert J 24 Jan 1866	BRIM, R(?) O	W	M	Mother BRIM, Martha
BROWDER, Henry 10 Aug 1868	Unmarried	B	M	Mother BROWDER, Rebecca
BROWN, Cora Lee 11 July 1868	BROWN, Hubert V (Tobacconist)	W	F	Father BROWN, Flora
BROWN, Emma S 14 July 1867	BROWN, John M	W	F	Mother BROWN, Mary E
BROWN, S A L 12 Dec 1869	BROWN, Samuel	W	M	Mother BROWN, Sarah Y

| CHILD'S NAME | | R | S | INFORMANT |
BIRTH DATE	FATHER			MOTHER
BRYAN, Abner J		W	M	Father
13 Nov 1868	BRYAN, Alexander N			BRYAN, Jane
BRYAN, John H		W	M	Father
15 Sept 1867	BRYAN, Richard			BRYAN, Julia A
BRYAN, John W		W	M	Father
15 July 1866	BRYAN, James			BRYAN, Mahala
BRYAN, Martha E		W	F	Father
18 June 1867	BRYAN, Alexander			BRYAN, Jane
BRYAN, Vinetta		W	F	Father
2 Feb 1868	BRYAN, James M			BRYAN, Rachael
BRYAN, William		W	M	Father
10 July 1867	BRYAN, Abner			BRYAN, Lucinda
BRYANT, Joel N		W	M	Father
10 Nov 1869	BRYANT, James M			BRYANT, Mahala
BRYANT, John H		W	M	Father
15 Oct 1869	BRYANT, John			BRYANT, Lucinda
BRYANT, Mahala A		W	F	Mother
3 June 1868	BRYANT, John			BRYANT, Lucinda
BRYANT, Malinda M		W	F	Father
20 Sept 1868	BRYANT, W J			BRYANT, Mahala
BRYANT, Martha Jane		W	F	William Corn, Neighbor
4 Nov 1869	BRYANT, George J			BRYANT, Louisa
BRYANT, Mary T		W	F	Mother
26 Feb 1867	BRYANT, John			BRYANT, Rachael
BRYANT, Mary T		W	F	Mother
27 July 1867	BRYANT, John			BRYANT, Lucinda
BURGE, Albert M		W	M	Father
6 Feb 1868	BURGE, Richard			BURGE, Ellen
BURGE, Not Named		B	M	Father
10 Mar 1868	Unmarried			BURGE, Mary
BURKHART, J T		W	M	Father
12 Mar 1869	BURKHART, Ephraim			BURKHART, Eliza
BURNETT, Aug M		W	M	Father
27 Aug 1866	BURNETT, John A			BURNETT, Mary E

7

```
CHILD'S NAME                             R  S  INFORMANT
BIRTH DATE         FATHER                      MOTHER
```

CHILD'S NAME / BIRTH DATE FATHER	R	S	INFORMANT / MOTHER
BURNETT, Dicey R 6 May 1869 BURNETT, Ferrell	B	F	Father BURNETT, Susan
BURNETT, John 10 Nov 1867 BURNETT, Jere	W	M	Grandfather BURNETT, Emeline
BURNETT, Not Named 1 Mar 1868 BURNETT, John A	W	M	Father BURNETT, Mary E
BURROUGHS, James Robert 20 Sept 1867 BURROUGHS, James B	W	M	Father BURROUGHS, Susan E
CAMPBELL, Charles F 16 Sept 1868 CAMPBELL, James W (Mechanic)	W	M	Father CAMPBELL, Mollie
CANNADAY, Andrew J -- Nov 1867 CANNADAY, Constant	W	M	Father CANNADAY, Elizabeth
CANNADAY, John B 20 Oct 1869 CANNADAY, Burwell	B	M	Father CANNADAY, Virginia
CANNADAY, Martha A 12 Apr 1868 CANNADAY, Constant	W	F	Father CANNADAY, Elizabeth
CARTER, Jesse B 29 Dec 1867 CARTER, John P	W	M	Father CARTER, America
CASSADAY, Cornelia 22 Aug 1867 Not Named	W	F	Mother CASSADAY, Ruth
CASSADAY, Not Named -- Nov 1867 Not Named	W	M	Mother CASSADAY, Nancy
CASSELL, Austin D 3 Mar 1869 CASSELL, Price	W	M	Father CASSELL, Martha J
CASSELL, Not Named 28 Sept 1867 CASSELL, Peter	W	M	Mother CASSELL, Nancy Jane
CHANDLER, Isaac (Twin) 9 Jan 1867 CHANDLER, W H	W	M	Father CHANDLER, Margaret Jane
CHANDLER, Martin (Twin) 9 Jan 1867 CHANDLER, W H	W	M	Father CHANDLER, Margaret Jane
CHANEY, Martha E 28 Feb 1869 CHANEY, Stephen B	W	F	Father CHANEY, Margaret E
CHAPMAN, J L 20 July 1869 CHAPMAN, A J	W	M	Father CHAPMAN, A

```
CHILD'S NAME                              R  S  INFORMANT
BIRTH DATE       FATHER                         MOTHER
```

```
CHAPMAN, Melissa                          W  F  Father
-- July 1867     CHAPMAN, A J                   CHAPMAN, Adaline

CLANTON, Not Named                        B  F  Father
10 Apr 1869      CLANTON, Wesley                CLANTON, Sallie

CLARK, Alice                              B  F  Friend
1 Feb 1868       Unmarried                      CLARK, Martha

CLARK, James                              B  M  Father
9 May 1867       CLARK, Jesse (F M)             CLARK, Letha

CLARK, James                              B  M  Father
-- Sept 1869     CLARK, John                    CLARK, Kate

CLARK, James M                            W  M  Not Given
1 July 1866      CLARK, John C                  CLARK, Susan A

CLARK, Joseph A Brown                     W  M  Father
7 Oct 1867       CLARK, Joseph H                CLARK, Mamie M Brown

CLARK, Joseph Jefferson                   W  M  Father
27 Oct 1867      CLARK, J M (Doctor)            CLARK, Ella

CLARK, Lucy                               B  F  James H Clark, Neighbor
20 Nov 1866      Not Known                      CLARK, Susan

CLARK, Not Named                          W  F  Father
30 July 1867     CLARK, R M                     CLARK, Exony E

CLARK, Not Named                          W  M  Father
21 Nov 1867      CLARK, Thomas (Clerk)          CLARK, Mattie

CLARK, Not Named                          B  F  Employer
1 Apr 1868       CLARK, Bob                     CLARK, Coatney

CLARK, Not Named                          W  F  Father
20 Dec 1869      CLARK, William                 CLARK, J

CLARK, Rebecca F                          W  F  Father
7 Apr 1868       CLARK, William Rufus           CLARK, Minerva A

CLARK, Ruth Virginia                      W  F  Father
-- Oct 1869      CLARK, Jesse                   CLARK, Leathy

CLARK, Sarah E                            W  F  Father
-- -- 1866       CLARK, William R               CLARK, Minerva

CLARK, Sue Harrison                       W  F  Father
5 Aug 1868       CLARK, George W                CLARK, Bettie
```

CHILD'S NAME BIRTH DATE	FATHER	R	S	INFORMANT MOTHER
CLARK, Susan A 20 Sept 1869	CLARK, J T (Merchant)	W	F	Father CLARK, Martha
CLARK, W T 25 June 1869	CLARK, Thomas J	W	M	Father CLARK, Mary J
CLEMENT, Eleanor 25 Feb 1868	CLEMENT, J W T	W	F	Father CLEMENT, Eliza A
CLIFTON, Carter F 7 Aug 1866	CLIFTON, Samuel	W	M	Not Given CLIFTON, Bolenada
CLIFTON, Not Named 28 May 1866	CLIFTON, James	W	M	Not Given CLIFTON, Eliza A
CLIFTON, Not Named 8 Feb 1868	CLIFTON, James	W	M	Father CLIFTON, Louisa A
CLIFTON, Rosa Allice 18 Aug 1868	CLIFTON, Samuel	W	F	Father CLIFTON, Melinda
COCKRAM, German S 30 July 1867	COCKRAM, Richard	W	M	Mother COCKRAM, Judith
COCKRAM, Leah E 9 Nov 1866	COCKRAM, Peter	W	F	Father COCKRAM, Elizabeth
COCKRAM, Mintoria T 19 Oct 1869	COCKRAM, John B	W	F	Father COCKRAM, Adeline
COCKRAM, Nancy E 17 May 1866	Not Given	W	F	Mother COCKRAM, E J
COCKRAM, Robert Lee 1 Oct 1866	COCKRAM, Isham	W	M	Father COCKRAM, Mahala
COCKRAM, William H 10 June 1866	COCKRAM, Alexander	W	M	Father COCKRAM, Sarah E
COCKRUM, Alvis R 6 June 1868	COCKRUM, Alex	W	M	Father COCKRUM, Sarah E
COCKRUM, Joseph S 26 Apr 1868	COCKRUM, John B	W	M	Father COCKRUM, M A
COCKRUM, Sarah L 5 Dec 1868	Not Given	W	F	Aunt COCKRUM, Elizabeth
COHEN, Asa A 13 July 1868	COHEN, John G	W	M	Father COHEN, Eda

```
CHILD'S NAME                            R  S  INFORMANT
BIRTH DATE        FATHER                      MOTHER
```

		R	S	INFORMANT / MOTHER

COLEMAN, Angeline   W   F   Not Given
3 Jan 1867   COLEMAN, Robert   COLEMAN, Mary

COLEMAN, Creed Jasper   W   M   Mother
25 July 1867   COLEMAN, William   COLEMAN, Finetta Nunn

COLEMAN, Ruth Ellen   W   F   Father
16 July 1868   COLEMAN, Samuel   COLEMAN, Martha

COLLINS, J T   W   M   Father
19 July 1869   COLLINS, J J   COLLINS, Mary

COLLINS, L (Twin) (Born Floyd)   W   M   Father
6 Jan 1869   COLLINS, Robert   COLLINS, Zeanna

COLLINS, N (Twin) (Born Floyd)   W   M   Father
6 Jan 1869   COLLINS, Robert   COLLINS, Zeanna

COLLINS, Not Named   W   F   Father
-- Jan 1868   COLLINS, J M (Blacksmith)   COLLINS, Tempy Jane

COLLINS, Not Named   W   F   Father
1 Jan 1868   COLLINS, James M   COLLINS, Temperance

COLLINS, Not Named   W   F   Mrs Bowling, Aunt
3 Mar 1869   COLLINS, Ab(?)   COLLINS, Mary

COLLINS, William James   W   M   Father
20 Dec 1868   COLLINS, Jesse   COLLINS, Nancy J

COMPTON, Annie H   W   F   Grandfather
30 Aug 1868   COMPTON, James R   COMPTON, Frances

COMPTON, Exony E   W   F   Father
9 Aug 1866   COMPTON, J R (Miller)   COMPTON, Frances

COMPTON, Louisa A   W   F   Father
3 Oct 1868   COMPTON, William   COMPTON, Louisa

CONNER, Charles C   W   M   Father
8 Dec 1868   CONNER, John   CONNER, Abigal

CONNER, Kesiah E   W   F   Father
26 Nov 1868   CONNER, David E   CONNER, Stattera

CONNER, Mary E R   W   F   Grandmother
20 June 1867   CONNER, Gabriel   CONNER, Mahala

CONNER, Mary Ruth   W   F   Father
25 July 1866   CONNER, William   CONNER, Jennie

CHILD'S NAME		R	S	INFORMANT
BIRTH DATE	FATHER			MOTHER

CHILD'S NAME / BIRTH DATE / FATHER	R	S	INFORMANT / MOTHER
CONNER, Melitia S 15 Nov 1867 CONNER, James	W	F	Uncle CONNER, Melitia
CONNER, Not Named 21 Nov 1867 CONNER, John	B	F	Neighbor CONNER, America
CONNER, Samuel R 6 June 1868 CONNER, William	W	M	Father CONNER, Elizabeth
CONNER, Sarah A 10 May 1867 CONNER, John	W	F	Uncle CONNER, Abigal
COOPER, J F 15 Jan 1869 COOPER, William H	W	M	Father COOPER, Ruth
COOPER, M E 17 July 1869 COOPER, J D	W	M	Father COOPER, M A
CORN, D C P J 5 Feb 1867 CORN, Peter	W	M	Father CORN, Nancy P
CORN, John Abram -- Sept 1867 CORN, Richard	W	M	Father CORN, Neomia
CORN, M E 28 Aug 1869 CORN, Jesse C	W	M	Father CORN, Sarah A
CORN, Nora A 4 July 1869 Unknown	B	F	Mother CORN, Sarah E
COX, J W 5 Nov 1869 COX, William	W	M	Father COX, Mary F
COX, Nancy E A 30 Apr 1868 COX, David R	W	F	Mother COX, Cynthia
CRAIG, Caroline 1 Aug 1869 CRAIG, Saunders	B	F	Father CRAIG, Henrietta
CRAIG, Emily V -- July 1867 CRAIG, John	W	F	Father CRAIG, Lucinda
CRAIG, Robert G 6 Feb 1867 CRAIG, James J	W	M	Father CRAIG, Mary J
CRAIG, Robert G 6 Feb 1868 CRAIG, James J	W	M	Brother CRAIG, Jane E
CRAIG, Sarah E 2 Dec 1867 CRAIG, Peter D	W	F	Father CRAIG, Sarah

```
CHILD'S NAME                              R   S   INFORMANT
BIRTH DATE      FATHER                             MOTHER
─────────────────────────────────────────────────────────────────

CRAIG, Susan A M                          W   F   Father
14 Nov 1869     CRAIG, Peter D                    CRAIG, Sarah A

CREASY, Lizzie Lee                        W   F   Father
15 July 1867    CREASY, James D                   CREASY, Caroline

CRITZ, Cora                               W   F   Not Given
14 May 1866     CRITZ, William                    CRITZ, Christine E

CRITZ, Harriett Alice                     W   F   Father
1 Dec 1868      CRITZ, Hamen                      CRITZ, Luvenia

CRITZ, John                               B   M   Employer
8 May 1868      CRITZ, Tobe                       CRITZ, Sallie

CRITZ, Not Named                          W   F   Father
4 Nov 1868      CRITZ, William D (Mechanic)       CRITZ, Christina

CRITZ, Not Named                          B   F   Employer
16 Oct 1868     Unmarried                         CRITZ, Eliza

CRITZ, Not Named                          B   M   Mother
10 Feb 1869     Unknown                           CRITZ, Jane

CRUISE, John B                            W   M   Mother
3 Feb 1869      Not Given                         CRUISE, Mary A

CRUISE, Leanna R                          W   F   Father
6 Feb 1867      CRUISE, David                     CRUISE, Sena

CRUISE, Mary A F J                        W   F   Father
26 Apr 1868     CRUISE, William B                 CRUISE, Elizabeth

CRUISE, Susan A                           W   F   Father
3 Feb 1868      CRUISE, Jno W                     CRUISE, Rosabeller

CRUISE, Ulisses S G                       W   M   Father
28 Feb 1869     CRUISE, David                     CRUISE, Sinea

CRUISE, Willie R                          W   M   Father
17 Mar 1868     CRUISE, Jackson                   CRUISE, Barbary

DALTON, Booker                            W   M   Father
-- Dec 1869     DALTON, Willis                    DALTON, Sallie

DALTON, M M                               W   M   Father
-- Apr 1869     DALTON, C J                       DALTON, Luvenia

DALTON, Martha Jane                       W   F   Father
11 June 1867    DALTON, Isham                     DALTON, Mary
```

13

```
CHILD'S NAME                              R  S  INFORMANT
BIRTH DATE        FATHER                        MOTHER
```


```
DALTON, Mary Ann                          W  F  Father
27 Oct 1869      DALTON, Isham                  DALTON, Mary J

DALTON, Melissa                           W  F  Father
25 Aug 1867      DALTON, Willis                 DALTON, Lucy Ann

DALTON, Minerva Emeline                   W  F  Father
15 Aug 1867      DALTON, Coleman G              DALTON, Luvenia

DALTON, Not Named                         W  M  Father
7 Sept 1867      DALTON, Joseph                 DALTON, Nancy

DALTON, Sibalto                           W  F  Father
29 Jan 1867      DALTON, W J                    DALTON, Sarah

DALTON, W H                               W  M  Father
13 Aug 1867      DALTON, Fred                   DALTON, Martha

DAVIS, Henry                              B  M  Father
20 Feb 1868      DAVIS, Allen                   DAVIS, Kitty

DAVIS, Jinnie                             B  F  Father
20 Dec 1869      DAVIS, Wash                    DAVIS, Ruth

DAVIS, John A                             W  M  Father
11 Aug 1866      DAVIS, S W                     DAVIS, Mary E

DAVIS, Patrick E                          B  M  Not Given
-- -- ----       DAVIS, Wash (F M)              DAVIS, Ruth

DAVIS, Robert Lee                         W  M  Father
24 Nov 1866      DAVIS, Charles E               DAVIS, Bettie B

DEAL, John Anderson                       W  M  Father
2 June 1867      DEAL, Gabriel                  DEAL, Martha

DEAL, Not Named                           W  M  Father
-- Nov 1867      DEAL, William                  DEAL, Mary

DEARMINE, John                            B  M  Not Given
15 Jan 1866      DEARMINE, Wash                 DEAMINE, Judy

DEATHERIDGE, James Phillip                W  M  Father
12 Jan 1867      DEATHERIDGE, W A (Wheelwright) DEATHERIDGE, Louisa Jane

DEEL, M                                   W  F  Father
13 Sept 1869     DEEL, Gabriel                  DEEL, M

DeHART, A M                               W  F  Father
13 Mar 1868      DeHART, John E                 DeHART, Millie
```

CHILD'S NAME BIRTH DATE	FATHER	R	S	INFORMANT MOTHER
DeHART, Angeline 16 May 1867	DeHART, John W	W	F	Father DeHART, Emilla
DeHART, B H 30 July 1867	DeHART, Joseph E	W	M	Father DeHART, Nancy
DeHART, Charles F 15 May 1868	DeHART, John W	W	M	Mother DeHART, Mahala
DeHART, Charles T 16 Nov 1867	DeHART, William	W	M	Father DeHART, Exony T
DeHART, Corsa A 25 May 1867	DeHART, Eli	W	F	Father DeHART, Leah
DeHART, Dillard P 15 Apr 1866	DeHART, Joseph	W	M	Mother DeHART, Nancy
DeHART, Green D 4 Aug 1868	DeHART, Eli	W	M	Father DeHART, Sarah E
DeHART, J C 24 July 1866	DeHART, Fleming	W	M	Mother DeHART, Milly J
DeHART, James W 1 June 1868	DeHART, Robert	W	M	Father DeHART, Maria E
DeHART, John W 3 Apr 1869	DeHART, William T	W	M	Father DeHART, Nancy F
DeHART, John W H 11 Jan 1869	DeHART, Aaron W	W	M	Father DeHART, Dolly
DeHART, Lucy L 25 May 1868	DeHART, William T	W	F	Mother DeHART, L T
DeHART, Mary E 20 Apr 1869	DeHART, Thomas J	W	F	Father DeHART, Malinda
DeHART, Mintoria J 19 Dec 1869	DeHART, Henry C	W	F	Father DeHART, Louisa
DeHART, Not Named 15 Dec 1867	DeHART, Henry	W	F	Father DeHART, Frances
DeHART, R D 11 July 1866	DeHART, Robert	W	M	Father DeHART, Elizabeth M
DeHART, Susan M 12 June 1866	DeHART, John C (Miller)	W	F	Father DeHART, Milly

```
CHILD'S NAME                                    R  S  INFORMANT
BIRTH DATE          FATHER                             MOTHER
```

		R	S	INFORMANT / MOTHER

DeHART, Tyler M   W M Father
10 Oct 1869   DeHART, Eleazer   DeHART, Mary J

DeHART, Virginia T   W F Father
30 Mar 1866   DeHART, Henry C   DeHART, Nancy F

DeHART, William G   W M Father
7 Feb 1866   DeHART, William T   DeHART, Louisa F

DeHART, Abram G   W M Father
10 Feb 1867   DeHART, Eleazar   DeHART, Mary J

DENT, Not Named   W F Father
9 Nov 1868   DENT, McHenry   DENT, Elmira

DENT, William H   W M Father
19 Feb 1867   DENT, McHenry   DENT, Elmira

DICKERSON, Lewis J C A (Born Henry Co)   W M Father
24 Aug 1869   DICKERSON, Martin   DICKERSON, Sarah J

DILLION, Edgar   W M Father
15 May 1869   DILLION, E S   DILLION, A N

DILLION, John H J   W M Father
15 Mar 1867   DILLION, C J   DILLION, Elizabeth

DILLION, Judith   W F Father
7 July 1867   DILLION, James D   DILLION, Exony

DILLION, Lucy D   W F Father
27 Aug 1868   DILLION, James D   DILLION, Exony

DILLION, Malinda G (Born Henry Co)   W F Father
14 July 1866   DILLION, A M   DILLION, Martha J

DILLION, Marietta   W F Father
27 June 1866   DILLION, James D   DILLION, Exony

DILLION, Rosa A   W F Mother
25 Aug 1867   Not Given   DILLION, Lucinda

DOSS, Martha T   W F Father
26 Jan 1867   DOSS, James A   DOSS, Rachael A

DOSS, Not Named   W F Not Given
26 Jan 1867   DOSS, Jack A   DOSS, R A

DUNKLEY, James S   W M Father
2 May 1869   DUNKLEY, Samuel H   DUNKLEY, Lucy F

CHILD'S NAME BIRTH DATE	FATHER	R	S	INFORMANT MOTHER
DUNKLEY, Nancy 13 Apr 1867	DUNKLEY, W H	W	F	Father DUNKLEY, Jane
DUNKLEY, Robert H 3 Oct 1867	DUNKLEY, Samuel H	W	M	Mother DUNKLEY, Lucy T
DURHAM, W A 21 June 1869	DURHAM, Frank	W	M	Father DURHAM, Mary
EANES, May S 24 Mar 1869	EANES, George W	W	F	Father EANES, Mary P
EATON, Mary L 3 Feb 1868	EATON, C H P	W	F	Father EATON, Lucinda
EATON, Thomas H 21 Jan 1868	EATON, Albert A	W	M	Father EATON, Margaret
EDWARDS, Isah 15 Dec 1868	EDWARDS, Jeff	B	M	Mother EDWARDS, Mahala
EDWARDS, Lucy A 23 Mar 1867	EDWARDS, Jeff	B	F	Father EDWARDS, Mahalia
EDWARDS, Lula 20 Feb 1868	Not Given	B	F	Former Master EDWARDS, Lucy
ELGIN, Martha 30 Jan 1869	ELGIN, Alfred	W	F	Father ELGIN, America
EMBERSON, Martha J 20 Jan 1868	EMBERSON, Wade A	W	F	Grandfather EMBERSON, E
EMMERSON, Lucinda 2 Feb 1866	EMMERSON, Wade	W	F	Father EMMERSON, Hetty J
EPPERLY, Laura A 8 Mar 1869	EPPERLY, Jesse P	W	F	Father EPPERLY, Caroline
EPPERLY, Mary A 25 May 1866	EPPERLY, Jesse P	W	F	Father EPPERLY, Caroline
EPPERLY, W E 15 Aug 1867	EPPERLY, Jesse P	W	M	Father EPPERLY, Caroline
EPPERSON, Not Named 24 May 1868	EPPERSON, Jno H	W	M	Father EPPERSON, Elizabeth
EPPERSON, Susannah 25 Dec 1868	EPPERSON, Y C T	W	F	Father EPPERSON, Matilda

CHILD'S NAME BIRTH DATE	FATHER	R	S	INFORMANT MOTHER
FAIN, Allimentia 5 Oct 1866	FAIN, Even	W	F	Not Given FAIN, Itura
FAIN, Andrew J 5 Nov 1868	FAIN, Eairn	W	M	Father FAIN, Plina
FAIN, Jno T 4 Apr 1868	FAIN, William	W	M	Father FAIN, Temperance
FAIN, Martha L 3 May 1866	FAIN, Richard	W	F	Not Given FAIN, Amanda
FINNEY, Cary L 9 Oct 1867	FINNEY, William	W	F	Father FINNEY, Ruth E
FINNEY, N 16 Mar 1869	FINNEY, Murphy	B	F	Father FINNEY, C
FINNEY, Sallie A 3 May 1866	FINNEY, William	W	F	Father FINNEY, Ruth E
FLIPPEN, Eliza 5 Apr 1867	FLIPPEN, Drewry	B	F	Father FLIPPEN, Mary Y
FLIPPEN, Flora (Born Surry Co) 23 Jan 1868	FLIPPEN, James W	W	F	Father FLIPPEN, Ruth
FLIPPIN, Mary Eliza 3 Aug 1866	FLIPPIN, J M	W	F	Not Given FLIPPIN, Ruth
FLOYD, Phebe Ann 25 Mar 1867	FLOYD, Montgomery	W	F	Father FLOYD, Emeline
FLOYD, S 20 Feb 1869	FLOYD, B H	W	M	Father FLOYD, W J
FOLEY, Alamenta 31 Jan 1866	FOLEY, William Lee	W	F	Father FOLEY, Mary
FOLEY, Jeremiah 28 Oct 1867	FOLEY, Reed	W	M	Mother FOLEY, Judith A
FOLEY, Lucinda R 20 Aug 1869	FOLEY, Bluford P	W	F	Father FOLEY, Esther
FOLEY, N E M K 23 Aug 1868	FOLEY, William Lee	W	F	Father FOLEY, Mary
FOLEY, Nancy A 1 Feb 1868	FOLEY, Bluford P	W	F	Father FOLEY, Hester A

CHILD'S NAME		R	S	INFORMANT
BIRTH DATE	FATHER			MOTHER

FOLEY, Not Named   W M Father
17 Mar 1868   FOLEY, James A   FOLEY, Letitia

FOLEY, Rozetta V   W F Father
23 Aug 1868   FOLEY, Peyton   FOLEY, Mahala

FOLEY, Samuel W J   W M Father
7 Oct 1869   FOLEY, William S   FOLEY, Mary

FOSTER, Abram (Born Henry)   B M Mother
1 Sept 1866   FOSTER, Preston   FOSTER, Mary

FOSTER, Charles P   W M Mother
1 June 1869   Not Given   FOSTER, Araminta

FOSTER, James   B M J G Tatum, Neighbor
15 Feb 1866   FOSTER, James   FOSTER, Caroline

FOSTER, William   W M Father
2 Apr 1869   FOSTER, John   FOSTER, Eliza

FRANCIS, Louisa   W F Not Given
30 Aug 1866   FRANCIS, William W   FRANCIS, Susan

FRY, Sarah A   W F Father
12 Oct 1869   FRY, James T   FRY, Susan

FULCHER, James T   W M Father
12 Nov 1866   FULCHER, John   FULCHER, Sarah A

FULCHER, James William   W M Father
4 Jan 1868   FULCHER, Edmond   FULCHER, Emere Catherine

FULCHER, Lucy H   W F G P Fulcher, Father
5 July 1866   FULCHER, G A(P?) (Shoemaker)   FULCHER, Ruth E

FULCHER, Martha A   W F Father
8 June 1868   FULCHER, George P (Mechanic)   FULCHER, Ruthe E

FULCHER, Martha A   W F Father
5 Oct 1866   FULCHER, William S   FULCHER, Mary S

FULCHER, N E   W M Father
12 Oct 1869   FULCHER, G P   FULCHER, Ruth

FULCHER, Nancy E   W F Father
15 Oct 1868   FULCHER, George W   FULCHER, Salvina

FULCHER, Nancy J   W F Grandfather
10 Feb 1868   FULCHER, William L   FULCHER, Susan E

CHILD'S NAME BIRTH DATE	FATHER	R	S	INFORMANT MOTHER
FULCHER, Not Named -- Sept 1867	FULCHER, W	W	F	Friend FULCHER, Susan G
FULCHER, Not Named 15 Sept 1868	Unmarried	W	F	Friend FULCHER, Sarah A
FULCHER, SALLIE -- Feb 1867	FULCHER, Harden	W	F	Father FULCHER, Luvenia
FULCHER, William Edgar 25 Oct 1867	FULCHER, Albert R	W	M	Father FULCHER, Ruth E
GALLANT, Not Named 20 Aug 1868	GALLANT, Daniel G	W	F	Father GALLANT, Ruth
GALLANT, Not Named 15 Jan 1869	GALLANT, D C	W	M	Father GALLANT, Ruth J
GAMMONS, E 3 May 1869	Unknown	W	M	Mother GAMMONS, M
GATES, Martha J 8 Dec 1868	GATES, William B	W	F	Father GATES, Zelphia
GATES, Tyler J 5 Mar 1866	GATES, William B	W	M	Not Given GATES, Zilpoh
GILBERT, Not Named 23 Dec 1868	GILBERT, Robert	W	F	Father GILBERT, Jane
GILBERT, Roberta 20 Apr 1868	GILBERT, Thomas J	W	F	Father GILBERT, Bettie
GILBERT, Rosa Lee 6 Apr 1868	GILBERT, William	W	F	Mother GILBERT, Lucinda
GILBERT, Tecoy 15 Oct 1866	GILBERT, S D	W	F	Father GILBERT, Viley W
GILHAM, Laura E 30 June 1867	GILHAM, John W	W	F	Father GILHAM, Mary A
GILHAM, William J 18 Feb 1869	GILHAM, Jno W	W	M	Father GILHAM, Mary A
GILL, Not Named 11 Dec 1869	GILL, John T	W	M	Father GILL, Sarepta
GLIDWELL, William Martin 3 Nov 1867	GLIDWELL, James A	W	M	Father GLIDWELL, Delila

```
CHILD'S NAME                              R  S  INFORMANT
BIRTH DATE        FATHER                        MOTHER
```

GOAD, Hattie -- Feb 1867	GOAD, William	W	F	Neighbor GOAD, Lettie
GOIN, Caroline 10 Apr 1867	GOIN, Amb	W	F	Father GOIN, Melissa
GOIN, Not Named 15 Mar 1867	GOIN, Ambrose	W	F	Father GOIN, Nancy Hooker
GOIN, Not Named 1 Aug 1868	Unmarried	W	F	Mother GOIN, Nancy M
GOIN, Susan 20 Sept 1869	GOIN, Lee	W	F	Father GOIN, P
GRADY, Charles 15 June 1869	GRADY, Leonard	W	M	Father GRADY, Emily
GRADY, James B 16 Apr 1866	GRADY, Len	W	M	Mother GRADY, Emily
GRANT, Frances A 10 Apr 1868	GRANT, John A (Dentist)	W	F	Mother GRANT, Iowa
GRANT, Mary R 4 May 1866	GRANT, John A	W	F	Mother GRANT, Iowa
GRAY, James Jackson 10 Oct 1867	GRAY, J T	W	M	Father GRAY, Mary Ann
GRAY, Not Named (Twin) 25 Dec 1869	GRAY, Jno F	W	F	Father GRAY, Mary Ann
GRAY, Not Named (Twin) 25 Dec 1869	GRAY, Jno F	W	M	Father GRAY, Mary Ann
GRIFFITH, Iowa A 4 July 1869	GRIFFITH, Sparrell T	W	F	Father GRIFFITH, Artiminey
GRIFFITH, Not Named 23 Sept 1867	GRIFFITH, G H	W	M	Father GRIFFITH, Nancy Jane
GRIFFITH, Not Named -- Jan 1867	GRIFFITH, David	W	M	Father GRIFFITH, Elizabeth
GUNNELL, George Washington -- May 1867	GUNNELL, James A	W	M	C C Clark GUNNELL, Jane
GUNTER, Columbus T 3 Oct 1866	GUNTER, W W	W	M	Not Given GUNTER, Mary

```
CHILD'S NAME                              R  S  INFORMANT
BIRTH DATE        FATHER                        MOTHER
_____

GUNTER, J A                               W  M  J M Foley, Grandfather
27 Dec 1866       GUNTER, G B                   GUNTER, S G

GUNTER, Not Named (Born NC)               W  M  Father
-- Oct 1869       GUNTER, B L                   GUNTER, E S

GUSLER, Exony L                           W  F  G Gusler
4 May 1867        GUSLER, Jacob G               GUSLER, Peggy S

GUSLER, M S                               W  M  Father
25 Apr 1869       GUSLER, J G                   GUSLER, P S

GUSLER, Samuel T                          W  M  Father
12 Jan 1868       GUSLER, Jacob J               GUSLER, Peggy S

HADEN, Not Named                          W  M  Father
3 Apr 1867        HADEN, William                HADEN, Lucy B

HAGOOD, L E                               W  F  Father
12 Apr 1866       HAGOOD, William R             HAGOOD, Ruth

HAIRSTON, Lafayette                       B  F  Father
1 Sept 1869       HAIRSTON, Isaac               HAIRSTON, Adeline

HAIRSTON, Marietta                        B  F  Mother
3 Nov 1869        HAIRSTON, Richard             HAIRSTON, Eliza

HAIRSTON, Richard                         B  M  Not Given
1 Dec 1866        Not Given                     HAIRSTON, Eva

HALEY, Joseph                             W  M  Father
25 July 1869      HALEY, James R                HALEY, Virginia

HALL, Celia                               W  F  Mother
6 July 1866       HALL, H E                     HALL, Nancy A

HALL, Lethea E                            W  F  Abe Hall, Father
15 Apr 1866       HALL, Absolem                 HALL, Elizabeth J

HALL, Lilly V                             W  F  Mother
22 Mar 1868       HALL, Elijah                  HALL, Nancy

HALL, Lucinda E                           W  F  Grandfather
27 Jan 1868       HALL, Crawford                HALL, Mahala

HALL, Martha E                            W  F  Father
17 June 1866      HALL, Jasper R                HALL, Lavinia

HALL, Martha V                            W  F  Father
22 Feb 1868       HALL, John C                  HALL, Nancy
```

CHILD'S NAME BIRTH DATE	FATHER	R	S	INFORMANT MOTHER
HALL, Mary E 23 Nov 1866	HALL, N R	W	F	Father HALL, Delila
HALL, Mary E 13 Dec 1869	HALL, Lewis P	W	F	Father HALL, Malinda V
HALL, Robert Lee 18 Apr 1868	HALL, Nathan R	W	M	Mother HALL, Delilah A
HALL, Tazewell G 14 Mar 1869	HALL, T G	W	M	Father HALL, Nancy
HALL, Thomas H 15 Mar 1868	HALL, Absolem	W	M	Father HALL, Elizabeth
HALL, W G 1 Sept 1867	HALL, B R	W	M	Father HALL, Martha J
HALLEY, Not Named 15 June 1866	HALLEY, Peyton	W	M	Father HALLEY, Sarah
HALLY, Alexander 20 July 1869	HALLY, Peyton	W	M	Mother HALLY, Sarah J
HAMBY, Harriett V 29 June 1866	HAMBY, D S	W	F	Not Given HAMBY, Susan
HANBY, James T 18 June 1867	HANBY, Samuel	B	M	Father HANBY, Rachael
HANBY, Nancy E 8 Aug 1867	HANBY, John R	W	F	Father HANBY, Mary J
HANBY, Sarah C 12 July 1868	HANBY, D S	W	F	Father HANBY, Susan C
HANCOCK, Eliza A 7 Apr 1868	HANCOCK, Fleming (Mechanic)	W	F	Father HANCOCK, Ruth
HANCOCK, Thomas G 16 May 1868	HANCOCK, John H	W	M	Father HANCOCK, E E
HANDY, John A 15 Dec 1868	HANDY, Jacob S	W	M	Grandfather HANDY, Mahala
HANDY, Lucinda Amella 1 Jan 1867	HANDY, Nath	W	F	Not Given HANDY, Sarah A
HANDY, Not Named 12 May 1867	HANDY, James H	W	M	Father HANDY, Ann Eliza

| CHILD'S NAME | | R | S | INFORMANT |
BIRTH DATE	FATHER			MOTHER
HANDY, Not Named 10 Nov 1868	Unmarried	W	M	Father HANDY, Mary
HANDY, Samuel J 15 Feb 1868	HANDY, William J	W	M	Friend HANDY, Virginia C
HANDY, Sarah A 3 Apr 1869	HANDY, J T	W	F	Father HANDY, Charity W
HARBOUR, Mary E 14 Dec 1866	HARBOUR, A J	W	F	Father HARBOUR, Martha A
HARBOUR, Stateria E 6 Feb 1868	HARBOUR, R H	W	F	Father HARBOUR, Frances
HARRELL, Hester A 20 Sept 1868	HARRELL, David K	W	F	Father HARRELL, Adeline
HARRELL, Mary S 4 Dec 1869	HARRELL, David D	W	F	Father HARRELL, Adeline
HARRIS, Exony R 3 Mar 1869	HARRIS, Samuel	W	F	Father HARRIS, Lavenia
HARRIS, German E 26 Mar 1867	HARRIS, John J	W	M	Father HARRIS, Nancy E
HARRIS, Isham L 13 Sept 1867	HARRIS, Samuel	W	M	Father HARRIS, Lavinia F
HARRIS, Jno W 27 Mar 1869	HARRIS, Jno J	W	M	Father HARRIS, Nancy
HARRIS, Lincoln 20 May 1867	HARRIS, William	W	M	Friend HARRIS, Catherine
HARRIS, Maria A 27 Nov 1868	HARRIS, Gabriel	B	F	Mother HARRIS, Jane
HARRIS, Martha A 30 Apr 1867	HARRIS, Samuel G	W	F	Father HARRIS, Mahala
HARRIS, Ori L 25 June 1866	Not Given	B	F	Mother HARRIS, Mary
HARRIS, William J 1 Apr 1866	HARRISS, M T	W	M	Father HARRIS, Mariah
HARSTON, John S 15 May 1868	HARSTON, Wilson	B	M	Mother HARSTON, Harriett

```
CHILD'S NAME                              R  S  INFORMANT
BIRTH DATE        FATHER                        MOTHER
```

```
HARSTON, William                          B  M  J M Jiles(Giles),Neighbor
15 Oct 1866       Not Known                      HARRISON, Minly

HASKINS, Jasper S                         W  M  Mother
7 Sept 1869       HASKINS, Jasper                HASKINS, Mary

HATCHER, H (Born Dead)                     W  M  Mother
3 Nov 1866        HATCHER, Elkanah               HATCHER, Judith

HATCHER, Jno A                            W  M  Father
25 Dec 1868       HATCHER, J W                   HATCHER, Martha J

HATCHER, Mollie                           W  F  Father
15 Jan 1868       HATCHER, Daniel G (Tobaccoist) HATCHER, Jennie

HAYNES, James R H T                       W  M  Mother
4 July 1869       HAYNES, Columbus               HAYNES, Lavinia

HAYNES, Mary S                            W  F  Father
14 Jan 1866       HAYNES, R  S                   HAYNES, Jemima

HAYNES, W J A J                           W  M  Mother
11 May 1867       HAYNES, Columbus               HAYNES, Lavinia M

HAZLE, Elvira                             B  F  Father
26 Sept 1868      HAZLE, William                 HAZLE, Jennie

HAZLEWOOD, Not Named                       W  F  Father
1 Oct 1868        HAZLEWOOD, Josiah              HAZLEWOOD, Ruth

HAZLEWOOD, Not Named                       W  F  Friend
27 May 1868       Unmarried                      HAZLEWOOD, Nancy J

HAZLEWOOD, Ruth T                         W  F  Mother
15 June 1867      Unmarried                      HAZLEWOOD, Nancy

HEADEN, Daniel H                          W  M  Father
4 Nov 1868        HEADEN, Leatin                 HEADEN, Matilda

HEADEN, Nannie E                          W  F  Father
13 Aug 1868       HEADEN, William                HEADEN, Lucy

HEILY, Luller Ann                         W  F  George Clark
-- Sept 1867      HEILY, S H                     HEILY, Luvenia

HELMS, Fleming                            W  M  Father
23 Apr 1868       HELMS, Adam                    HELMS, Luvena

HELMS, Mary E                             W  F  Father
5 Nov 1868        HELMS, Joseph                  HELMS, Malissa
```

CHILD'S NAME		R	S	INFORMANT
BIRTH DATE	FATHER			MOTHER

HELMS, Mary J — W F — Mother
17 Oct 1869 — HELMS, George T — HELMS, Martha M

HENDRIC, Sampson — W M — Father
15 Nov 1868 — HENDRIC, R D — HENDRIC, Victoria

HENLIN, Not Named — W M — Not Given
13 Jan 1866 — HENLIN, William — HENLIN, Lucy V

HENSLEY, Cainy — W F — Father
13 Nov 1867 — HENSLEY, John — HENSLEY, Matilda

HENSLEY, Samuel — W M — Father
4 Apr 1866 — HENSLEY, John — NORMAN, Matilda

HIAT, Gusty — W F — John Scott
25 Dec 1867 — HIAT, Jesse — HIAT, Elizabeth

HIAT, Laura Ann — W F — Father
-- Aug 1867 — HIAT, Ephraim — HIAT, Lucinda

HIAT, Not Named — W M — Father
26 Feb 1868 — HIAT, William F — HIAT, Catherine

HICKMAN, Jane — B F — Employer
1 Apr 1868 — HICKMAN, Peter — HICKMAN, Caroline

HILL, John W — W M — Father
4 May 1866 — HILL, John R — HILL, Inna

HILL, Mary A R — W F — Mother
27 Sept 1868 — HILL, John — HILL, Irena

HINES, James C — W M — Mother
29 Apr 1869 — HINES, J H — HINES, Rachael

HINES, Not Named — W M — Father
13 May 1868 — HINES, James H — HINES, Rachael

HODGE, Caroline — W F — Father
5 Apr 1868 — HODGE, J B — HODGE, Jane

HOLT, John — W M — Father
20 Dec 1868 — HOLT, William — HOLT, Elizabeth

HOOKER, George R — W M — Father
10 May 1869 — HOOKER, Lee P — HOOKER, Lucy A

HOOKER, John A — W M — Father
29 Apr 1867 — HOOKER, J W — HOOKER, Derency

CHILD'S NAME BIRTH DATE	FATHER	R	S	INFORMANT MOTHER
HOOKER, Not Named 20 June 1868	Not Given	B	F	Neighbor HOOKER, America
HOOKER, Robert Lee 17 Apr 1869	HOOKER, Jno W(?)	W	M	Father HOOKER, Margaret
HOPKINS, George E 12 Nov 1869	HOPKINS, Samuel A	W	M	Father HOPKINS, Mary
HOPKINS, John D 6 Aug 1868	HOPKINS, David T	W	M	Father HOPKINS, Susan E
HOPKINS, Joseph S 5 May 1869	HOPKINS, James M	W	M	Father HOPKINS, Hester V
HOPKINS, Not Named 11 May 1866	HOPKINS, W T	W	F	Father HOPKINS, Nancy
HOPKINS, Thomas H 10 May 1866	HOPKINS, Jo	W	M	Father HOPKINS, Aleany C
HOPKINS, Thomas J 8 July 1868	HOPKINS, W T	W	M	Father HOPKINS, Nancy A
HOPKINS, William L 3 Sept 1868	HOPKINS, James M	W	M	Father HOPKINS, Hester V
HOUCHENS, Charles C 30 Jan 1867	HOUCHENS, J C	W	M	Father HOUCHENS, Jathina T
HOUCHENS, Marshall R 25 Mar 1868	HOUCHENS, Jeff	W	M	Neighbor HOUCHENS, Malinda
HOUCHENS, Mary 7 Oct 1868	HOUCHENS, Isaac	W	F	Father HOUCHENS, Jathena
HOUCHINS, Eora (Twin) 3 Feb 1869	HOUCHINS, John T	W	F	Father HOUCHINS, Sarah A
HOUCHINS, Mary E (Born NC) 17 May 1869	HOUCHINS, John	W	F	Mother HOUCHINS, Martha H
HOUCHINS, Thomas (Twin) 3 Feb 1869	HOUCHINS, John T	W	M	Father HOUCHINS, Sarah A
HOUCHINS, W A 2 Nov 1866	HOUCHINS, John T	W	M	Not Given HOUCHINS, Sarah A
HOWELL, Charles F 25 Mar 1866	HOWELL, E D	W	M	Mother HOWELL, Martha J

| CHILD'S NAME | | R | S | INFORMANT |
BIRTH DATE	FATHER			MOTHER
HOWELL, Elizabeth		W	F	Father
2 Oct 1869	HOWELL, Thomas D			HOWELL, Fannie
HOWELL, Everett		W	M	Father
1 July 1868	HOWELL, Henry B			HOWELL, Angeline
HOWELL, Harry		B	M	Father
1 June 1868	HOWELL, Harry			HOWELL, Nancy
HOWELL, Homer		W	M	Father
1 June 1868	HOWELL, John W			HOWELL, Lucinda
HOWELL, James M		W	M	Mother
22 Dec 1866	HOWELL, Thomas			HOWELL, Virginia
HOWELL, John		W	M	Father
13 Dec 1868	HOWELL, Thomas			HOWELL, Virginia
HOWELL, Louisa		W	F	Friend
10 June 1868	Unmarried			HOWELL, Mollie
HOWELL, Luther D		W	M	John Howell, Grandfather
16 Apr 1866	HOWELL, John W			HOWELL, Lucinda
HOWELL, Not Named (Born Lee Co)		W	F	Friend
12 Aug 1868	Unmarried			HOWELL, Louisa
HOWELL, Prince Ella		W	F	Father
28 June 1867	HOWELL, T D (Deputy Sheriff)			HOWELL, Fannie
HOWELL, William H		W	M	Mother
13 Apr 1867	HOWELL, H B			HOWELL, Angalina
HUBBARD, Benjamin T		W	M	Father
17 Sept 1866	HUBBARD, James W			HUBBARD, Milly
HUBBARD, Johnny Reb		W	M	Father
1 Apr 1866	HUBBARD, J W			HUBBARD, S L
HUBBARD, Louisa E		W	F	Father
12 Sept 1867	HUBBARD, James W			HUBBARD, Emilla
HUBBARD, Lucinda		W	F	Father
8 Nov 1868	HUBBARD, James W			HUBBARD, Milly
HUDNAL, John D		W	M	Father
-- July 1867	HUDNAL, C B			HUDNAL, Eliza J
HURD, John P		W	M	Father
5 June 1869	HURD, Samuel			HURD, R E

CHILD'S NAME BIRTH DATE	FATHER	R	S	INFORMANT MOTHER
HURT, William H 25 Dec 1869	HURT, James B	W	M	Father HURT, Martha
HYLTON, Alice (Born Henry Co) 3 Jan 1868	HYLTON, James	B	F	Employer HYLTON, Ruth
HYLTON, Gabriel S 3 June 1869	HYLTON, Gabriel	W	M	Father HYLTON, Lucy A
HYLTON, George B 6 July 1868	HYLTON, George	W	M	Father HYLTON, Annie
HYLTON, James 3 Jan 1868	HYLTON, Mat	B	M	Father HYLTON, Mariah
HYLTON, James W 13 June 1867	HYLTON, Valentine	W	M	Father HYLTON, Mary A
HYLTON, Mary E 18 Oct 1867	HYLTON, Edmond (Blacksmith)	B	F	Father HYLTON, Mary
HYLTON, Not Named 27 Sept 1869	HYLTON, Val	W	M	Father HYLTON, Mary
HYLTON, Pleasant Emmett 17 Aug 1867	HYLTON, James G	W	M	Father HYLTON, Nancy Jane
HYLTON, Sanuel G 25 Feb 1868	HYLTON, James	W	M	Father HYLTON, Nancy
HYLTON, Sarah R 4 Jan 1868	HYLTON, Isaac	W	F	Father HYLTON, Lucinda
HYLTON, William J 23 May 1866	HYLTON, William B	W	M	Mother HYLTON, Eliza A
INGRAM, Carter Braxton 25 Dec 1869	Not Given	B	M	Mother INGRAM, Sarah E
INGRAM, Susan J 25 May 1868	INGRAM, William G C	W	F	Grandfather INGRAM, Martha F
INGRAM, Susan W 1 May 1867	INGRAM, R S	W	F	Father INGRAM, Petna (?)
IROLER, Elizabeth C 2 Feb 1866	IROLER, Emmanuel	W	F	Not Given IROLER, Emily
IRVIN, Nancy J 15 Jan 1868	Unmarried	B	F	Mother IRVIN, Matilda

CHILD'S NAME BIRTH DATE	FATHER	R	S	INFORMANT MOTHER
JEFFERSON, John W 30 Dec 1866	JEFFERSON, Peyton G	W	M	Father JEFFERSON, Louisa J
JEFFERSON, Mary S 20 Oct 1869	JEFFERSON, John P	W	F	Father JEFFERSON, Lucinda
JEFFERSON, Nancy E 19 Sept 1867	JEFFERSON, J T (Mechanic)	W	F	Father JEFFERSON, Louisa
JEFFERSON, Nannie J 9 Aug 1868	JEFFERSON, Peyton G	W	F	Father JEFFERSON, Louisa
JEFFERSON, Not Named 7 Oct 1866	JEFFERSON, M P	W	F	Father JEFFERSON, L J
JEFFERSON, Peter D 17 Apr 1869	JEFFERSON, William J	W	M	Jane Hall, Grandmother JEFFERSON, Lurinda C
JEFFERSON, William H 30 June 1866	JEFFERSON, T T	W	M	Father JEFFERSON, L A
JEFFERSON, William J 6 Feb 1868	JEFFERSON, Moses P	W	M	Father JEFFERSON, Luvenia
JEFFERSON, William M J 14 Dec 1867	JEFFERSON, J T	W	M	Not Given Not Given
JESSUP, Ambus T 17 June 1866	JESSUP, E S	W	M	Father JESSUP, Delilah
JESSUP, Not Named 7 June 1868	JESSUP, William H	W	M	Father JESSUP, Harriett
JESSUP, U S 11 June 1869	JESSUP, William	W	M	Father JESSUP, Harriett
JONES, James Abram 14 Nov 1867	JONES, Peter D	W	M	Father JONES, Nancy Joyce
JONES, Martha 5 Mar 1869	JONES, Peter D	W	F	Father JONES, Nancy
JONES, Mary E 14 May 1866	JONES, Isaac	W	F	Father JONES, Sally
JONES, Nancy J 9 Feb 1868	JONES, Isaac	W	F	Father JONES, Sally
JOYCE, Charlie 3 Feb 1867	JOYCE, Hamilton	W	M	Father JOYCE, Lizzie

```
CHILD'S NAME                                  R  S  INFORMANT
BIRTH DATE        FATHER                             MOTHER
```

		R	S	
JOYCE, Martha E		W	F	Mother
18 June 1867	JOYCE, James			JOYCE, Mary E
JOYCE, Martha E		W	F	Mother
8 Apr 1868	JOYCE, L G			JOYCE, Martha J
JOYCE, Milia A		W	F	Neighbor
10 Sept 1868	JOYCE, R			JOYCE, Sarah A
JOYCE, Thomas C		B	M	Father
1 Mar 1868	JOYCE, Samuel			JOYCE, Letha
KASEY, George N		W	M	Father
16 May 1868	KASEY, William A R			KASEY, Florantine
KASEY, John W S		W	M	Father
11 Jan 1866	KASEY, William T			KASEY, Florentine
KEATTS, James W		W	M	Father
6 Nov 1868	KEATTS, William C (Mechanic)			KEATTS, Mary C
KENNERLY, Betty L		W	F	Father
10 Oct 1866	KENNERLY, Joseph			KENNERLY, Eliza
KENNERLY, J B		W	M	Father
17 May 1869	KENNERLY, Joseph			KENNERLY, E J
KING, E B		W	M	Father
12 Sept 1869	KING, William			KING, Eliza A
KING, E B (Born Rockingham, NC)		W	M	Father
12 Sept 1868	KING, William			KING, Eliza J
KING, Emma A		W	F	Father
10 July 1868	KING, John			KING, Eliza J
KING, J D		W	M	Father
15 Apr 1869	KING, Gus(?)			KING, S J
KING, Not Named		B	M	Neighbor
-- Apr 1867	KING, Isaac			KING, Elizabeth
KING, Sallie H		W	F	Father
-- Feb 1867	KING, John			KING, Eliza
KIZER, S		B	M	Father
15 June 1869	KIZER, Sandy			KIZER, Victoria
KOGER, Jno M		B	M	Father
7 May 1868	KOGER, Sandy			KOGER, Victoria

CHILD'S NAME BIRTH DATE	FATHER	R	S	INFORMANT MOTHER
LACKEY, William E 3 Jan 1869	LACKEY, W C	W	M	Father LACKEY, Martha J
LAND, Joseph H 18 Mar 1868	LAND, John	W	M	Father LAND, Catharine
LAWLESS, Luella 14 Apr 1866	LAWLESS, Thomas	W	F	Father LAWLESS, Sally
LAWLESS, Martha J 11 July 1868	LAWLESS, Thomas	W	F	Father LAWLESS, Sally
LAWLESS, Virginia Bell 27 Oct 1867	LAWLESS, George W	W	F	Father LAWLESS, Roseanner
LAWRENCE, Mollie F 8 June 1868	LAWRENCE, John	W	F	Father LAWRENCE, Lacy
LAWRENCE, Thomas H 15 June 1867	LAWRENCE, Robert	W	M	Father LAWRENCE, Emily
LAWSON, Amanda 1 Jan 1866	Not Given	W	F	Not Given LAWSON, Elizabeth
LAWSON, Anna C J 21 Apr 1869	LAWSON, Claiborne L	W	F	Father LAWSON, Sina V
LAWSON, Armstead L 25 Nov 1868	LAWSON, William D	W	M	Father LAWSON, Annie
LAWSON, B M (Twin) 2 Nov 1866	LAWSON, James	W	M	Father LAWSON, Mahala
LAWSON, James W I 5 Apr 1868	LAWSON, John C	W	M	Father LAWSON, Luvenia A
LAWSON, Keziah Jane 23 Oct 1867	LAWSON, William D	W	F	Father LAWSON, Annie
LAWSON, Keziah V A 28 Aug 1869	LAWSON, Jno C	W	F	Father LAWSON, Lavenia A
LAWSON, Lucinda E (Twin) 11 Nov 1869	LAWSON, James M	W	F	Father LAWSON, Mahala
LAWSON, Lucinda J 20 Apr 1866	LAWSON, M T	W	F	Father LAWSON, Ruth
LAWSON, Lurinda A (Twin) 11 Nov 1869	LAWSON, James M	W	F	Father LAWSON, Mahala

CHILD'S NAME BIRTH DATE	FATHER	R	S	INFORMANT MOTHER
LAWSON, Nancy R 6 Jan 1869	LAWSON, Mat T	W	F	Father LAWSON, Ruth
LAWSON, Not Named 20 Sept 1868	LAWSON, James M	W	F	Father LAWSON, Mahala
LAWSON, T J (Twin) 2 Nov 1866	LAWSON, James	W	M	Father LAWSON, Mahala
LAWSON, Tyrrhus M A 25 May 1869	LAWSON, Jeff T	W	M	Father LAWSON, Rosabelle F
LAWSON, Wiilliam B 29 Oct 1866	LAWSON, William S	W	M	Father LAWSON, Anna
LAYMAN, Not Named 6 Dec 1867	LAYMAN, W C	W	M	Father LAYMAN, Eveline
LAYMAN, Not Named 18 Dec 1866	LAYMAN, David	W	M	Father INGRAM, Sarah
LAYMAN, Thomas M 18 Dec 1867	LAYMAN, David	W	M	Father LAYMAN, Sarah
LEE, William E 27 July 1868	LEE, Jackson	B	N	Mother LEE, Candice
LEE, William S 27 May 1868	LEE, John	W	M	Father LEE, Elizabeth A
LEWIS, Ailey E 10 Dec 1867	LEWIS, W J	W	F	Father LEWIS, Mary J
LEWIS, Daniel P 25 Aug 1867	LEWIS, Samuel	W	M	Father LEWIS, Malinda C
LEWIS, James E 20 Oct 1869	LEWIS, Martin E	W	M	William Lewis, GFather LEWIS, Letitia A
LEWIS, King E 15 Dec 1869	LEWIS, Andrew J	W	M	Father LEWIS, Mary J
LEWIS, Mary E 20 Oct 1869	LEWIS, Samuel	W	F	Father LEWIS, Malinda
LEWIS, Not Named 15 Dec 1866	LEWIS, A J	W	M	Father LEWIS, Mary
LIGHT, Charles C 18 Sept 1868	LIGHT, Henry C	W	M	Father LIGHT, Mary E

```
CHILD'S NAME                                     R  S  INFORMANT
BIRTH DATE        FATHER                               MOTHER
```

CHILD'S NAME / BIRTH DATE	FATHER	R	S	INFORMANT / MOTHER
LIGHT, Green A 1 Aug 1868	LIGHT, John G	W	M	Father LIGHT, Lucinda
LIGHT, Jack Anderson 28 Mar 1867	LIGHT, James	W	M	Father LIGHT, Lucinda
LYBROOK, Philip H 26 Jan 1868	LYBROOK, A M (Lawyer)	W	M	Father LYBROOK, Mary
LYON, Levona M 28 Sept 1867	LYON, Silas T	W	F	Mother LYON, Caroline
LYONG, George M 10 Dec 1869	LYON, Silas T	W	M	J P Epperly, Neighbor LYON, Caroline
MABE, S J 20 May 1869	MABE, William	W	M	Father MABE, S A
MAIZE, Waller J 20 Oct 1868	MAIZE, John W	W	M	Neighbor MAIZE, Fannie
MARSHALL, A J 24 July 1869	MARSHALL, Lee	W	M	Father MARSHALL, S
MARSHALL, Not Named 7 June 1867	MARSHALL, William	W	M	Father MARSHALL, Lucy
MARSHALL, Sydney 12 May 1869	MARSHALL, John	W	M	Father MARSHALL, Araminta
MARTIN, G R 14 Nov 1869	MARTIN, J H	W	M	Father MARTIN, Martha
MARTIN, James A -- July 1867	MARTIN, W A	W	M	Neighbor MARTIN, Mary A
MARTIN, James L 10 Aug 1868	MARTIN, Charles J	W	M	Father MARTIN, Adeline
MARTIN, James W 15 June 1866	MARTIN, William A	W	M	Isaac Martin, Grandfather MARTIN, Mary A
MARTIN, John -- Aug 1867	MARTIN, John	W	M	Father MARTIN, Martha
MARTIN, John J 23 Dec 1867	MARTIN, A J (Miller)	W	M	Father MARTIN, Lucinda
MARTIN, John J 24 Dec 1868	MARTIN, W J	W	M	Father MARTIN, Lucinda

```
CHILD'S NAME                              R  S  INFORMANT
BIRTH DATE      FATHER                           MOTHER
```

		R	S	
MARTIN, John M 11 Mar 1866 MARTIN, James P		W	M	Father MARTIN, Martha J
MARTIN, John Robert 26 May 1867 MARTIN, John (Blacksmith)		W	M	Father MARTIN, Elizabeth Ann
MARTIN, Louise E 2 Jan 1868 MARTIN, William A		W	M?	Father MARTIN, Mary
MARTIN, Mary E 4 Sept 1867 Not Given		W	F	Mother MARTIN, Aramartha E
MARTIN, Mary J 1 Dec 1869 Not Given		W	F	W G Wright, Neighbor MARTIN, Louisa
MARTIN, Minerva A 17 July 1869 MARTIN, David H		W	F	Father MARTIN, Harriett E
MARTIN, N D 19 Sept 1869 MARTIN, Charles T Jr		W	M	Mother MARTIN, Texas
MARTIN, Not Named 9 Sept 1867 MARTIN, William B		W	F	Father MARTIN, Martha A
MARTIN, Robert S 29 June 1868 MARTIN, John H		W	M	Father MARTIN, Martha
MARTIN, Saroda 20 Feb 1867 MARTIN, J G		W	F	Father MARTIN, Mary Ann
MARTIN, Susan -- Aug 1867 MARTIN, Henry L		W	F	Neighbor MARTIN, Jane
MARTIN, Walker Edward 1 Sept 1866 MARTIN, Edward N		W	M	Father MARTIN, Sarah
MARTIN, William A 3 Mar 1867 MARTIN, Charles J		W	M	Father MARTIN, Adaline
MARTIN, William Thomas 25 May 1867 MARTIN, C T (Plasterer)		W	M	Father MARTIN, Texas
MASSEY, James 31 May 1869 Not Given		W	M	Mother MASSEY, Exony
MASSEY, Louisa 10 Nov 1869 MASSEY, James M		W	F	Father MASSEY, Frances E
MASSEY, Nancy J 18 Oct 1866 MASSEY, James M		W	F	Father MASSEY, Frances E

```
CHILD'S NAME                          R  S  INFORMANT
BIRTH DATE        FATHER                     MOTHER
```

CHILD'S NAME / BIRTH DATE / FATHER	R	S	INFORMANT / MOTHER
MASSEY, Thomas B 2 June 1869 MASSEY, James A	W	M	Mother MASSEY, Elizabeth
MAYBE, C R 26 Mar 1869 MAYBE, M	W	M	Father MAYBE, L J
MAYS, Martha L 18 Sept 1866 MAYS, J W	W	F	Father MAYS, Martha F
McALEXANDER, George L 5 Oct 1867 McALEXANDER, David	W	M	Father McALEXANDER, Mary
McALEXANDER, John W 8 June 1867 McALEXANDER, Charles	W	M	Mother McALEXANDER, Tamas
McALEXANDER, Mary E 15 July 1867 McALEXANDER, David	W	F	Father McALEXANDER, Lucinda
McALEXANDER, Nancy 8 May 1868 McALEXANDER, William	W	F	Mother McALEXANDER, Susannah
McARTHUR, Susan -- July 1867 McARTHUR, Perry	W	F	Father McARTHUR, Elizabeth
McBRIDE, Alice 13 June 1867 McBRIDE, Henry (?)	W	F	Mother McBRIDE, Mary Jane
McBRIDE, T B 12 Aug 1869 McBRIDE, Jefferson	W	M	Father McBRIDE, N A
McGEE, M A L 15 Jan 1868 McGEE, William (Mechanic)	W	F	Father McGEE, Martha A
McGEE, William T 17 June 1866 McGEE, John P	W	M	Father McGEE, Judith
McINTOSH, Paul 10 Sept 1867 McINTOSH, Bluford (Mechanic)	W	M	Father McINTOSH, Sarah
McMELON, W D Fletcher 28 Apr 1867 McMELON, John	W	M	Father McMELON, Elizabeth
McMILLON, Crawford 15 June 1868 McMILLON, L D	W	M	Father McMILLON, Bethania
McPEAK, E 25 Nov 1869 McPEAK, Bluford	W	M	Father McPEAK, S A
McPEAK, Paul 12 Sept 1868 McPEAK, Bluford	W	M	Father McPEAK, Sarah

CHILD'S NAME		R	S	INFORMANT
BIRTH DATE	FATHER			MOTHER

MIDKIFF, Elizabeth		W	F	Father
19 Aug 1866	MIDKIFF, Green			MIDKIFF, Rhoda
MIDKIFF, Elizabeth		W	F	Grandfather
13 Mar 1868	MIDKIFF, Joseph			MIDKIFF, Mary
MIDKIFF, George W		W	M	Father
10 Jan 1866	MIDKIFF, Joseph			MIDKIFF, Lavinia
MIDKIFF, Lucinda		W	F	Father
6 Feb 1869	MIDKIFF, James			MIDKIFF, Malinda
MIDKIFF, Rosabell		W	F	Father
15 July 1868	MIDKIFF, Joseph			MIDKIFF, Lavinia
MILLS, James		B	M	Mother
10 May 1868	MILLS, Green			MILLS, Harriet
MILLS, M E		W	M	Father
3 Mar 1869	MILLS, James			MILLS, Fannie
MITCHELL, E		W	M	Father
12 Mar 1869	MITCHELL, George W			MITCHELL, E J
MITCHELL, Lucy Ann		W	F	Father
15 May 1867	MITCHELL, James M			MITCHELL, Elizabeth
MITCHELL, Martha Frances		W	F	father
22 July 1867	MITCHELL, George W			MITCHELL, Eliza Jane
MITCHELL, Not Named		W	?	Father
15 June 1868	MITCHELL, John			MITCHELL, Martha
MIZE, Ellen M		W	F	Father
1 Mar 1868	MIZE, William B			MIZE, Lucinda
MOIR, Mary (Born Danbury, Stokes Co, NC)		W	F	Father
29 May 1866	MOIR, W W (Merchant)			MOIR, C (?) V
MOIR, Thomas A		W	M	Grandmother
19 May 1868	MOIR, William W (Merchant)			MOIR, C V
MOIR, W M		W	M	Not Given
21 Sept 1866	Unknown (Wagoner?)			MOIR, Beckie
MONTGOMERY, Mat		W	M	Father
18 July 1869	MONTGOMERY, Floyd			MONTGOMERY, E
MONTGOMERY, Susan		W	F	Father
18 June 1868	MONTGOMERY, Floyd			MONTGOMERY, Emeline

CHILD'S NAME		R	S	INFORMANT
BIRTH DATE	FATHER			MOTHER

MOOR, Margaret E		W	F	Mother
7 Oct 1869	Not Given			MOOR, Adeline
MOOR, Not Named		W	F	A Moor, Grandfather
15 May 1866	Not Given			MOOR, Adaline
MOOR, Not Named		W	F	Mother
27 May 1869	Not Given			MOOR, Nancy
MOORE, Jesse		W	M	Not Given
25 Aug 1866	MOORE, H J			MOORE, Caroline M
MOORE, Marion		W	F	Not Given
10 Sept 1866	MOORE, E E			MOORE, Lidy A
MOORE, Mary S (Born Henry Co)		W	F	Father
10 Sept 1866	MOORE, J E (Millwright)			MOORE, Sarah A
MOORE, Mollie S		W	F	Father
10 Sept 1867	MOORE, James E			MOORE, Sallie A
MOORE, Ulysses C		W	M	Not Given
6 June 1866	MOORE, W T			MOORE, Pauline A
MORAN, E A		B	F	Mother
1 Nov 1869	Not Given			MORAN, Amanda A
MORAN, James D		W	M	Father
5 Feb 1869	MORAN, Crawford			MORAN, Sarah C
MORAN, Laura J		W	F	Mother
10 Jan 1868	Not Given			MORAN, May
MORAN, Martha E		W	F	Father
1 Feb 1868	MORAN, John J			MORAN, Exony A
MORAN, Not Named		W	F	Grandfather
15 Mar 1868	MORAN, John			MORAN, Ruth
MORRIS, Not Named		W	M	Not Given
6 Mar 1866	MORRIS, Coleman G			MORRIS, Sukey
MORRIS, Not Named		W	M	Father
10 July 1868	MORRIS, G L			MORRIS, Lakey
MORRIS, Not Named		W	F	Father ?
18 May 1868	Unmarried			MORRIS, Sallie
MORRIS, Not Named		W	M	Father
23 Dec 1869	MORRIS, C G			MORRIS, S

CHILD'S NAME BIRTH DATE	FATHER	R	S	INFORMANT MOTHER
MORRISON, Aaron B S 15 Sept 1869	MORRISON, Joseph	W	M	Father MORRISON, Exony
MORRISON, Charles C 15 Mar 1868	MORRISON, David J	W	M	Grandfather MORRISON, Susan J
MORRISON, Mary E 9 Mar 1868	MORRISON, Andrew T	W	F	Father MORRISON, Sena M
MORRISON, Mary J 30 Jan 1869	MORRISON, David	W	F	Father MORRISON, Susan J
MORRISON, Not Named 4 Apr 1867	MORRISON, Joseph	W	M	Father MORRISON, Exony
MORRISON, Tazewell 20 Aug 1866	Not Given	W	M	J T Morrison, Grandfather MORRISON, Sarah J
MORRISON, William B 14 Aug 1866	MORRISON, David J	W	M	J T Morrison, Grandfather MORRISON, Susan J
MURPHY, Gusta M 25 Aug 1867	MURPHY, Edmund	B	F	Father MURPHY, Jestine
NEWMAN, Ballard M 12 May 1869	NEWMAN, Jno	W	M	Father NEWMAN, Milly
NEWMAN, Haman 24 Aug 1868	NEWMAN, Joseph E	W	M	Father NEWMAN, Sarah
NEWMAN, James 24 Mar 1869	NEWMAN, John	W	M	Father NEWMAN, Lucinda
NEWMAN, Not Named -- Dec 1867	NEWMAN, Samuel	W	M	Father NEWMAN, Ruth
NEWMAN, Not Named 9 Jan 1867	NEWMAN, John	W	M	Father NEWMAN, Milly
NEWMAN, Tempy Adeline 14 Nov 1867	NEWMAN, James	W	F	Mother NEWMAN, Ruth
NOEL, Julia 11 May 1868	NOEL, W T (Merchant)	W	F	Father NOEL, Cybella
NOLEN, Mary A 31 July 1866	NOLEN, Charles M	W	F	Father NOLEN, Lucinda
NOLEN, Not Named 14 June 1866	NOLEN, David	W	M	Father NOLEN, Catherine

```
CHILD'S NAME                               R  S  INFORMANT
BIRTH DATE        FATHER                         MOTHER
```

		R	S	
NOLEN, Sarah J		W	F	Father
30 Oct 1867	NOLEN, Charles N			NOLEN, Lucinda
NORMAN, Not Named		W	F	Father
15 Aug 1868	NORMAN, James			NEWMAN (?), Esther
NOWLIN, Edward		B	M	Former Master
9 June 1868	Unmarried			NOWLIN, Josephine
NOWLIN, Fanny L		-	-	Not Given
15 Nov 1866	NOWLIN, C C			Not Given
NOWLIN, Lucy E		W	F	Father
25 Nov 1869	NOWLIN, Arch F (Mechanic)			NOWLIN, Jennie
NOWLIN, Not Named		W	M	Father
7 Feb 1868	NOWLIN, C C (Mechanic)			NOWLIN, Esther
NUNN, Judy A		W	F	Not Given
29 Apr 1866	NUNN, William			NUNN, Nancy
NUNN, Major Jefferson		W	M	Mother
30 July 1867	NUNN, _____			NUNN, Nancy
NUNN, Tecora		W	F	Father
25 Oct 1867	NUNN, Ed			NUNN, America
OAKLEY, E J		W	F	Father
11 Sept 1869	OAKLEY, William M			OAKLEY, A J
OAKLEY, Sarah L		W	F	Father
-- July 1867	OAKLEY, William M			OAKLEY, Amanda G
OMARA, Daniel S		W	M	Father
4 Aug 1867	OMARA, Daniel			OMARA, Leona
OMARA, Margaret		W	F	Father
18 Apr 1866	OMARA, Daniel			OMARA, Leona
OMARA, Sarah C		W	F	Father
5 Mar 1869	OMARA, Daniel			OMARA, Leona
ORENDER, Not Named		W	M	Father
-- Oct 1867	ORENDER, G W			ORENDER, Susan
ORENDER, Not Named (Dead)		W	M	Father
20 Jan 1868	ORENDER, John H			Not Given
ORRENDER, Sarah		W	F	Father
29 May 1869	ORRENDER, John			ORRENDER, Eliza

CHILD'S NAME BIRTH DATE	FATHER	R	S	INFORMANT MOTHER
OSENELER, James Matthew 12 Aug 1867	OSENELER, W T	W	M	Father OSENELER, Mary E
OWEN, H S J 8 Sept 1867	OWEN, Samuel	W	M	Father OWEN, Sarah A
PACK, Thomas L 30 Aug 1867	PACK, Greenville	W	M	Father PACK, Rebecca
PADGET, James W 28 June 1869	PADGET, Pleasant H	W	M	Father PADGET, Mary A
PALMER, Not Named 30 Oct 1867	PALMER, James (Miller)	W	F	Father PALMER, Rachael
PARKER, James W 6 July 1867	PARKER, Smith	W	M	Father PARKER, E T
PATRISO, Mary 5 Oct 1869	PATRISO, James	W	F	Father PATRISO, Julia
PEDIGO, Amanda R 15 June 1868	PEDIGO, Bluford	W	F	Neighbor PEDIGO, Lucy
PEDIGO, Josephine W 11 Dec 1866	PEDIGO, Rufus C	W	F	Father PEDIGO, Ruth P
PENDLETON, George E 14 Nov 1869	PENDLETON, John	W	M	Father PENDLETON, Mary J
PENDLETON, L F 16 Sept 1866	PENDLETON, V H	W	F	Father PENDLETON, Mary
PENDLETON, Not Named 6 Dec 1868	PENDLETON, V H	W	F	Father PENDLETON, Mary
PENDLETON, Not Named 22 July 1869	PENDLETON, John	W	M	Father PENDLETON, Mary
PENN, Ada 19 Jan 1868	PENN, John E (Lawyer)	W	F	Father PENN, Alice
PENN, Charles A 29 Nov 1868	PENN, Frank R (Merchant)	W	M	Father PENN, Annie
PENN, Davis H 23 Oct 1868	PENN, Rufus	W	M	Father PENN, Lizzie
PENN, Frank 1 Apr 1867	PENN, William	B	M	Father PENN, Catherine

CHILD'S NAME		R	S	INFORMANT
BIRTH DATE	FATHER			MOTHER

PENN, Gabriel H   W M Father
12 May 1869   PENN, John E (Sawyer)   PENN, Alice

PENN, Hattie M   W F Father
2 Sept 1867   PENN, W L   PENN, Jane

PENN, Kelly   B M Friend
-- July 1867   PENN, Kemp   PENN, Ann

PENN, L   W M Father
12 Apr 1869   PENN, Jno A   PENN, L

PENN, Lillie   W F Grandmother
-- Dec 1867   PENN, Dallas   PENN, Edna Ann

PENN, Lizzie   B F Father
-- Oct 1867   PENN, Pleasant   PENN, Mary

PENN, Not Named   B F Neighbor
25 Aug 1868   PENN, Henry   PENN, Fannie

PENN, Not Named   W M Father
1 Sept 1868   PENN, Greenville (Merchant)   PENN, Kate M

PENN, Not Named   B M Father
15 Oct 1869   PENN, Dallas   PENN, Eaney

PENN, Sally (Born Henry Co)   B F Father
1 Apr 1866   PENN, John   PENN, Rose

PENN, Thomas B   W M Father
25 Mar 1868   PENN, William A   PENN, Mary L

PENNELL, Peter S   W M Father
-- Oct 1867   PANNELL, James   PANNELL, Sarah M

PICKERALL, Thomas   W M Father
19 Mar 1869   PICKERALL, Thomas   PICKERALL, Margaret

PICKERELL, Not Named   W M Father
5 Mar 1869   PICKERELL, Richard   PICKERELL, Cynthia

PIGG, J A   W M Father
15 Sept 1869   PIGG, Paul C Jr   PIGG, Lucinda

PIGG, Lucy Tecoa   W F Father
11 Sept 1867   PIGG, Thomas C   PIGG, Susan Jane

PIGG, William F   W M Father
11 Nov 1868   PIGG, Thomas C   PIGG, Susan

```
CHILD'S NAME                            R  S  INFORMANT
BIRTH DATE       FATHER                        MOTHER
```

		R	S	INFORMANT MOTHER
PIKE, Anner Staples -- June 1867	PIKE, Jacob	W	F	John Bennett PIKE, Milly Ann
PIKE, R F 8 Mar 1869	PIKE, Jack	W	M	Father PIKE, W A
PIKE, Ranson P 17 Mar 1866	PIKE, Jacob	W	M	Not Given PIKE, Willis A
PLASTERS, Lavenia E 18 July 1869	PLASTERS, T J	W	F	Father PLASTERS, Mary J
PLASTERS, Not Named 20 June 1869	PLASTERS, A H	W	M	Father PLASTERS, Martha
POTICE, Tiney Jane 1 Mar 1866	POTICE, James	W	F	Not Given POTICE, Julia A
PRICE, Caraville 15 Sept 1866	PRICE, Peter	W	F	Father PRICE, Polina
PRICE, Osborne D 26 Oct 1866	PRICE, William J (Miller)	W	M	Father PRICE, Mary E
PRICE, Rosa L 12 Oct 1868	PRICE, John	B	F	Grandfather PRICE, Milly
PRICE, William G 12 Apr 1868	PRICE, Peter W	B	M	Father PRICE, Rolena
PROPHET, Joseph A 29 Oct 1867	PROPHET, Thomas	W	M	Father PROPHET, Nancy M
PUCKET, George W 18 May 1869	PUCKET, Robert	W	M	Father PUCKET, Louisa
PUCKET, Louisa 23 July 1869	PUCKETT, Elijah	W	F	Father PUCKETT, Sarah
PUCKET, Sallie A 7 Jan 1867	PUCKET, Elijah	W	F	Not Given PUCKET, Sallie
PUCKET, U L G 11 May 1869	PUCKET, Hosea	W	M	Mother PUCKET, Sally Ann
PUCKETT, General Marion 9 Jan 1868	PUCKETT, John	W	M	Father PUCKETT, Nancy Caroline
PUCKETT, James C 10 Sept 1868	PUCKETT, Read A	W	M	Father PUCKETT, Matilda

```
CHILD'S NAME                                    R  S  INFORMANT
BIRTH DATE      FATHER                                MOTHER
_____

PUCKETT, Not Named                              W  M  Father
10 Aug 1867     PUCKETT, H (?)                        PUCKETT, Sallie

PUCKETT, Not Named                              W  F  Father
24 Sept 1868    PUCKETT, Rily                         PUCKETT, Matilda

PUCKETT, Not Named (Born Dead)                  W  M  Father
-- Sept 1867    PUCKETT, John                         PUCKETT, Alena

PUCKETT, Not Named (Dead)                       W  F  Father
18 Feb 1868     PUCKETT, John                         PUCKETT, Aulenia

PUGH, Elvira                                    W  F  Mother
12 July 1869    PUGH, Pleasant                        PUGH, Sarah

PUGH, Sarah                                     W  F  Father
12 Apr 1867     PUGH, Pleasant                        PUGH, Sally

RADFORD, Sallie A                               W  F  Neighbor
1 Nov 1868      RADFORD, Fleming                      RADFORD, Hester

RAKES, Israel G                                 W  M  Father
2 Mar 1868      RAKES, Richard                        RAKES, S D

RAKES, James C                                  W  M  Mother
15 Mar 1869     RAKES, Thomas T                       RAKES, Elizabeth

RAKES, John T                                   W  M  Father
28 Dec 1868     RAKES, William H                      RAKES, Lucinda

RAKES, M E                                      W  F  Father
12 Nov 1866     RAKES, Alex                           RAKES, V A

RAKES, Martha J                                 W  F  Father
20 Sept 1867    RAKES, Alexander                      RAKES, Violet J

RAKES, Rosa A                                   W  F  Father
14 May 1867     RAKES, Thomas T                       RAKES, Elizabeth

RAKES, Sarah M                                  W  F  Father
2 Jan 1869      RAKES, William H                      RAKES, Lucinda

RAKES, William E F                              W  M  Father
6 Apr 1866      RAKES, R R                            RAKES, Sarah D

RANGELY, Walter                                 W  M  Father
8 July 1868     RANGELY, James H (Merchant)           RANGELY, Alice

RANGLEY, A J                                    W  M  Father
30 Dec 1869     RANGLEY, James H (Merchant)           RANGLEY, Alice
```

CHILD'S NAME BIRTH DATE	FATHER	R	S	INFORMANT MOTHER
RATLIFF, A L 1 Sept 1866	RATLIFF, C C	W	C	Father RATLIFF, Milly
RAY, Charles C 4 Aug 1869	Not Given	W	M	Mother RAY, Martha A
RAY, James A 9 Mar 1867	Not Given	W	M	Grandmother RAY, Martha
REYNOLDS, Margaret (Twin) 27 June 1867	REYNOLDS, Dick	W	F	Mother REYNOLDS, Lucille
REYNOLDS, Mattie Jane (Twin) 27 June 1867	REYNOLDS, Dick	W	F	Mother REYNOLDS, Lucille
REYNOLDS, Nancy J 15 Sept 1866	REYNOLDS, Unick	B	F	Not Given REYNOLDS, Eady
RICKMAN, Adolphus 4 Mar 1868	RICKMAN, William	W	M	Father RICKMAN, Emily
ROBERSON, John W 22 Mar 1868	ROBERSON, Landon	W	M	Father ROBERSON, N V
ROBERTSON, James W 23 May 1867	ROBERTSON, Abram	W	M	Father ROBERTSON, Emmerzetta
ROBERTSON, Not Named 26 Aug 1866	ROBERTSON, A H	W	M	Father ROBERTSON, Mary E
ROBERTSON, Not Named 25 Jan 1867	ROBERTSON, E F	W	M	Not Given ROBERTSON, Sarah E
ROBERTSON, S 19 Aug 1869	ROBERTSON, Abram	W	M	Father ROBERTSON, Emberzetta
ROBERTSON, Uriah S 10 Apr 1869	ROBERTSON, Abram H	W	M	Father ROBERTSON, Mary E
ROGERS, Flora 16 Apr 1869	ROGERS, Joseph	W	F	Father ROGERS, Mary
ROGERS, Malisa 12 June 1868	ROGERS, George S	W	F	Father ROGERS, Sallie
ROGERS, Not Named 12 Apr 1868	ROGERS, Clement	W	M	Father ROGERS, Ruth
ROGERS, Not Named 15 Feb 1868	ROGERS, Joseph	W	F	Father ROGERS, Adaline

```
CHILD'S NAME                              R   S   INFORMANT
BIRTH DATE         FATHER                         MOTHER
```

CHILD'S NAME / BIRTH DATE / FATHER	R	S	INFORMANT / MOTHER
ROGERS, Robert 30 Oct 1868 ROGERS, Andrew J	W	M	Father ROGERS, Elizabeth
RORER, Abram A 23 July 1866 RORER, D C	W	M	Father RORER, Sarah A
RORER, Flora 22 Dec 1869 RORER, William A	W	F	Father RORER, Catherine
RORER, G 12 Apr 1869 RORER, M A	W	M	Father RORER, Louisa
RORER, Samuel G 26 Mar 1866 RORER, J W	W	M	Father RORER, Adeline
RORER, T R 29 Apr 1869 RORER, Jno W	W	M	Father RORER, Avaline
RORRER, Mary J 14 Sept 1868 RORRER, Peter T	W	F	Father RORRER, Nancy J
RORRER, Not Named -- Sept 1867 RORRER, J W	W	M	Neighbor RORRER, Adeline
RORRER, Not Named 10 Mar 1868 RORRER, William A	W	M	Father RORRER, Catherine
RORRER, Not Named 10 Mar 1868 RORRER, Michael A	W	M	Father RORRER, Louisa
RORRER, Pernina E 8 Oct 1868 RORRER, David C	W	F	Father RORRER, Sarah A
RORRER, Samuel G 26 Mar 1866 RORRER, John W	W	M	Not Given RORRER, Adaline
RORRER, Thomas L 30 Jan 1868 RORRER, William R	W	M	Father RORRER, Mary A
RORRER, Thomas R 4 May 1868 RORRER, John W	W	M	Father RORRER, Adaline
ROSS, A A 8 Feb 1868 ROSS, Peyton	W	M	Father ROSS, Judith V
ROSS, Daniel C 12 Mar 1869 ROSS, Hardin D	W	M	Father ROSS, Martha J
ROSS, Elizabeth D C 31 Aug 1866 ROSS, Peyton R	W	F	Father ROSS, Judith

CHILD'S NAME BIRTH DATE	FATHER	R	S	INFORMANT MOTHER
ROSS, Fanny 15 Nov 1869	ROSS, D Lee	W	F	Father ROSS, Elizabeth A
ROSS, James D 26 Sept 1868	ROSS, McD	W	M	Father ROSS, Elisheba G
ROSS, Lucinda 8 July 1868	ROSS, Barth	B	F	Father ROSS, Matilda
ROSS, Not Named 13 Jan 1866	ROSS, H D	W	M	Father ROSS, Martha
ROSS, Not Named 15 Mar 1867	ROSS, Butt	B	M	Neighbor ROSS, Maheda
ROSS, O J 27 Oct 1867	ROSS, Charles A	W	M	Father ROSS, Dicy L
ROSS, Robert Lee 7 Mar 1868	ROSS, Lewis T	W	M	Father ROSS, Stella
ROSS, William 29 Apr 1866	Not Given	W	M	Not Given ROSS, Jane
SALMONS, Martha A 24 Feb 1868	SALMONS, John	W	F	Father SALMONS, Nancy
SANDERS, James 25 Mar 1869	SANDERS, Samuel	W	M	Father SANDERS, Polly
SAUNDERS, Emily J 10 Oct 1866	SAUNDERS, Silas	W	F	Dr. Lewis, Neighbor SAUNDERS, Martha
SCALES, John 15 May 1868	SCALES, John	B	M	Mother SCALES, Ann
SCALES, Not Named 25 July 1867	SCALES, W H	W	M	Not Given SCALES, Elizabeth
SCALES, Not Named 25 Sept 1868	SCALES, Nat H	W	M	Father SCALES, Bettie
SCALES, Not Named 15 July 1868	SCALES, Jerry	B	F	Father SCALES, Catharine
SCOTT, Stephen M 24 Nov 1866	SCOTT, Thomas D	W	M	Father SCOTT, Lucinda
SCOTT, Susan J 22 Dec 1868	SCOTT, John W	W	F	Father SCOTT, Sarah

```
CHILD'S NAME                              R  S  INFORMANT
BIRTH DATE        FATHER                        MOTHER
```

```
SCOTT, Susan M                            W  F  Father
2 Aug 1868        SCOTT, Thomas D               SCOTT, Lucinda E

SHELTON, A V                              W  M  Father
20 Feb 1867       SHELTON, Fred                 SHELTON, Rebecca

SHELTON, Allice                           W  F  Father
4 June 1867       SHELTON, A W                  Not Given

SHELTON, Dora Lee                         W  F  Father
2 Sept 1868       SHELTON, Arch C               SHELTON, Octavia

SHELTON, Effa Lille                       W  F  Father
12 Nov 1867       SHELTON, Peter W              SHELTON, Mary A

SHELTON, G T                              W  M  Mother
19 Nov 1869       Not Given                     SHELTON, S J

SHELTON, George T                         W  M  Father
12 Nov 1869       SHELTON, Peter M              SHELTON, Mary A

SHELTON, J G                              W  M  Father
10 Nov 1869       SHELTON, Green                SHELTON, Nancy

SHELTON, Martin L                         W  M  Father
26 Oct 1869       SHELTON, Thomas H             SHELTON, Barbara A

SHELTON, Mary E                           W  F  Father
13 Feb 1868       SHELTON, William J            SHELTON, Lucinda

SHELTON, Murry Turner                     B  M  Father
-- Aug 1867       SHELTON, King                 SHELTON, Frances

SHELTON, N E (Born Floyd)                 W  M  Father
20 Oct 1869       SHELTON, William L            SHELTON, Sally

SHELTON, Nancy E                          W  F  Father
13 Dec 1868       SHELTON, Charles M            SHELTON, Fannie

SHELTON, Robert Walter                    W  M  Father
9 June 1867       SHELTON, G W                  SHELTON, Marth A

SHELTON, Ruth F                           W  F  Father
21 Aug 1866       SHELTON, A  A (Carpenter)     SHELTON, Nancy

SHOCKLEY, Alverda                         W  F  Grandmother
-- Dec 1867       Not Married                   SHOCKLEY, Martha

SHOCKLEY, Sarah E                         W  F  Father
10 Sept 1868      SHOCKLEY, James M (Mechanic)  SHOCKLEY, Ruth
```

CHILD'S NAME		R	S	INFORMANT
BIRTH DATE	FATHER			MOTHER

SIMPSON, H H N   W M Father
1 Sept 1866   SIMPSON, William H (Physician)   SIMPSON, Anliza Spencer

SLATE, John   W M Father
18 July 1869   SLATE, S M   SLATE, Mary A

SLUSHER, David T   W M Father
2 Feb 1868   SLUSHER, Sparrel G   SLUSHER, Margaret

SMART, Alaminta   W F Father
-- July 1869   SMART, William C   SMART, Malinda

SMITH, Ellis   W M Father
15 July 1868   SMITH, Lewis   SMITH, Martha

SMITH, H B   W M Father
15 Mar 1867   SMITH, Daniel   SMITH, Martha A

SMITH, Harriett   W F Not Given
5 May 1866   SMITH, Hardin M   SMITH, Elizabeth

SMITH, Jerrey   W M Father
12 July 1868   SMITH, Isaac   SMITH, Jane A

SMITH, Lavinia   W F Father
10 Nov 1869   SMITH, James A   SMITH, L

SMITH, Martha A (Born Surry Co, NC)   W F Father
30 July 1866   SMITH, Albert   SMITH, Lemina J

SMITH, Not Named   B F Father
-- Jan 1868   SMITH, Dick (F M)   SMITH, Mary Ann

SMITH, Not Named   W F Father
-- Dec 1867   SMITH, Hardin W   SMITH, Elizabeth P

SMITH, P A   W F Bartlett Smith, GFather
4 Oct 1866   SMITH, Burwell   SMITH, M A

SMITH, Ruth Matilda   W F Father
26 Mar 1867   SMITH, Joseph W   SMITH, Sarah

SMITH, Susan Frances   W F Father
19 Dec 1867   SMITH, John W   SMITH, Susan

SMITH, Walter C   W M Father
16 June 1867   SMITH, Isaac   SMITH, Martha

SMITH, William L   W M Father
19 Feb 1868   SMITH, Marshall L   SMITH, Mary A

```
CHILD'S NAME                              R  S  INFORMANT
BIRTH DATE        FATHER                        MOTHER
```

CHILD'S NAME / BIRTH DATE FATHER	R	S	INFORMANT / MOTHER
SOYARS, Jennie 1 Jan 1869 SOYARS, Mark	W	F	Father SOYARS, Mary
SPAIN, Eliza A 10 July 1868 SPAIN, James	W	F	Father SPAIN, Jane
SPANGLER, Mary Jane 29 Aug 1867 SPANGLER, James W	W	F	Father SPANGLER, Cicily A
SPANGLER, Not Named 20 Sept 1868 SPANGLER, George W	W	M	Father SPANGLER, Sicily
SPENCER, Lucinda E 30 Dec 1867 SPENCER, James M	W	F	Fathr SPENCER, Elizabeth
SPENCER, M E 29 Dec 1869 SPENCER, L G	W	M	Father SPENCER, H E
SPENCER, Mahala 22 Sept 1869 SPENCER, J T	W	F	Father SPENCER, M
SPENCER, Martha B 18 Feb 1867 SPENCER, H D	W	F	Father SPENCER, Martha J
SPENCER, Mary 2 Mar 1869 SPENCER, A J	W	F	Father SPENCER, A
SPENCER, Mary M 4 Feb 1866 SPENCER, Abram J	W	F	Father SPENCER, Adeline
SPENCER, N E 23 May 1869 SPENCER, John R	W	M	M L Spencer, Grandfather SPENCER, Alberta
SPENCER, Paul W 10 Apr 1868 SPENCER, Joshua T	W	M	Father SPENCER, Mahala
SPENCER, Thomas P 9 Nov 1868 SPENCER, D G	W	M	Father SPENCER, Henrietta
STAPLES, Catharine 24 Oct 1866 STAPLES, Gabe	B	F	W H Shelton, Neighbor STAPLES, Susan
STAPLES, Gabriel 10 Aug 1868 STAPLES, Gabriel	B	M	Father STAPLES, Susan
STAPLES, Jerry -- July 1867 STAPLES, Lee (F M)	B	M	Dock Staples STAPLES, Louisa
STAPLES, Lilia 10 July 1868 STAPLES, John S	B	F	Employer STAPLES, Nancy

```
CHILD'S NAME                                 R  S  INFORMANT
BIRTH DATE         FATHER                           MOTHER
```

```
STAPLES, William G                           B  M  William A Napier,Neighbor
20 Sept 1866       TATUM, Henry                     STAPLES, Catharine

STEGALL, John W                              W  M  Mother
27 July 1866       STEGALL, William                 STEGALL, Susan E

STEIN, George B                              W  M  Not Given
-- -- (1866)       STEIN, Jacob J (Merchant/res.)   Not Given

STERN, G Benjamin                            W  M  Father
3 Feb 1867         STERN, G  G (Merchant)           STERN, Mary

STUART, Ollie                                B  F  Father
-- Feb 1869        STUART, Green                    STUART, Minerva

SUTPHIN, J S                                 W  M  Father
15 June 1869       SUTPHIN, J G                     SUTPHIN, M J

SUTPHIN, Levinia Jane                        W  F  Father
5 Jan 1868         SUTPHIN, Marion                  SUTPHIN, Nancy Elizabeth

TATUM, C D                                   W  M  Father
9 Jan 1869         TATUM, Thomas H                  TATUM, Ruth S

TATUM, Chris M                               B  M  Father
21 Sept 1869       TATUM, Price                     TATUM, Ann

TATUM, John                                  B  M  J G Tatum, Neighbor
1 Mar 1866         TATUM, Charles                   TATUM, Charlotte

TATUM, Not Named                             W  F  Father
18 Oct 1867        TATUM, A T                       TATUM, Mary

TATUM, Not Named (Born Rockingham, NC)       B  M  Father
8 Nov 1868         TATUM, Henry                     TATUM, Catherine

TATUM, Samuel M                              B  M  Neighbor
5 Sept 1868        TATUM, Price                     TATUM, Ann

TATUM, Walter                                W  M  Father
20 Dec 1868        TATUM, John P                    TATUM, Martha

TATUN, Jno F                                 W  M  Father
22 Feb 1869        TATUM, William F                 TATUM, Mary A

TAYLOR, Charles R                            W  M  Father
9 July 1966        TAYLOR, James M                  TAYLOR, Mary E

TAYLOR, Emma M                               W  F  Father
18 Jan 1868        TAYLOR, William B (Physician)    TAYLOR, Frances M
```

```
CHILD'S NAME                              R   S   INFORMANT
BIRTH DATE        FATHER                          MOTHER
```

TAYLOR, George L	W M	Father
17 Sept 1869 TAYLOR, James A		TAYLOR, Statira E
TAYLOR, Laura A	W F	Father
14 Apr 1868 TAYLOR, James A		TAYLOR, Statira E
TAYLOR, Mary Etter	B F	Father
-- June 1867 TAYLOR, Lemly (F M)		TAYLOR, Rachael
TAYLOR, Mary J	W F	Father
26 Apr 1868 TAYLOR, George S		TAYLOR, Parthenia
TAYLOR, Mary S A	W F	Father
21 Nov 1869 TAYLOR, William A		TAYLOR, Adeline
TAYLOR, Not Named	W F	Father
26 Jan 1866 TAYLOR, James B		TAYLOR, Mary
TAYLOR, Not Named	W M	Father
-- Jan 1869 TAYLOR, James B		TAYLOR, Mary
TAYLOR, Oregon C	W M	Father
7 Aug 1869 TAYLOR, George S		TAYLOR, Parthenia
TAYLOR, Rufus F	W M	Mother
15 Oct 1866 Unknown		TAYLOR, Charlotte T
TERRY, Martha E	W F	Mother
21 Oct 1866 TERRY, John J		TERRY, Mary A
TERRY, Mary H	W F	Mother
19 June 1869 TERRY, Jno J		TERRY, Mary A
TERRY, Not Named	W M	Father
22 July 1869 TERRY, James G		TERRY, Mary
TERRY, Reuben H B	W M	Father
30 June 1868 TERRY, Joseph G		TERRY, Mary
TERRY, Sarah	W F	Father
10 Dec 1867 TERRY, N B (Mechanic)		TERRY, E Y
TERRY, Susan J	W F	Mother
20 Jan 1868 TERRY, John J		TERRY, Mary A
TERRY, T A A	W F	Father
6 Apr 1866 TERRY, James G		TERRY, Mary
TERRY, Ulysses G	W M	Father
1 Mar 1869 TERRY, Nathan B		TERRY, E J

CHILD'S NAME		R	S	INFORMANT
BIRTH DATE	FATHER			MOTHER

THOMAS, Arazona A		W	F	Mother
12 Jan 1868	THOMAS, Walter H			THOMAS, Judith V
THOMAS, Benjamin T		W	M	Father
28 Apr 1867	THOMAS, James W			THOMAS, Nancy A
THOMAS, Frances A		W	F	Mother
15 Oct 1868	THOMAS, Lewis T			THOMAS, Amanda A
THOMAS, Frances A		W	F	Father
26 Oct 1869	THOMAS, Lewis T			THOMAS, Amanda A
THOMAS, Frances E		W	F	Father
6 Dec 1866	THOMAS, Tazewell			THOMAS, Louisa
THOMAS, John A		W	M	Father
30 Oct 1869	THOMAS, Charles			THOMAS, Lavinia
THOMAS, M E R E		B	F	Neighbor
15 Nov 1868	THOMAS, Robin			THOMAS, Ruth
THOMAS, Not Named		B	F	W T Thomas, Neighbor
15 Oct 1866	Not Given			THOMAS, Mollie
THOMAS, Penceanna		W	F	Father
17 Sept 1868	THOMAS, Claiborne			THOMAS, Milly J
THOMAS, Pleasant C		W	M	Father
25 May 1866	THOMAS, L T			THOMAS, Amanda A
THOMAS, Q E A C		W	F	Grandmother
14 Aug 1868	THOMAS, Tazewell			THOMAS, Louisa
THOMAS, Richard		W	M	Father
28 Sept 1867	THOMAS, Tazewell			THOMAS, Letitia
THOMAS, Rosabell		W	F	Father
15 Sept 1868	THOMAS, Franklin P			THOMAS, Mary
THOMAS, Sparrell T		W	M	Mother
24 May 1866	THOMAS, Peter J			THOMAS, Mary J
THOMAS, Victoria E		W	F	Mother
2 Feb 1868	THOMAS, Taylor L			THOMAS, Malinda M
THOMAS, Wellington A J		W	M	Father
29 July 1869	THOMAS, Tazewell			THOMAS, Letitia J
THOMAS, William E		W	M	Mother
19 Apr 1869	THOMAS, Peter J			THOMAS, Mary J

| CHILD'S NAME | | R | S | INFORMANT |
| BIRTH DATE | FATHER | | | MOTHER |

THOMPSON, Not Named (Deformed)   W M Father
15 Mar 1867   THOMPSON, Hiram   THOMPSON, Martha

THOMPSON, Samuel A   W M Mother
18 Nov 1869   THOMPSON, William P   THOMPSON, Sarah A

THOMPSON, William R   W M Father
-- Oct 1869   THOMPSON, Hiram   THOMPSON, Martha

TOWNLEY, Alamenta   W F Grandmother
28 Apr 1868   TOWNLEY, Josiah   TOWNLEY, Martha

TRENT, John H   W M Father
10 Oct 1868   TRENT, David   TRENT, Lavinia

TRENT, Laura A   W F Mother
9 Mar 1869   TRENT, William H   TRENT, Alamenta A

TRENT, Louisa A   W F Mother
3 Mar 1869   TRENT, David   TRENT, Lavinia

TRENT, Sarah J   W F Father
25 Nov 1868   TRENT, William H   TRENT, Allaminta A

TUDOR, Virginia A   W F Father
9 Oct 1866   TUDOR, John   TUDOR, Nancy A

TURNER, Bruce   W M Father
12 July 1867   TURNER, T A (Mechanic)   TURNER, Mary Jane

TURNER, Cynthia R   W F Father
10 Apr 1869   TURNER, Jeremiah   TURNER, Martha J

TURNER, George S   W M Father
9 June 1867   TURNER, Samuel C   TURNER, N M

TURNER, James A J   W M Mother
30 July 1867   TURNER, John   TURNER, Martha J

TURNER, Joe   B M Friend
15 Oct 1867   TURNER, Nelson   TURNER, Rhoda

TURNER, John B   W M Father
14 Aug 1866   TURNER, Jeremiah   TURNER, M Jane

TURNER, John T   W M Father
24 Nov 1868   TURNER, Samuel C   TURNER, Nancy M

TURNER, Judith P   W F Father
20 Dec 1866   TURNER, Samuel C   TURNER, Nancy M

CHILD'S NAME		R	S	INFORMANT
BIRTH DATE	FATHER			MOTHER

TURNER, Lilliam E   W F Father
13 Oct 1866   TURNER, Mury   TURNER, Sarah

TURNER, Lillian Emma   W F Not Given
3 Oct 1866   TURNER, Murry   TURNER, Sarah P

TURNER, Melissa   B F Neighbor
12 May 1867   Not Given   TURNER, Harriett

TURNER, Not Named   W F Not Given
29 Jan 1867   TURNER, W G   TURNER, Mary J

TURNER, Not Named   W F Father
28 Feb 1868   TURNER, William G   TURNER, Mary G

TURNER, Pink   B M Father
15 Mar 1867   TURNER, Michael   TURNER, Senia

TURNER, Samuel A   W M Father
2 Aug 1868   TURNER, Fleming   TURNER, Nancy E

TURNER, Thomas J (Born Floyd Co)   W M Father
23 Feb 1866   TURNER, Fleming   TURNER, Nancy

TURNER, V C J   W F Father
15 Oct 1866   TURNER, George T   TURNER, Mary A

TURNER, William L   W M Father
17 Apr 1866   TURNER, James R   TURNER, Sabrina

UNDERWOOD, R E   W M Father
22 July 1869   UNDERWOOD, I W   UNDERWOOD, Mary S

VARNER, Mollie   W F Father
2 Sept 1869   VARNER, William   VARNER, Ruth

VAUGHN, Minca A   B F Father
15 Apr 1869   VAUGHN, Samuel   VAUGHN, Rhoda

VIA, Charles G   W M Father
2 May 1866   VIA, James E   VIA, Louisa V

VIA, Exony E   W F Mother
15 Apr 1866   Not Given   VIA, Elizabeth

VIA, George W   W M Mother
24 Apr 1868   VIA, James E   VIA, Louisa

VIA, James J   W M Mother
17 Apr 1869   VIA, Sparrel   VIA, Mary J

CHILD'S NAME BIRTH DATE	FATHER	R	S	INFORMANT MOTHER
VIA, James T 28 Sept 1868	Not Given	W	M	Mother VIA, Mary E
VIA, Lillian 5 Nov 1869	VIA, James E	W	F	Father VIA, Louisa V
VIA, Mary 15 Aug 1868	VIA, Booker	B	F	Mother VIA, Lucy
VIA, Mary 14 May 1868	VIA, Micajah	B	F	Father VIA, Martha
VIA, Not Named 11 Dec 1868	VIA, Elijah D	W	F	Father VIA, Nancy
WASHINGTON, Mary A E 16 Nov 1869	WASHINGTON, Robert(?) P	W	F	Mother WASHINGTON, Mary E
WASHINGTON, Virginia A 27 Aug 1868	WASHINGTON, Reed P	W	F	Mother WASHINGTON, Mary E
WEAVER, William A 19 Sept 1867	WEAVER, James T	W	M	Father WEAVER, Elizabeth
WEBB, Emma A 11 Feb 1867	WEBB, Henry	W	F	Father WEBB, Susan M
WEST, N J E 6 May 1866	WEST, Wilson J	W	F	Father WEST, Elizabeth
WHITE, Joseph 14 Jan 1869	WHITE, Joseph	W	M	Father WHITE, Mary
WHITE, Mary E 11 Mar 1866	WHITE, Joseph	W	F	Not Given WHITE, Mary A
WHITE, William M 18 Dec 1866	WHITE, James	W	M	Not Given WHITE, Harriett
WHITLOCK, Not Named 1 July 1867	WHITLOCK, J R	W	F	Father WHITLOCK, Susan
WIGGENTON, George W 29 Aug 1868	WIGGENTON, A J (Mechanic)	W	M	Father WIGGENTON, Nancy G (J)
WIGGENTON, Not Named 21 Nov 1866	WIGGENSTON, W J(G?)	W	F	W G Wiggenton, Father WIGGENTON, Sarah E
WIGGINGTON, Thomas S H 26 May 1867	WIGGINGTON, W J	W	M	Father WIGGINGTON, Nancy Jane

```
CHILD'S NAME                              R  S  INFORMANT
BIRTH DATE        FATHER                        MOTHER
_____

WIGGINGTON, William J                     W  M  Father
26 Jan 1869       WIGGINGTON, W J               WIGGINGTON, S C

WILLARD, Mary                             W  F  Father
24 Mar 1866       WILLARD, James M              WILLARD, Ruth

WILLIAMS, James S (Twin)                  W  M  Father
18 June 1868      WILLIAMS, Robert S            WILLIAMS, Mary C

WILLIAMS, John T (Twin)                   W  M  Father
18 June 1868      WILLIAMS, Robert S            WILLIAMS, Mary C

WILLIAMS, Mary                            W  F  Father
25 Feb 1868       WILLIAMS, Sparrel             WILLIAMS, Onia

WILLIAMS, Mary S                          W  F  Father
15 Mar 1868       WILLIAMS, Jacob W             WILLIAMS, Lucinda

WILLIAMS, Sally R                         W  F  Mother
25 Apr 1866       WILLIAMS, Creed               WILLIAMS, E A

WILSON, Francis                           B  M  J M Jiles(Giles),Neighbor
10 Sept 1866      Not Known                     WILSON, Betty

WILSON, Green                             B  M  Father
-- July 1867      WILSON, Pleasant              WILSON, Winna

WIMBISH, J H L                            W  M  Father
24 Oct 1869       WIMBISH, George W             WIMBISH, Prudence

WOOD, Alverda Clementine                  W  F  Father
21 May 1867       WOOD, Martin                  WOOD, Ellen

WOOD, David G                             W  M  Father
9 Mar 1867        WOOD, Alexander               WOOD, M J

WOOD, David J                             W  M  Father
8 Mar 1866        WOOD, Alex                    WOOD, M Jane

WOOD, E  T                                W  M  Father
-- June 1867      WOOD, John                    WOOD, Martha

WOOD, Flora S                             W  F  Father
26 Oct 1867       WOOD, German                  WOOD, Ruth

WOOD, Greenville                          W  M  Father
9 Nov 1866        WOOD, P J                     WOOD, Judith

WOOD, Iowa                                W  F  William F Hall, Neighbor
15 June 1869      WOOD, James                   WOOD, Betsey
```

```
CHILD'S NAME                                  R  S  INFORMANT
BIRTH DATE        FATHER                             MOTHER
```

```
WOOD, J J D (Born in W VA)                    W  M  Mother
13 Sept 1867      WOOD, John B                       WOOD, Lucy A

WOOD, Jefferson B                             W  M  Father
18 July 1869      WOOD, Stephen H                    WOOD, Richard(?)

WOOD, Not Named                               W  M  Mother
23 July 1869      WOOD, Lee                          WOOD, Elizabeth

WOOD, Not Named (Born Dead)                   W  M  Mother
4 Aug 1868        WOOD, Lee                          WOOD, Elizabeth

WOOD, Sarah L                                 W  F  Father
11 Feb 1869       WOOD, Alexander                    WOOD, Mary J

WOOD, Tazewell M                              W  M  Father
27 Nov 1866       WOOD, Wingfield                    WOOD, Lydia

WOOD, Violet A                                W  F  Mother
15 Aug 1868       WOOD, Winfield S                   WOOD, Mahala

WOODWELL, Rufus Albert                        W  M  Father
10 Apr 1867       WOODWELL, James W                  WOODWELL, Mary Ann

WOOLWINE, Sallie Wharton                      W  F  Father
23 July 1869      WOOLWINE, Rufus J                  WOOLWINE, Sarah R

WORTH, S J                                    W  M  Father
20 Sept 1869      WORTH, William H                   WORTH, S J

WORTH, Victoria                               W  F  Father
-- Oct 1867       WORTH, William H (Lawyer)          WORTH, Susan Jane

WRIGHT, Albuest                               W  M  Father
31 Dec 1867       WRIGHT, Robert M                   WRIGHT, Letha

WRIGHT, Andrew Fuller                         W  M  Father
17 May 1867       WRIGHT, Henry S                    WRIGHT, Lucy E T

WRIGHT, Charles                               W  M  Father
14 Feb 1868       WRIGHT, Columbus J                 WRIGHT, Elizabeth

WRIGHT, James J                               W  M  Father
11 Oct 1868       WRIGHT, Jeff N                     WRIGHT, Nancy J

WRIGHT, Mary A                                W  F  Father
30 Aug 1867       WRIGHT, M E                        WRIGHT, America

WRIGHT, Not Named                             W  M  Father
10 Mar 1866       WRIGHT, Columbus J                 WRIGHT, Elizabeth
```

CHILD'S NAME BIRTH DATE	FATHER	R	S	INFORMANT MOTHER
WRIGHT, S E H E F 30 Sept 1868	WRIGHT, William G	W	M	Father WRIGHT, Temperance
WRIGHT, William B R M A 26 Dec 1869	WRIGHT, William G	W	M	Father WRIGHT, Tempy
YATES, Rosalie 7 Jan 1869	YATES, George W	W	F	Father YATES, Mary J
YEATES, Not Named -- July 1867	YEATES, Henry T	W	M	G W Spangler YEATES, Karen R
YEATTS, Charles Y 29 Nov 1867	YEATTS, George W	W	M	Father YEATTS, Mary
YEATTS, Rosa Lee 7 Jan 1868	YEATTS, George W	W	F	Father YEATTS, Mary G
YOUNG, Margaret H -- May 1869	YOUNG, John	W	F	Father YOUNG, Ruth E
YOUNG, Peter 10 Apr 1868	YOUNG, Patrick	B	M	Father YOUNG, Hannah
ZIGLER, Mary 19 Dec 1868	ZIGLER, William	W	F	Father Zigler, Sally
ZIGLER, Sarah 1 Apr 1868	Unmarried	B	F	Physician ZIGLER, Sophia

Heritage Books by Barbara C. Baughan and Betty A. Pilson:

Miscellaneous Records of Patrick County, Virginia

Patrick County, Virginia 1880 Census

Patrick County, Virginia Birth Records: 1853–1869, Volume I

Patrick County, Virginia Birth Records: 1870–1880, Volume II

Patrick County, Virginia Birth Records: 1881–1889, Volume III

Patrick County, Virginia Birth Records: 1890–1896, Volume IV

Patrick County, Virginia Death Records: 1868, 1869, and 1871–1896

Patrick County, Virginia Land Entry Book: July 1791–February 1796

Patrick County, Virginia Superior Court Order Book: May 1809–May 1831

Patrick County, Virginia Unrecorded Documents, 1791–1920

Patrick County, Virginia Will Book, No. 2

www.ingramcontent.com/pod-product-compliance
Lightning Source LLC
Chambersburg PA
CBHW070752270326
41927CB00010B/2121